HERALDRY
Customs, Rules and Styles

To Diana, my wife, in gratitude for
her patience and moral support.

HERALDRY
Customs, Rules and Styles

Written and Illustrated by

CARL-ALEXANDER VON VOLBORTH

Membre de l'Académie Internationale d'Héraldique

NEW ORCHARD EDITIONS
Poole Dorset

First published in the U.K. 1981 by Blandford Press
ISBN 1 85079 037 X

This edition published by
NEW ORCHARD EDITIONS
POOLE DORSET

NEW ORCHARD EDITIONS LTD
ROBERT ROGERS HOUSE
NEW ORCHARD, POOLE
DORSET BH15 1LU, ENGLAND

Printed in Hong Kong by South China Printing Co.

CONTENTS

INTRODUCTION

Heraldry is a phenomenon of European history that is very much alive more than eight hundred years after its inception. It is alive not only in Europe but also in the other continents where it was introduced by migrating and colonizing Europeans. Originally a means of identification for the warrior class, the heraldic shield came to be used on the seals needed to authenticate documents, and the practice of using armorial devices as cognizances soon spread to burghers, municipal governments, craft guilds and the Church. Gradually the arms became hereditary and it became the custom to display armorial bearings. After their disappearance from the battlefield, they lived on, deeply rooted in the culture and traditions of European society.

Times have changed and yet with the exception of France, Italy and most communist countries, the different states in Europe, whether monarchies or republics, still use coats of arms in perfect heraldic tradition. The thousands of civic arms are proof of the heraldic awareness of our time. Family heraldry continues to survive and its popularity is even on the increase in some countries. Man seems to need to place himself into a relationship with society. He wants to be able to identify himself as belonging to a family, a clan, a community or a nation, and this can be pictorially expressed by a coat of arms, a badge or a flag.

Coats of arms can be found in portraits, on banners, monuments, tombstones and above the gates of towns and castles. Coats of arms appear in stained-glass windows and as hatchments in churches. They are engraved on silverware and signet rings and are widely used in bookplates. Knowledge of heraldry is an enrichment for anybody interested in history or genealogy and can be of great help in dating and identifying objects of art, craft and architecture.

Any friend of heraldry will eventually run into difficulties when trying to become acquainted with the customary heraldic practice of foreign countries. There is the problem of discovering which books to study and where to find them, and there is the frustrating experience of seeing one's efforts handicapped by language barriers.

I have been collecting information about international heraldry for many years, with emphasis on its pictorial peculiarities and the peculiarities of customs, rules and styles, excepting those regions in the Balkans which underwent different trends of development during their occupation by the Turks (these include Greece, Bulgaria and the Yugoslav section of Macedonia). This book is the result. It is far from being encyclopaedic but should be of value to anyone wishing to gain a more international view of the subject. It should also serve as an introduction to heraldry for a newcomer to the field.

There is an important point which must be made: the right to arms is not the privilege of any particular group of society and anyone may assume new arms for himself or for his family, unless it is not considered legal or customary in his country. But the rights of others should be respected, and since a coat of arms is the property of its bearer, to adopt the armorial bearings of another family that happens to have the same or a similar name, without having proof of the necessary genealogical connection, is misleading and could be called theft. Unfortunately there are individuals and firms who prey on the vanity of people desiring a coat of arms. They compile lists of family names, find arms that seem to go with the name and try to sell the arms to a customer, who then genuinely believes that these are the arms to which he is entitled. Since there is no such thing as 'arms of a family name', it should be obvious that such an offer is fraudulent. Anybody who wants to assume armorial bearings should obtain information and advice from a reputable heraldist or, in the case of Great Britain, Ireland and Spain, he should contact the official heraldic institution.

Carl-Alexander von Volborth, Antwerp, 1981.

An Imaginary Achievement of Arms

containing most of the characteristic accessories to a shield of arms which appear in European heraldry. In addition to these, insignia of office and badges may be displayed in conjunction with arms, as may insignia of Orders of Chivalry (O). An achievement as shown in the illustration would belong to a member of the high aristocracy of Europe. A normal achievement consists of shield, helm with crest and mantling and sometimes a motto.

1 SHIELD. **2** HELM or HELMET. **3** CREST. **4** MANTLING. **5** CREST-CORONET. **6** CREST-WREATH or TORSE. **7** SUPPORTER. **8** BANNER. **9** CRI-DE-GUERRE or WAR CRY. **10** MOTTO. **11** COMPARTMENT. **12** MANTEAU or ROBE OF ESTATE. **13** CROWN or CORONET OF RANK.

INTRODUCTION IN PICTURES

1. Free lance herald, Northern Italy, c 1450. The white staff was borne by heralds as a symbol of their office.

2. Pursuivant, early 15th century. While the tabard of a herald consisted of front and back panels joined above the shoulders, the panels of a pursuivant's tabard covered the arms.

3. Herald of the Holy Roman Empire, 16th century, wearing a tabard emblazoned with the double-headed eagle of the empire charged with the arms of Austria and Burgundy ancient. The red bordure of Burgundy was often omitted in the imperial arms.

It is through the mediaeval tournament in the last decades of the 12th century, in which knights tested their skill in combat, that we meet the first heralds. They marshalled the combatants, announced them when they were entering the lists and finally proclaimed the winner of the contest. Heralds had to be well informed about all the armorial devices likely to be present at such an event, since a participant's face was hidden under the protection of his pot helm. So it is hardly surprising that the heralds compiled painted records of all the arms they encountered on such occasions, and also collected the armorial bearings of sovereign princes and their vassals.

Heralds were in the service of kings and princes, they were also employed by tournament societies and towns, and sometimes even by simple knights. They were also used as official messengers in peace and war and had the immunity of ambassadors. Heralds had to perform ceremonial duties at state affairs and in several countries they were later in charge of issuing the certificates of new grants of arms.

There were three grades of herald: senior heralds called 'Kings of Arms', the actual 'Heralds', and aspirants to the office of herald called 'Pursuivants'. These grades still exist in Great Britain today. Their names of office were normally territorial designations: Romreich (Roman Empire) for the King of Arms of the Emperor. Jutland and Zealand for Danish heralds. Monjoy, named after the war-cry of the French kings. Harcourt, from the Norman noble family, Savoie from the house of Savoy. Garter is still used in England and Lyon in Scotland, one named after the English order, the other after the lion in the arms of Scotland. Several countries have official heraldic services. Some of these are concerned only with civic arms, others only with heraldic matters of the noblesse, some with both (and corporate arms). A Cronista de Armas in Spain may even grant and register burgher-arms.

4. A crusader from the 13th century, wearing chain mail and a pot helm with a flat top.

5. Two knights ready for the tournament. Adaptation from the *Codex Manesse,* c 1300. The shield and crested helm together form a complete coat of arms.

6. The Earl of Warwick.

7. The Earl of Oxford.

8. John de Vesci.

9. Henry de Hastings.

Both shield and helm belonged to the defensive part of a mediaeval warrior's equipment, and both were suitable for decoration. Particular devices were used to distinguish one knight from another. This was necessary as once in full armour a knight became unrecognizable to both his friends and enemies. Heraldry was born of necessity in the first decades of the 12th century. The idea of decorating shield and helm for the purpose of identification was not new, but these armorial devices were soon used in civil life and became hereditary.

10. In early heraldry shield and helm could be displayed separately in opposite corners of a design or be placed next to each other. The shield placed on the left (dexter in heraldry) and the helm on the right (sinister). These are the arms of two minne singers from the *Codex Manesse.*

Some Ancient Italian, French, Scottish and German Arms

11. Pallavicini.

12. Imperiali.

13. Spinola.

14. Vivaldi.

15. de Villiers.

16. de Monfort.

17. de Tilly.

18. de Mallet.

19. Hay.

20. Douglas.

21. Bruce.

22. Campbell.

23. von Berlichingen.

24. von Metternich.

25. von Sickingen.

26. von Frundsberg.

The devices painted on the shield were also used on banners. They had to be simple and clear in design, with strong contrasting colours, so they could be recognized at a distance of at least 250 metres.

27. Belmont. 28. Lochen. 29. Schenk von Basel. 30. Spiegelberg.

Swiss coats of arms from the *Zürcher Wappenrolle* c 1340.

The term 'coat of arms' signifies an armorial achievement which consists of a shield with helm, crest and mantling. It is derived from the surcoat of a knight (worn over his armour), on which the charges of his shield were repeated. The word crest designates the figure which is placed on the helm.

31. Sir Alexander Stewart. 32. Sir Alexander Ramsay. 33. Sir Robert Erskine.

Scottish coats of arms from the *Armorial de Gelre,* 14th century.

The shield is the only indispensable part of an armorial achievement. It can be used by itself without helm, crest or any other heraldic appurtenance. Moreover, there are a great number of arms which do not have a helm, for instance, the majority of civic arms. And in most European countries women are not supposed to use a helm. In more modern times the Roman Catholic clergy renounced the helm and now use only ecclesiastical accessories with their arms.
Several possibilities of how arms can be displayed without helm are illustrated here and on the following two pages.

34. Finland.

35. Switzerland.

36. Poland.

37. Baden-Baden (West Germany). Civic arms are sometimes ensigned with a mural crown.

38. Dom William Wilfrid Bayne. This is a typical achievement of a simple priest in the Roman Catholic Church.

39. von Steuben. In general, the arms of noblemen can be displayed with just their coronet of rank.

40. Archbishop Bruno Bernard Heim. Archbishops and bishops of the Roman Catholic Church may indicate their status in the hierarchy by use of the cross alone.

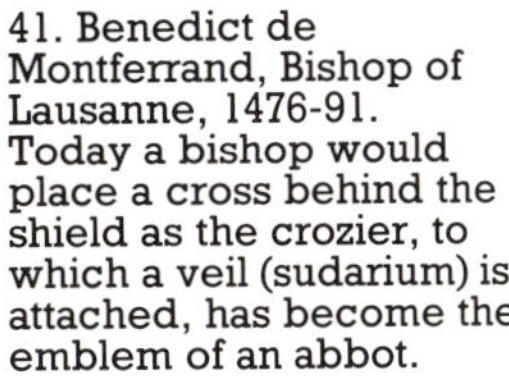

41. Benedict de Montferrand, Bishop of Lausanne, 1476-91. Today a bishop would place a cross behind the shield as the crozier, to which a veil (sudarium) is attached, has become the emblem of an abbot.

Christian, of Unerigg and Milntown, Cumberland.

42. The city of Cologne in West Germany. By the 15th century the shield of the 'free imperial city' was placed on the imperial double-headed eagle.

Hiram Kennedy Douglass, of Florence, Alabama, U.S.A. (an English grant of 1957).

43. *Above, left* and *right:* in British heraldry, helm and mantling are sometimes omitted, though this practice is discouraged nowadays.

44. Pope Pius XI, 1922-1939. The shield is ensigned with the papal tiara and the keys of St Peter crossed in saltire.

45. Count de Segur. This is a normal armorial composition for a count-senator of the French empire. Helms were never used in the heraldry created by Napoleon I.

46. Baron van Delft. The Belgian family of van Delft was ennobled by the Empress Maria Theresa. The family uses a helm with a crest. One member of the family was created a baron in 1858 by the King of the Belgians. An illustration of his arms in the *Armorial Général de la Noblesse Belge, 1957,* shows the same basic arms but with supporters and motto; helm and crest replaced by a baronial coronet. Titled families of Belgium often use a coronet of rank and omit helm and crest, this is also customary in France.

47. Prince of Croy. The armorial bearings of this ancient house are illustrated in the *Armorial Général de la Noblesse Belge, 1957* in a form that has become customary in Europe since the 17th century. The antiquity of the family is expressed in the simple shield, while the manteau and the bonnet of a prince of the Holy Roman Empire indicate the nobiliary rank.

Tinctures

The tinctures generally used in heraldry are red, blue, black, green and purple – they are termed gules, azure, sable, vert and purpure. Yellow and white are considered metals and are blazoned Or and argent. In British heraldry, the colours orange (or tawny) and reddish purple are also used. The first one is called tenné, the second one murrey or sanguine.
In the heraldry of more modern times we also find charges of natural colours (called proper), for example, a brown stag or a flesh-coloured human figure. In practical use a coat of arms can be engraved on silver or appear as a black and white drawing on book-plates, stationery, etc. Since the tinctures are essential, they should be indicated.

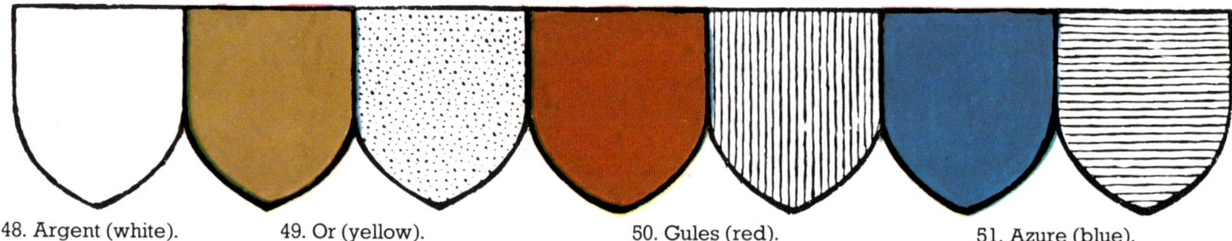

48. Argent (white). 49. Or (yellow). 50. Gules (red). 51. Azure (blue).

Tincturing is possible through a system of dots and hatching invented by Pietra Santa who used it in his *Tesserae Gentilitiae* (1638). This system has its artistic shortcomings but is nevertheless internationally known, and anyone who is used to it will 'read' tinctures the way a musician reads the music in a score.

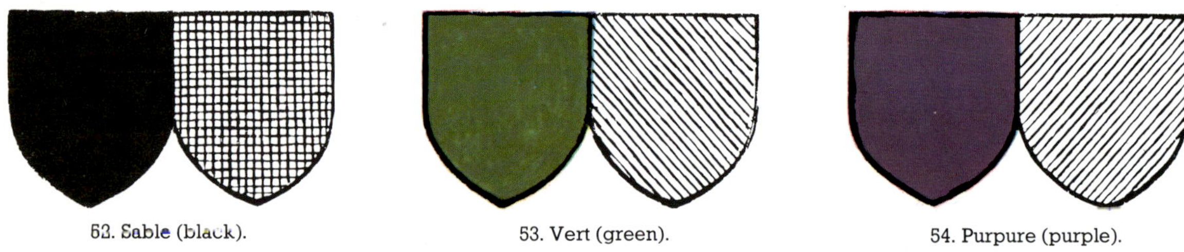

52. Sable (black). 53. Vert (green). 54. Purpure (purple).

Pietra Santa's method is used throughout this book, except for natural colours which are left white. These can be recognized, since a charge that is not hatched placed in a field Or or argent, must be of natural colour. Human supporters are normally proper, and lion supporters are in most cases gold or of natural colour (proper).

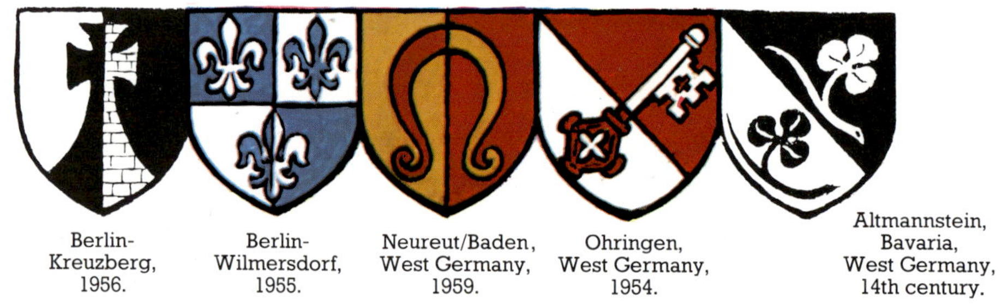

Berlin-Kreuzberg, 1956. Berlin-Wilmersdorf, 1955. Neureut/Baden, West Germany, 1959. Ohringen, West Germany, 1954. Altmannstein, Bavaria, West Germany, 14th century.

55. Counterchanged means that the charge of a divided shield is divided by the same line, its halves being tinctured of the colour or the metal of the opposite field.

Nyborg, Denmark, c 1300.

Przemyśl, Poland, 14th century.

56. To place colour on colour or metal on metal is bad heraldry. There are, however, many exceptions to this rule.

Kingdom of Galicia in the Austro-Hungarian monarchy.

St Pölten, Austria, 1538.

57. Brabant.

The tinctures of a coat of arms are of great importance. Therefore, in black and white drawings, they should always be indicated, unless a description (blazon) accompanies the arms. For example, the shields of Brabant and of Flanders are easily distinguished. The first one is: 'sable, a lion rampant Or' while the second one is blazoned: 'Or, a lion rampant sable'. But if no tinctures were indicated the arms could belong to anybody who had a lion rampant as the sole charge of his shield.
The arms displayed on this page are taken from a relatively small area. They belong to noble families of the Kingdom of Belgium.
The larger the circle on the map, the more one finds identical arms. For example, 'gules, a cross argent' is the description not only of the arms of Vienna, but also of the city-arms of Pavia, the arms of the Order of Malta, of the dynastic house of Savoy, and of many others.

58. Flanders.

59. de Cunchy.

60. de Patoul.

61. Lallemant de Levignen.

62. Mince du Fontbaré.

63. de Bousles.

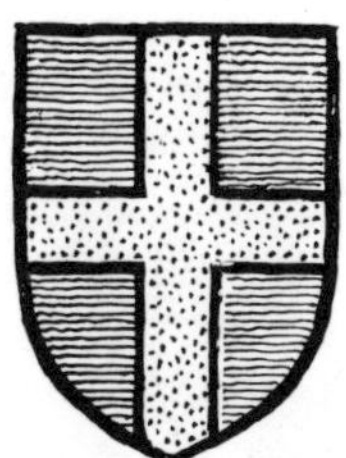

64. de Labeville.

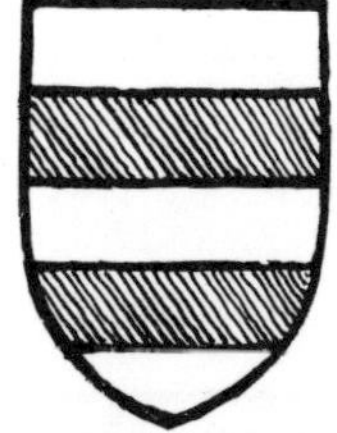

65. de Cocqueau des Mottes.

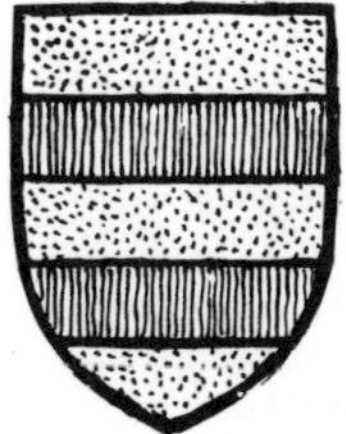

66. van Gameren.

67. de Viller.

68. de Lalaing.

69. de Rasse.

70. de Bassompierre.

71. van Borsselen van der Hooge.

72. Caïmo.

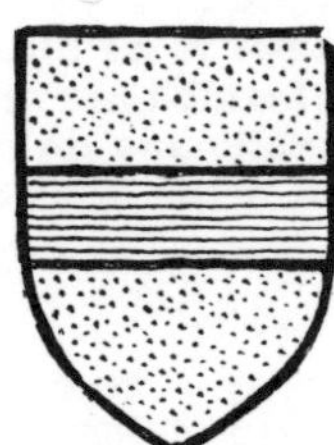

73. de Spangen.

74. de Blondel de Schiers.

75. de Nédonchel.

76. de Blondel de Beauregard de Viane.

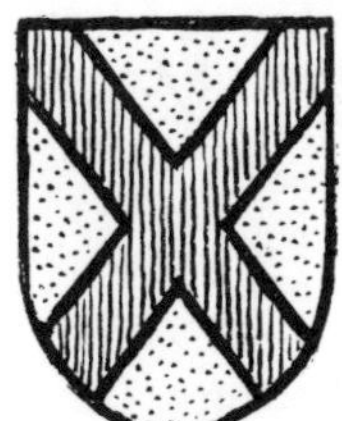

77. de Surlet de Chockier.

78. de le Vingne.

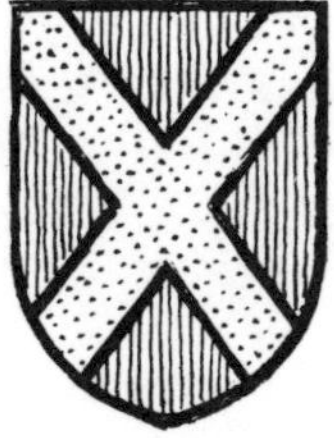

79. de Vischer de Celles.

80. Iweins.

81. de Feller.

82. d'Espiennes.

Furs

Ermine, quite common in English heraldry, is rare in Scandinavian arms, and in the unique heraldry of Poland, seemingly neither ermine nor vair are used.

83. Ermine.

84. Ermines.

85. Erminois.

86. Pean.

Ermine tails, fastened to the white skin, can be depicted in a couple of stylized versions. In continental heraldry they are normally used in their natural form outside the shield, for example, the lining of a royal pavilion or the trimming of the various chapeaux or caps of the high nobility.

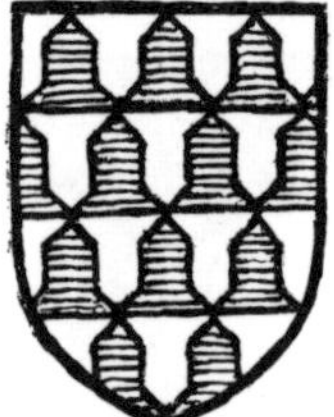
87. Vair.

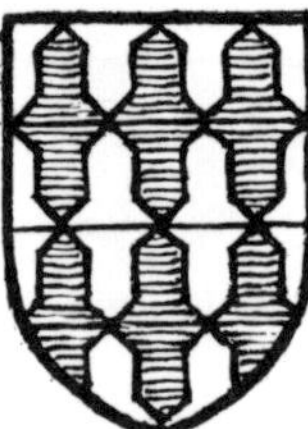
88. Counter-vair.

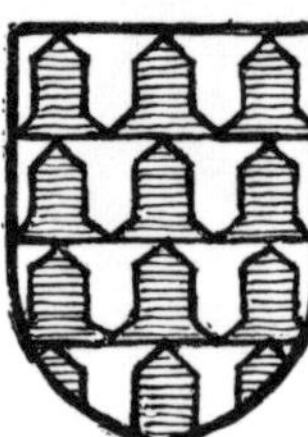
89. Vair in pale.

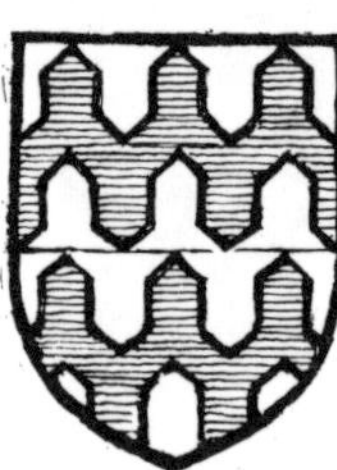
90. Vair en point.

91. Vairy (of four tinctures).

92. Natural fur.

93. Potent.

Vair, a stylized pattern of blue and white pieces, represents the skin of the grey squirrel, or more precisely the light fur of its belly and the darker fur of its back. If it is of any other colour or metal, it should be blazoned as vairy and the tinctures given.
Vair ancient is represented by lines undy or nebuly, separated by straight lines in fess. Originally it did not make a difference whether pieces of vair were rounded or angular. See fig. 114.
In Germanic countries one finds Buntfeh, a vair pattern of two colours and two metals that would have to be blazoned as vairy. There is also natural fur, the pieces of which are arranged like the scales of a fish. These are normally white and light brown around the edges. Natural fur is mainly found in the arms of furriers.

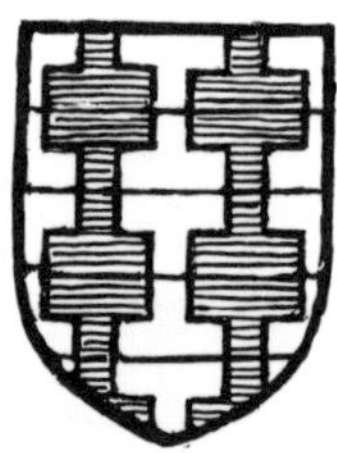
94. Counter-potent.

95. Bregenz, Austria.

96. Ypres, Belgium.

97. Cologne, West Germany.

98. Birmingham, England.

99. Brest, France.

The rule that colour should not be placed on colour nor metal on metal does not apply to furs.

THE SHIELD

Most shields were made from light wood and covered with parchment or leather. An overlay of canvas was stretched over this. The canvas was then sized with glue and white chalk, on which the charges of the shield were sometimes lightly moulded before painting.

100. Ireland.

101. England.

102. Wales.

To justify the term 'arms' or 'coat of arms', the device, by which a man, family, town or country is known, must be painted on a shield. It must show a connection with the mediaeval origin of the heraldic cognizances which were painted on a shield. It is therefore incorrect to call non-heraldic symbols, such as the national emblems of Italy, the Soviet Union or Yugoslavia, by the word 'arms'. There is nothing in these designs reminiscent of the essential part of an armorial achievement, namely the shield. Such emblems have been intentionally created in new forms that are contrary to heraldic traditions.

103. Italy. 104. Soviet Union. 105. Yugoslavia.

106. For accurate description of complicated arms it is necessary to know the different parts and points of the shield.

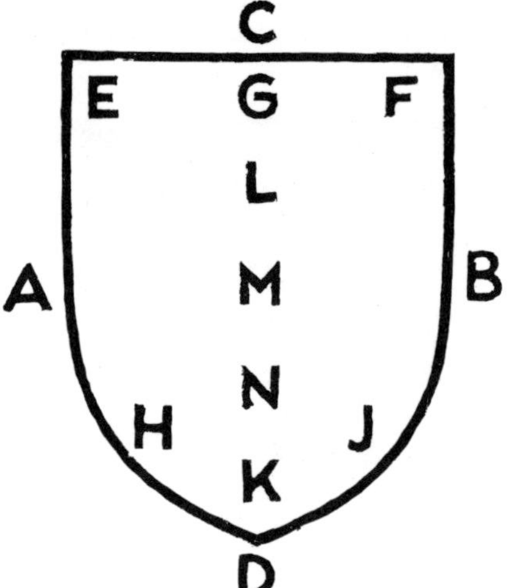

A The dexter, or right-hand side.
B The sinister, or left-hand side
C Chief.
D Base.
E Dexter chief.
F Sinister chief.
G Middle chief.
H Dexter base.
J Sinister base.
K Middle base (or 'the point').
L Honour point.
M Fess point.
N Nombril or navel point.

107. A shield is described from the bearer's position behind it. The heraldic right is where his right arm is. Thus the heraldic right, which is called dexter, and the heraldic left, called sinister, are the opposite to the normal right and left.

108. In today's heraldry the most popular forms of shield are the heater-shaped escutcheon and the shield rounded at the bottom. The diamond-shaped lozenge is used for women, mainly in the western countries of Europe and in Italy. It has never been generally accepted in Germany or the eastern countries. The oval shield is sometimes preferred by married women. This is the case in the Netherlands.

Various Forms of Shield

109. In the beginning the shields of heraldic art were patterned on the shields actually used in battle or tournament. The shield became obsolete in the 14th century when plated armour replaced chain mail, and the strongbow and the cannon appeared on the battlefield. Shields continued to be used in tournaments until tournaments fell from favour after the death of Emperor Maximilian I in 1519, and they were discredited by the accident in 1559 which cost the life of King Henry II of France.

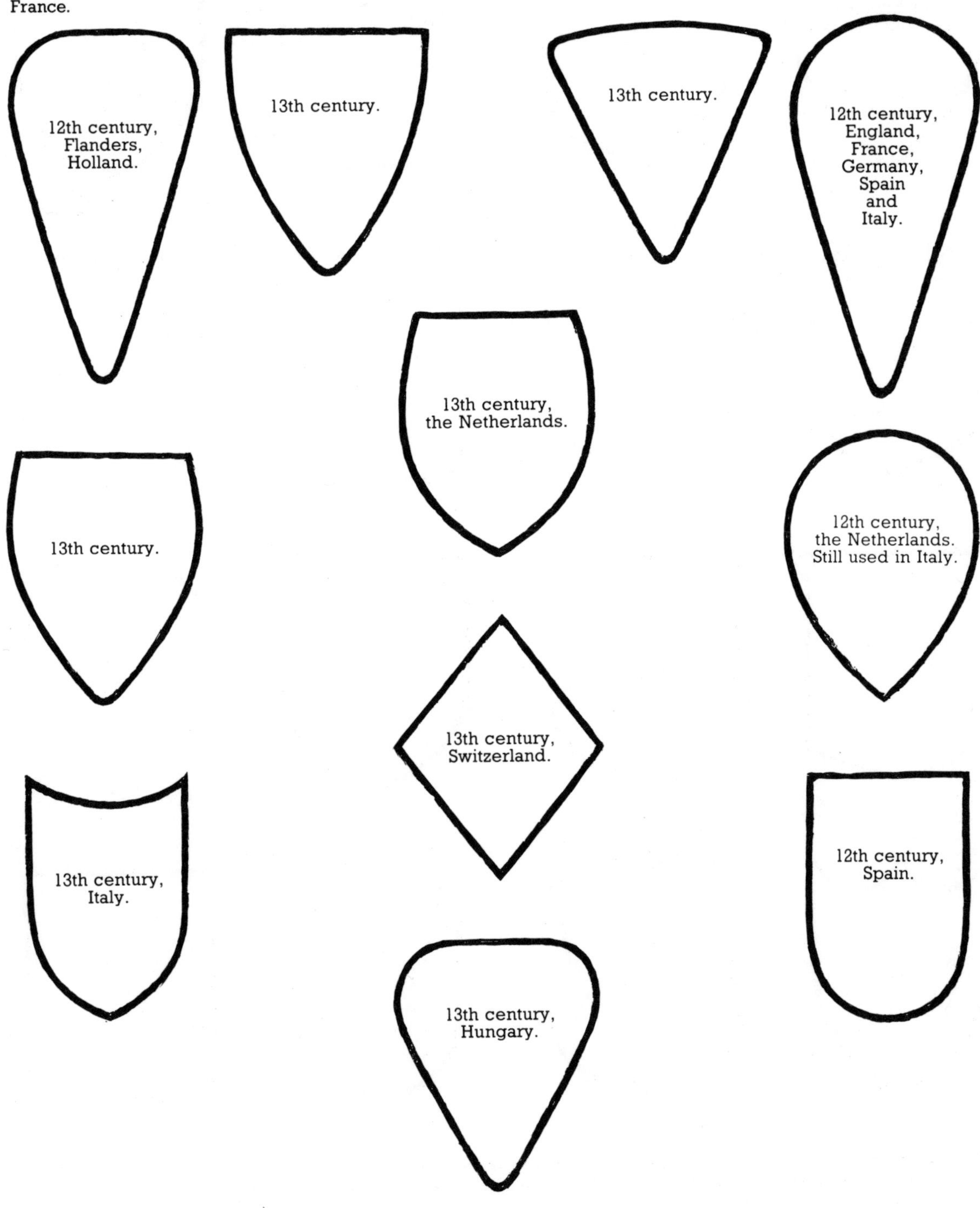

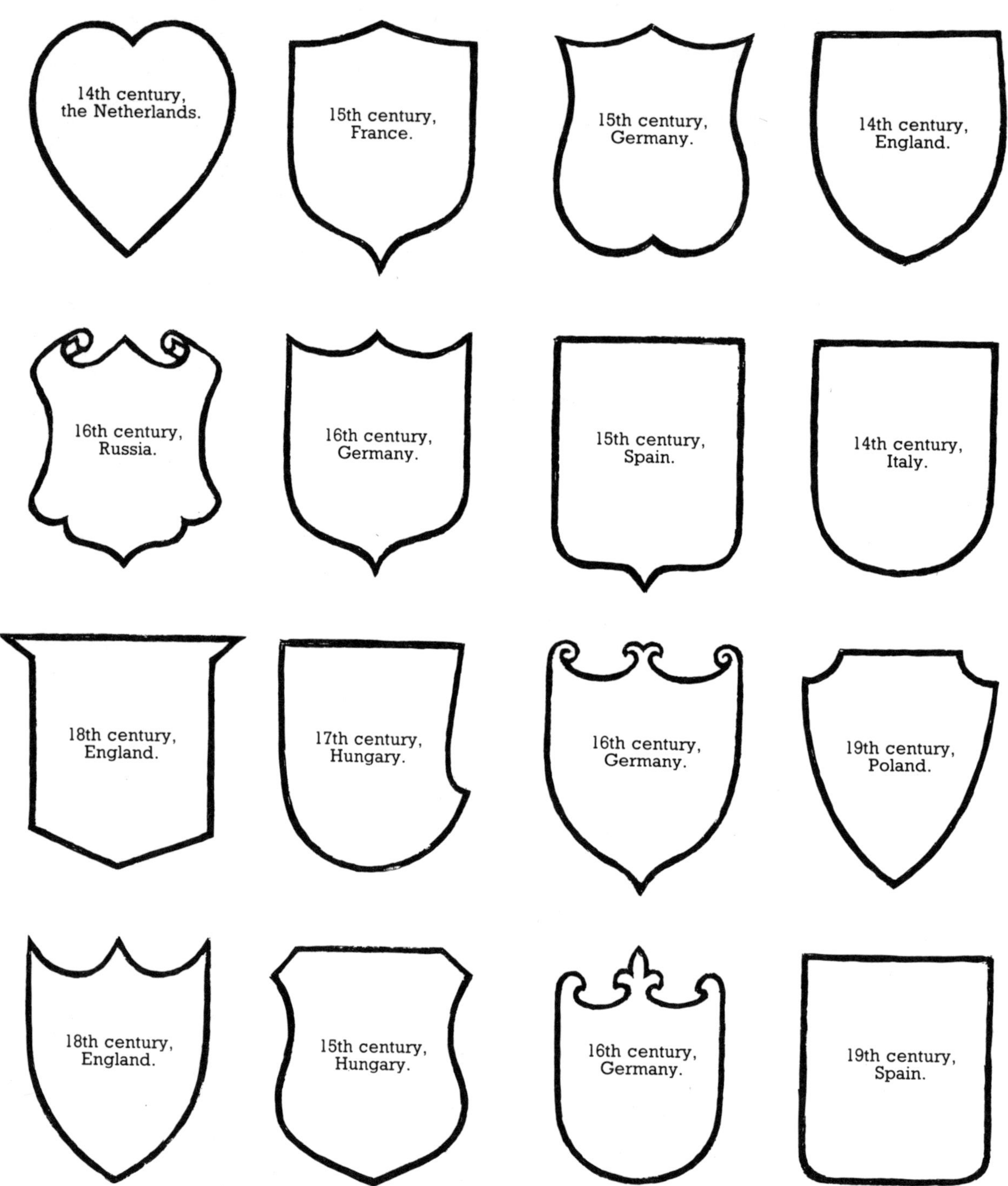

The painted shield and the crested helm disappeared from military life, but armorial bearings continued as representative markings of individuals, families, towns, guilds and other corporations.
The coat of arms, without any relationship to the then current military equipment, remained an emblem of identification and gained importance as a symbol of tradition and status. This was the beginning of 'paper-heraldry', in which the form of a shield depended on the taste of the artist, and heraldry was influenced by artistic fashion and style.

110. Pope Paul VI

The shield above and the one on its left are typical creations of the Italian Renaissance. They are called horse-head shields and are still used today. The shields with a curved notch for the lance are called à bouche but in French the word targe is used, Tartsche in German.

The four shields shown below are characteristic of the beginning of decadence of heraldry in the second half of the 16th century.

Divisions and Lines of Partition

The simplest way of creating new arms was to draw a line on the surface of the shield, dividing it into two parts and painting one part with a colour the other with a metal. By using the colours, metals and furs of heraldry, a great number of arms could thus be designed. All would be different from each other and yet have the same basic structure. A partition line does not have to be plain, it may be ornamental and thus the number of possibilities increases.

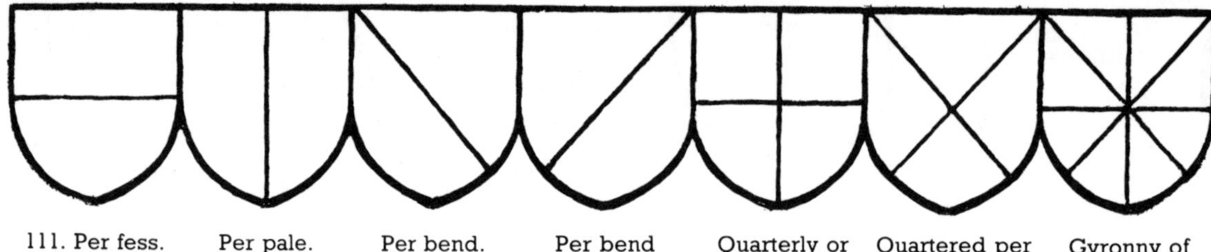

111. Per fess. Per pale. Per bend. Per bend sinister. Quarterly or per cross. Quartered per saltire. Gyronny of eight.

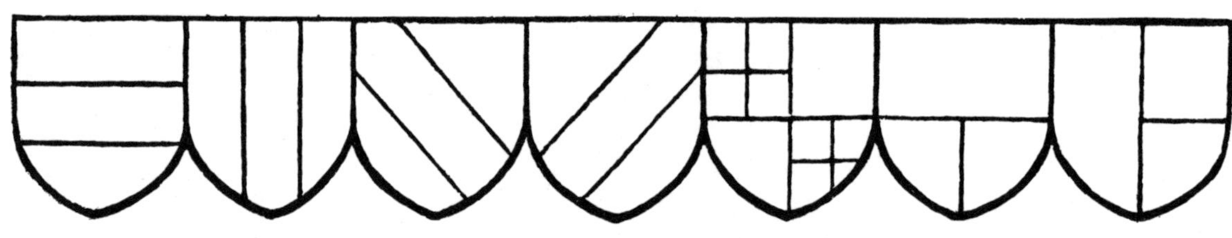

112. Tierced in fess. Tierced in pale. Tierced in bend. Tierced in bend sinister. Counter-quartered. Per fess, the base per pale. Per pale, the sinister half per fess.

113. Per pall. Per pale, the sinister half also per pale. Per fess, the base also per fess. Per chevron. Gyronny of ten. Gyronny of twelve. Quarterly 'en énquerre'.

114. Per fess wavy or undy. Per fess dovetailed. Per fess urdy or palisado. Per pale indented. Embattled per bend sinister. Raguly per bend sinister. Per fess nebuly.

Partition and Border Lines, Fields

115. Per fess potenty. Per fess rayonny or radiant. Per fess battled embattled or embattled grady. Per pale angled. Per bend sinister bevilled. Per fess arched or enarched. Per fess nowy.

116. Bordure engrailed. Bordure invected. Barry. Paly. Bendy sinister. Bendy. Chevronny.

117. Checky. Lozengy. Fusily. Barry-bendy. Paly-bendy. Paly-wavy. Barry dancetty.

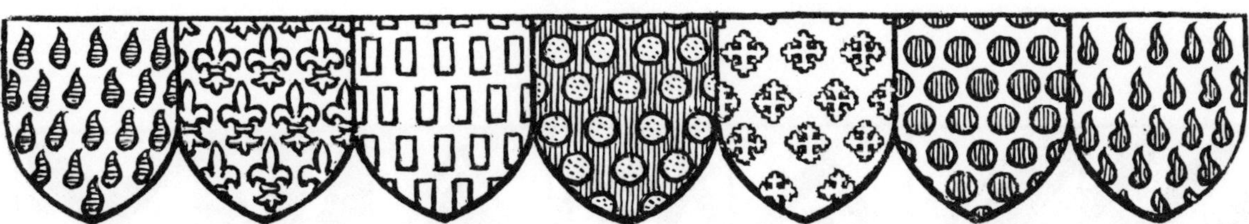

118. Goutté de larmes. Semé-de-lis. Billety. Bezanty. Crusily. Semé of torteaux. Goutté de sang.

119. A diaper is a decorative design which has nothing to do with the devices forming the arms. It was often used, especially during the Renaissance, to increase the vividness of a field, and we may still find this purely ornamental accessory even in modern arms, painted, for instance, on glass. It is often executed in a different tint but of the same tincture as the field. It has to be kept subdued so that it does not compete with the tinctures or the charges of the arms.

Ordinaries and Subordinaries

In the early days of heraldry, very simple easily distinguished forms were painted on the shield. They were not difficult to paint, could readily be recognized, even at some distance, and could easily be remembered. Because of their common usage they came to be called ordinaries. To a certain extent the classification is arbitrary and opinions vary as to which figures should be included. The same is true of the subordinaries which are secondary devices of a simple character.

120. Chief. Fess. Bars. Pale. Bend. Bend sinister. Chevron.

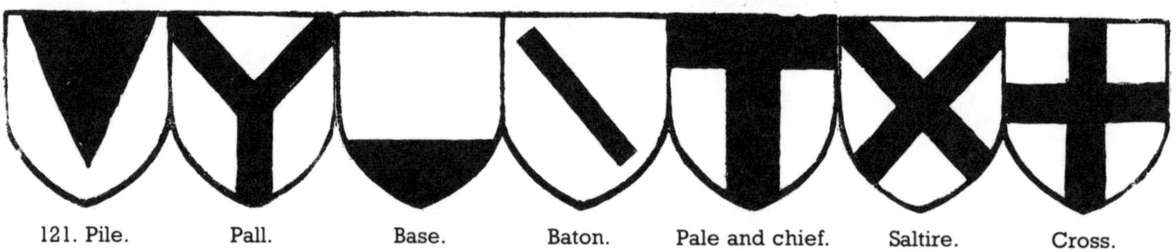

121. Pile. Pall. Base. Baton. Pale and chief. Saltire. Cross.

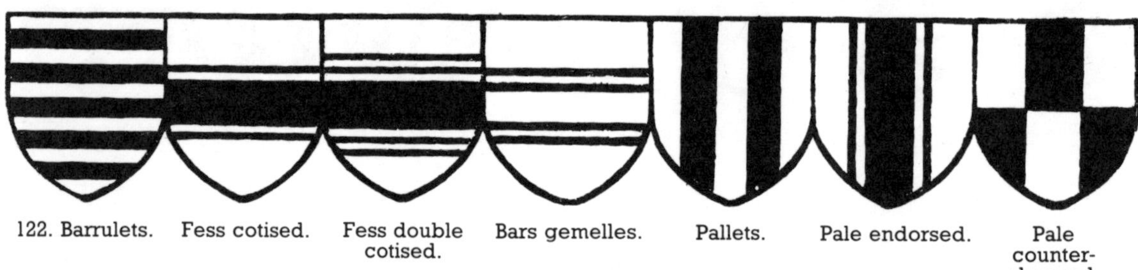

122. Barrulets. Fess cotised. Fess double cotised. Bars gemelles. Pallets. Pale endorsed. Pale counter-changed.

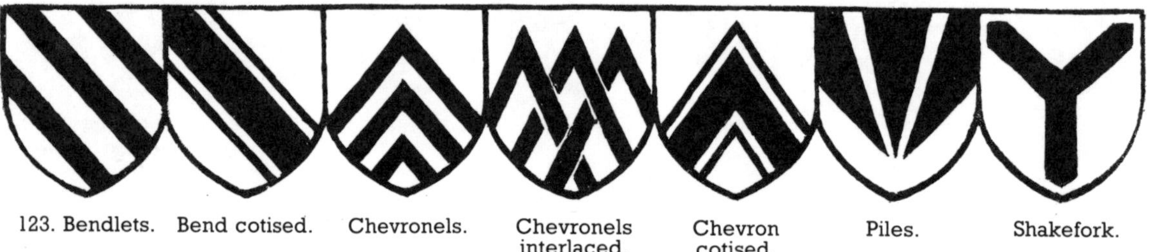

123. Bendlets. Bend cotised. Chevronels. Chevronels interlaced. Chevron cotised. Piles. Shakefork.

The chief, pale, bend, fess, chevron, cross and saltire are definitely ordinaries. An ordinary is often the only or predominant charge of the shield. Probably because of their ancient origin, ordinaries are also called honourable ordinaries, in French pièces honorables. In German heraldry they are called Heroldstücke or Heroldsbilder.

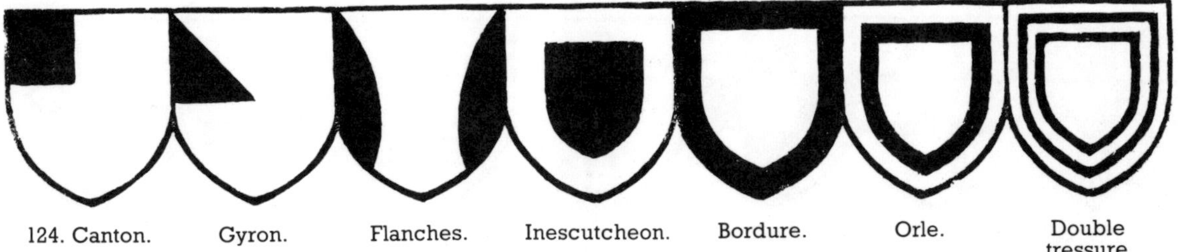

124. Canton. Gyron. Flanches. Inescutcheon. Bordure. Orle. Double tressure.

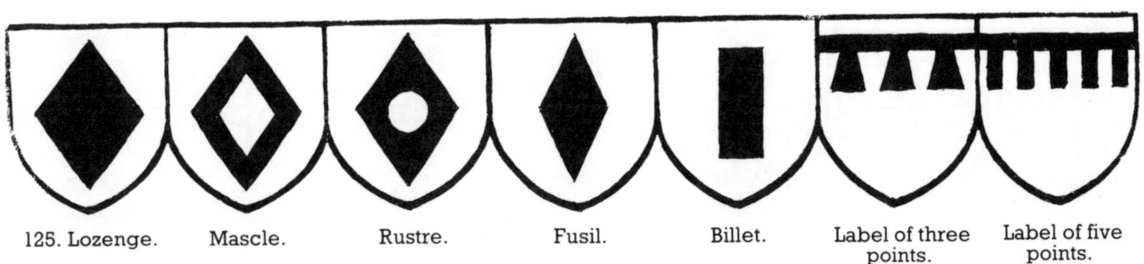

125. Lozenge. Mascle. Rustre. Fusil. Billet. Label of three points. Label of five points.

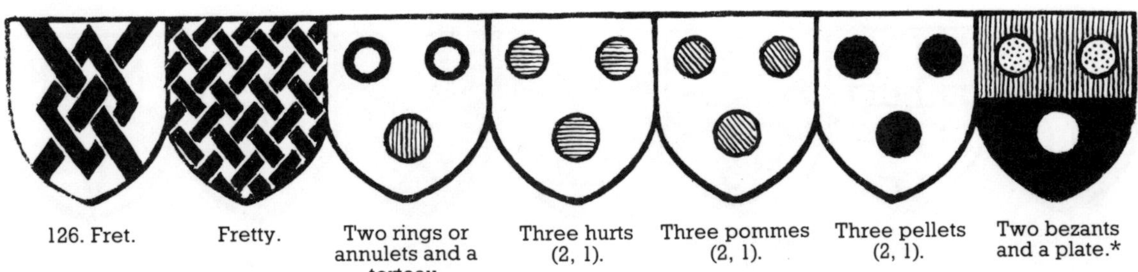

126. Fret. Fretty. Two rings or annulets and a torteau. Three hurts (2, 1). Three pommes (2, 1). Three pellets (2, 1). Two bezants and a plate.*

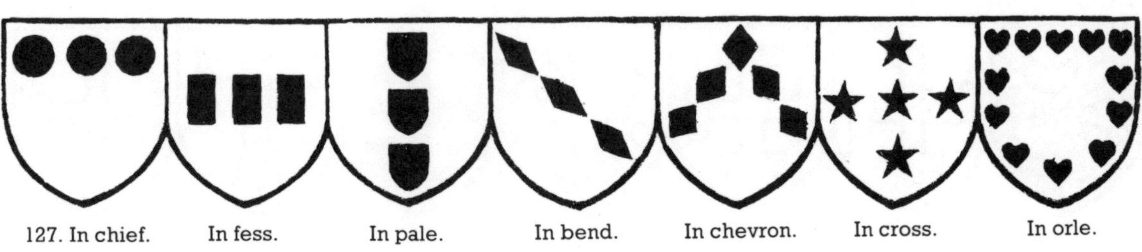

127. In chief. In fess. In pale. In bend. In chevron. In cross. In orle.

* Roundles of different tinctures have distinctive names.

The Cross

The cross, being a simple form, was one of the most common charges to be painted on a shield, and it occurs in a great variety of ornamentally stylized shapes.
As a religious emblem and heraldic symbol of Christian armies in the crusades, the cross belonged to the most important devices of heraldry. As one of the ordinaries, it is subject to all the forms of borderline, such as indented, invected, engrailed, etc.

128. Cross fimbriated. | Cross voided. | Cross quarter-pierced. | Latin cross. | Calvary cross. | Patriarchal cross or cross of Lorraine. | Cross pointed.

129. Cross fourché. | Cross moline. | Cross recercelé. | Cross of Aviz. | Cross of Sant'Jago. | Cross patonce. | Cross flory.

130. Cross floretty. | Cross crosslet. | Cross botonny or treflé. | Cross formy or paty (patté). | Cross of Malta. | Cross formy fitchy. | Cross formy fitchy at the foot.

131. Cross of Toulouse. | Cross cramponned or fylfot. | Cross potent. | Cross millrind. | Cross couped and voided throughout. | Tau cross or St Anthony cross. | Cross pommelled or bourdonné.

132. Cross indented. | Cross wavy or undy. | Cross engrailed. | Cross raguly. | Quarterly a cross counter-changed or cross counter-quartered. | Cross gobony. | Cross counter-gobony.

133. Cross double-parted. | Cross double-parted and fretted. | Cross treble-parted. | Cross triparted and fretted. | Cross fillet. | Cross lozengy-nowed. | Cross nowy.

134. Cross nowy-lozengy. | Cross nowy-quadrat. | Cross cablé. | Cross lozengy, properly or a cross of nine lozenges. | Cross mascle or four mascles conjoined in cross. | Cross of bezants. | Cross of chains.

135. Cross nowy-quadrat couped. | Cross patté double sarcelled at bottom. | Cross couped and fitché at all points. | Cross couped treble-fitché | Cross coronated. | Cross fer-de-moline, pierced lozengy. | Cross avelane.

CHARGES

Human Beings

136. Fortuna, the goddess of good fortune, in the canting arms of Glückstadt (Glück is German for good luck), Schleswig-Holstein, West Germany, 1903.

137. Monk in the canting arms of Munich (München in German: Mönch is a monk), Bavaria, West Germany, 14th century.

138. Justitia, the goddess of law and justice, in the arms of Ilshofen, Württemberg, West Germany, 16th century.

139. The figure of Hope.

140. A king's head couped at the neck, in the arms of Stockholm, Sweden. This is supposed to be King Eric IX, who reigned from 1150 to 1160.

141. A king on his throne could be depicted in many different ways.

142. A Norse warrior on his skis, in the arms of Lillehammer, Norway, confirmed 1898.

143. Moor's head as the crest of pot helm, the arms of Pappenheim, Bavaria, West Germany. This is a version of the crest of the Counts von Pappenheim. These arms are derived from a 14th century seal.

144. A Frisian warrior, in the arms of Wilhelmshaven, Lower Saxony, West Germany, 1949.

Parts of the Human Body

145. Jean de la Champagne, Normandy, France, 15th century.

146. Villiers de L'Isle-Adam, France, 15th century.

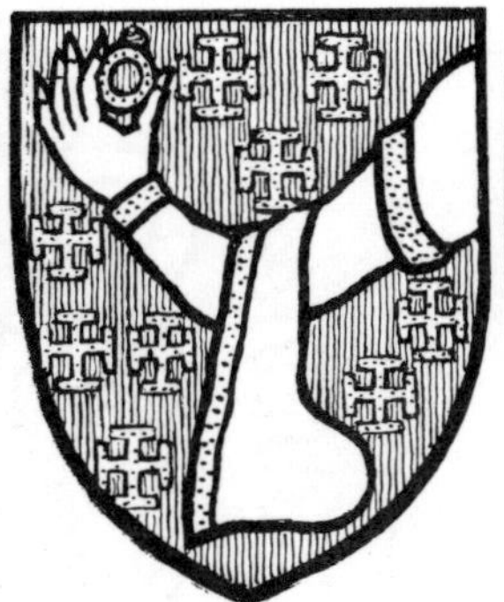

147. Konrad von Lövenich, Germany, 14th century.

148. Jan Raspe, Poland, 15th century, originally from Austria.

Shields of knights from the 14th and 15th century charged with hands and arms.

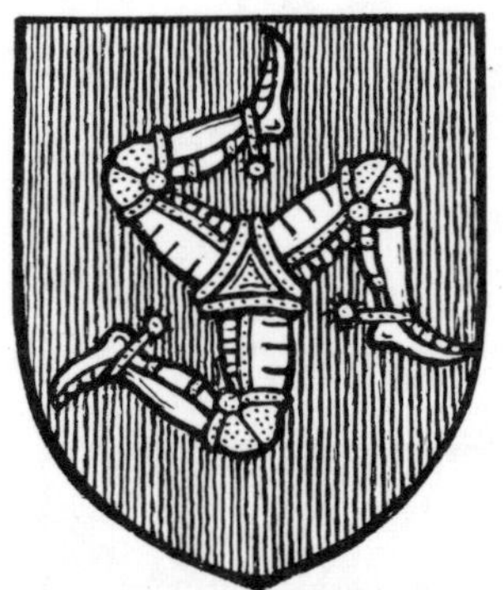

149. Three legs in armour, flexed at the knee and conjoined at the fess point, in the arms of the Isle of Man in the Irish Sea.

150. The crowned bust of a moor, in the arms of Lauingen (Danube), Bavaria, West Germany, 16th century.

151. Three legs flexed at the knee and disposed in triangle, in the arms of Füssen, Bavaria, West Germany, 14th century. Canting arms, since the German word Füsse (pl) means feet in English.

152. Three dexter arms flexed and conjoined at the shoulders, vested and cuffed, the fists clenched.

153. An arm in armour (vambraced). A hand holding a club or a sword often appeared as a crest. This one is embowed fess-wise and couped at the shoulder.

154. A cubit arm erect, habited and cuffed, in the hand a pen.

155. Saracen's head affronté erased at the neck and wreathed about the temples.

156. Janus's head.

Divine Beings, Saints, Religious Symbolism

157. Virgin and Child, in the arms of Altötting, Bavaria, West Germany, 1845.

158. The artists of the Middle Ages often represented Our Lady as surrounded by a flaming glory, wearing a celestial crown and standing on a moon crescent. This was inspired by St John's vision in the Apocalypse. The lily of the sceptre is a symbol of the Holy Virgin.

159. St Christopher bearing the Divine Child, in the arms of Kappeln, Schleswig-Holstein, West Germany, 1959.

160. St Andrew, in the arms of Teisendorf, Bavaria, West Germany.

161. St Hallvard in 1043 tried to save a girl from her pursuers but was killed with arrows. His body, weighted down with a mill-stone, was thrown in the water. The arms of Oslo, capital of Norway, relate to the story.

162. St Vitus, in the arms of Veitshöchheim, Bavaria, West Germany.

163. *Left:* a representation of St Tydfil, in the arms of Merthyr Tydfil, Wales, 1906.

164. *Right:* a cherub, in the arms of Taunton, Somerset, England, 1934.

165. St Sebastian, in the arms of Blonhofen, Bavaria, West Germany, 1836.

166. Our Lord upon the cross, in the arms of Inverness, Scotland, 1900, based upon the obverse of an old seal from 1439.

167. St Martin and the beggar, in the arms of Edingen, Baden, West Germany, 1900, based on a seal c 1600.

168. St Laurentius, in the arms of Bobenheim am Rhein, Rhineland-Palatinate, West Germany, 1928.

169. Our Lord seated upon a throne, a sword issuant from his mouth, in the arms of the see of Chichester, England.

170. St Peter, in the arms of Trier, Rhineland-Palatinate, West Germany, originating in the 15th century.

171. The horseman slaying a dragon, in the arms of Moscow, Russia, has been defined as St George since 1730. The version illustrated is from 1856. See fig. 309.

172. Archangel Michael with a flaming sword, in the arms of the Ukrainian capital Kiev, 1782. See figs. 948 and 949.

173. St Catherine, in the arms of Altena, North Rhine-Westphalia, West Germany, 1928, based on a seal from the 15th century.

174. Cherub.

176. Seraphim.

175. Paschal Lamb (Agnus Dei), in the arms of Brixen (Bressanone), Tirol, Italy. In the arms of Perth, Scotland, the lamb is shown without a halo and the banner is blue, bearing the white cross of St Andrew. The lamb in the arms of Debrecen, Hungary, bears a red banner with a white cross. Such lambs need not be reguardant.

177. A winged bull with a halo is the symbol of St Luke, who was a physician. Legend also made him a painter. See fig. 1075.

178. An eagle with a halo about its head is the symbol of St John the Apostle, it is best known as the badge of Aragon. See fig. 556.

179. A winged lion with a halo about its head is the symbol of St Mark and appears in the arms of Venice.

180. The Archangel Michael holding a balance, in the lower bowl a naked man, in the other the devil. These are the arms of Ludwigsstadt, Bavaria, West Germany, derived from a 14th century seal, the tinctures are since 1819.

181. The winged bull of St Luke issuant from the lower half of an eight-pointed star, in the arms of Sachsenberg, Hesse, West Germany, based on a seal from 1349.

182. The head of St John the Baptist in a cup, in the arms of Künzelsau, Württemberg, West Germany, derived from seals.

The Lion

183. Lion rampant.

The lion has always been the most popular quadruped in heraldry. The king of beasts appears all over Europe in innumerable arms as a charge, also as a crest; and as supporter he probably outnumbers all the other beasts and birds.
The heraldic terms describing its different poses are applied to other beasts as well, unless some different expression is indicated. In British heraldry the lion is supposed to be langued and armed gules, but if it is itself of that tincture or on a red field, tongue and claws should be azure, or of any other colour specified in the blazon. In continental heraldry tongues and claws are often not of a different tincture.

184. The original attitude of the heraldic lion was rampant, and in good heraldry its appearance is rather more stylized than true to nature.
Adaptation from an illustration by René De Cramer, 1913.

185. Lion rampant double-tailed.

186. Lion rampant reguardant.

187. Lion rampant guardant. The French call this a léopard lionné.

188. Lion rampant coward.

189. Lion rampant defamed.

190. Lion passant reguardant.

191. Lion passant. In French heraldry this could also be called a lion léopardé.

192. Lion passant guardant. The French call this a léopard.

193. Lion statant.

194. Lion naissant.

195. Two lions addorsed.

196. Lion issuant.

197. Lion's head contourné and couped.

198. Lion's head erased.

199. Lion's face (in early heraldry this was blazoned a leopard's face).

200. Lions combatant or counter-rampant.

201. A lion's face. Jessant-de-lis.

202. Lion sejant.

203. Lion couchant.

204. Lion dormant.

205. Lion sejant affronté.

206. Three leopards' faces, in the arms of Michael de la Pole, Earl of Suffolk, 1330-1388.

207. Lion tri-corporate. Edmund, Earl of Lancaster, 1245-1296, used a tri-corporate lion on a seal that had two lions in base.

208. Three lions' heads erased, in the arms of Sir Christopher Wren, 1632-1723.

209. Lion in the style of the herald Gelre (Claes Heinen). End of the 14th century.

210. Lion double-headed.

211. Three lions' gambs erased, the putative arms of Jane Austen's father.

212. Crowned lion in the arms of Henry, Landgrave of Thuringia, (+1298). After a drawing by E. Doepler the Younger, 1879.

213. Lion bi-corporate.

214. Crowned lion of the arms of Conrad, Landgrave of Thuringia, (+1241). After a drawing by E. Doepler the Younger, 1879.

Be it as supporters for the shield or as charges, lions have always been very popular in the heraldry of the Low Countries (Belgium and the Netherlands). Of the nine provinces of Belgium only Antwerp has no lion in her arms.

215. West Flanders.

216. East Flanders.

217. Antwerp.

218. Luxemburg.

219. Limburg.

220. Liège.

221. Namur.

222. Hainaut.

223. Brabant.

Other Beasts

224. Greyhound salient, crowned and collared, in the arms of Burgwindheim, Bavaria, West Germany, 1966.

225. Talbot's head erased.

226. Squirrel sejant on a ragged staff holding a nut.

227. Wolf rampant, the arms of Passau, Bavaria, West Germany, 15th century.

228. A boar's head couped close.

229. Bear rampant, muzzled.

230. A boar's head couped at the neck.

231. A hare rampant, in the arms of Hassfurt, Bavaria, West Germany, 1544.

232. A climbing boar, the arms of Ebersberg, Bavaria, West Germany, 1830. Canting arms: Eber is German for boar, Berg for mountain.

233. A beaver rampant, crowned, the arms of Biberach an der Riss, Württemberg, West Germany, 1488. The arms are allusive to the town's name. Biber is the German word for beaver.

The term armed is applied to the horns, claws and teeth of beasts and monsters, and also to the beaks and talons of birds. Thus the animal in fig. 238 would be blazoned an ox passant gules, armed and unguled Or.
Unguled is a term which applies to the hoofs of the bull, horse, stag, etc., if they are of a different tincture from the body of the animal.

234. A horse forcené, in the arms of Stuttgart, Württemberg, West Germany. In its present form the arms originate from the 15th century. The horse is allusive to the name, the German word Stute meaning a mare.

235. An ox passant, suspended from his neck by a ribbon an escutcheon, the arms of Auerbach (Upper Palatinate), Bavaria, West Germany, 1963, based on seals from the 15th century.

236. Buck rampant, the arms of Boxberg, Baden, West Germany, 1959, based upon arms from 1594. The arms are canting as Bock means a buck in German and Berg means mountain.

237. The front part of a horse in gallop, bridled, in the arms of Pardubice, Czechoslovakia, used since the 14th century and alluding to a story about an ancestor of the lords of Pardubice, whose horse was cut in half by a portcullis in the attack on Milan in 1158.

238. Ox passant (ox fording a stream), in the canting arms of Oxford, England. Recorded at the visitation in 1634.

239. A buck rampant, in the arms of Chur, Switzerland. Animals in Swiss heraldry are usually 'over-sexed'.

240. A horse passant, in the allusive arms of Horsens, Denmark, c 1300. The ancient Danish word hors had the same meaning as the English word horse.

241. A bull or steer rampant, in the canting arms of Torino, Italy. The Italian word toro means bull.

242. Bull rampant guardant, in the arms of Tyrstrup, Denmark, 1951. Tyr is the Danish word for bull.

243. A stag's head cabossed, in the arms of Hørsholm, Denmark, 1938. The Danish name is probably derived from the German Hirsch, meaning a stag and the Danish holm, meaning a small peninsula.

244. A stag springing (or salient) charged on the shoulder with an escutcheon, in the arms of Hirschau, Bavaria, West Germany. The German word Hirsch means stag and Au means meadow.

245. A bear's head erased, in the arms of Sjöbo, Sweden, 1969.

246. A stag trippant, in the arms of Gérardmer, Lorraine, France. A running animal of the deer type is termed at speed, in full chase or courant. A stag statant and looking at the spectator is not statant guardant but at gaze.

247. A bear's face, crowned, in the arms of Pori, Finland, derived from a 17th century seal. A canting charge since the Swedish name of the town is Björneborg. Björn means bear and borg means a fortified castle.

248. A polar bear sejant, the arms of Greenland, this also appears in the royal arms of Denmark. See fig. 967.

249. Ram rampant, crowned with an eastern crown, in the arms of the Canton Schaffhausen, Switzerland. The arms evolved from the arms of the town of Schaffhausen (known from the 13th century) in which a sheep (Schaf in German) is coming out of a building (Haus).

250. Ram's head affronté, in the arms of Assing, Denmark, 1965.

251. Bear rampant, in the arms of the Swiss Canton Appenzell Innerrhoden, derived from the arms of the ancient monastery of Saint Gall, 13th century.

Fish

252. Dolphin hauriant.

253. Dolphin naiant embowed.

254. Dolphin hauriant.

The heraldic dolphin has little in common with the fish thus named. It appears in various decoratively stylized forms and is shaped like a question mark (?). In French heraldry it is usually shaped like an increscent (fig. 252).

255. Fish hauriant, (palewise, head upwards).

256. Fish naiant, (fesswise).

257. Fish urinant, (palewise, head in base).

A fish may be finned or scaled of different tinctures. The famous arms of the Dauphins of Viennois were: Or, a dolphin hauriant azure, finned gules. See fig. 578.

258. Two fish respecting. Back to back they would be two fish addorsed. See fig. 262.

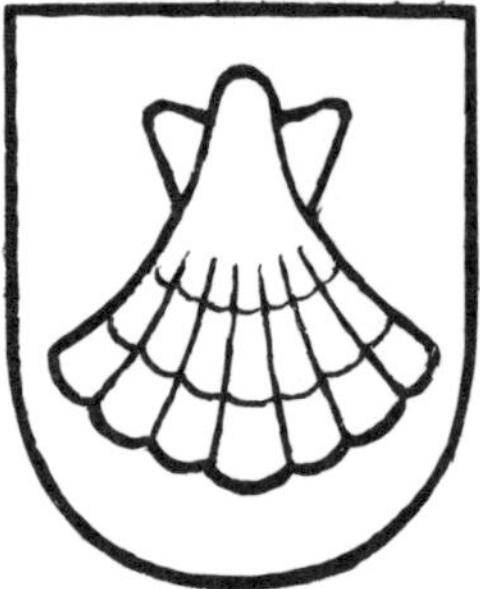

259. The escallop, a cockle-shell, is the emblem of St James, patron of pilgrims.

260. A lobster.

261. Three fish interchangeably posed.

262. Two pikes addorsed, the arms of the family de la Chappelle, followers of the Count of Flanders, 15th century.

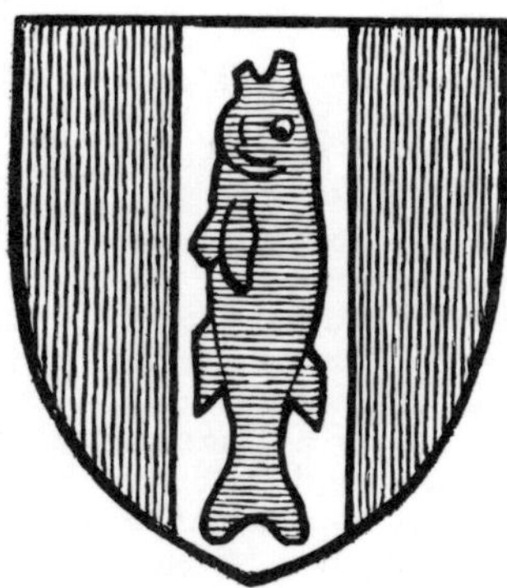

263. A fish hauriant, in the arms of Kaiserslautern, Rhineland-Palatinate, West Germany, derived from a seal of the 17th century.

264. Three turbots hauriant, the arms of a Dutch knight, Bott Dezeme, 15th century.

265. Two fish naiant, the arms of Forchheim, Bavaria, West Germany, 13th century. The name of the town is traced back to Forchen (pl), an ancient word meaning trout in English.

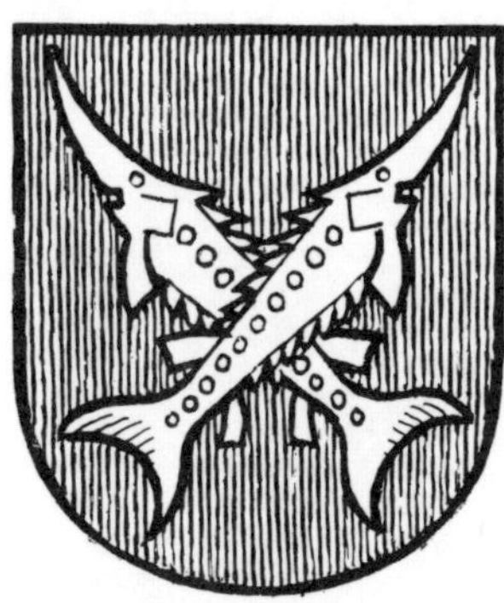

266. Two sturgeons crossed in saltire, the arms of Tsaritsyn, Russia, 1857. From 1925 to 1961 the city's name was Stalingrad and since then it has been Volgograd.

267. A salmon embowed hauriant, in the arms of Tørring, Denmark, 1953.

268. Three fish in pale counter-naiant, the arms of the Dutch commune Enkhuizen, North Holland, Netherlands, 1816.

269. Two barbels hauriant and addorsed, in the arms of Freudenstadt, Württemberg, West Germany, 1601.

270. A dolphin naiant, the arms of Vejlby-Strib, Denmark, 1939.

271. An eel hauriant embowed, crowned and winged. The wrongly canting arms of Ahlen, North Rhine-Westphalia. Developed from a 13th century seal, granted in its present form in 1910. An eel is Aal in German.

The Eagle and the Falcon

272. Eagle displayed.

The eagle holds the same pre-eminent position among the birds that the lion holds among other animals. The terms used to describe the eagle's poses are used for the other birds, unless some special expression is indicated. Usually the beak, tongue and talons are in a tincture different from that of the body but not always, for instance not in Italian heraldry. If they are, the eagle is blazoned as langued and armed of a particular colour.

277. The original attitude of the heraldic eagle was displayed, and in good heraldry its appearance is rather more stylized than true to nature.

273. Double-headed eagle.

274. Eagle rising or rousant.

275. Eagle displayed, wings inverted.

276. Eagle close or trussed.

278. Double-headed eagle.

Figs. 273 and 275 are from a design by Gerald Cobb. Figs. 277 and 278 are from a design by René De Cramer, 1913.

The double-headed eagles of the Austrian and Russian monarchies disappeared in 1918 and 1917. The Yugoslavian double-headed eagle disappeared during World War II. Today Albania is the only country to have a double-headed eagle as its state emblem.

279. Eagle from about 1300. Montbrison (Loire), France.

280. Eagle in the style of the *Armorial Wijnbergen,* 1265-1288.

281. Eagle in the style of the *Armorial Bellenville,* from c 1364-1386.

282. Eagle rising, head turned to sinister, the arms of the German knight Richard von Blankenburg, in an armorial document from 1361 in Mantua, Italy.

283. The Polish eagle, 14th century.

284. Eagle from the second half of the 12th century, time of Emperor Frederick I Barbarossa.

285. Napoleon I chose the eagle of Jupiter standing on a thunderbolt as his imperial arms. In ancient Rome this appeared in the signa of the legions.

286. The double-headed eagle of the Holy Roman Empire, an adaptation from a woodcut by Albrecht Dürer c 1520. The inescutcheon is per pale Austria and Burgundy ancient.

287. Another form of Napoleonic eagle. These arms were used a second time under Napoleon III. They are still the arms of la Maison Napoléon.

288. Wings conjoined in lure. Arms of Seymour: gules, a pair of wings inverted conjoined in lure Or.

289. The American or bald eagle in the seal of the United States is proper, meaning of natural colours (brown with a white head). These arms were created in 1782.

290. A vol (wings conjoined in base).

291. An alerion (without beak and legs). Arms of Lorraine: Or, on a bend gules three alerions argent.

292. The eagle in the state seal of Mexico, model of 1968, shows the influence of native art and has little in common with heraldic forms in Europe. The design relates to the foundation of Tenochtitlan in the mythology of the Aztecs.

293. A falcon close, belled and jessed.

294. An eagle's head couped.

295. An eagle's leg erased at the thigh.

296. Two wings endorsed.

297. An eagle's head erased.

298. Falcon's leg erased at the thigh, belled, jessed and varvelled.

299. The eagle of the German empire, 1871-1918, charged on the breast with an escutcheon of Prussia. If it was displayed on a (golden) shield, the crown above the head and the collar of the Order of the Black Eagle were left out. Instead the shield was encircled with the collar and ensigned with the imperial crown. See fig. 311.

300. Falcon's head erased. In heraldry the eagle's head and neck are tufted, while the falcon's are smooth.

301. Arms of the Kingdom of Serbia (the Kingdom of the Serbs, Croats and Slovenes, 1918, Yugoslavia, 1929). The double-headed eagle and the inescutcheon relate to a historical connection with the Byzantine empire.*

302. Arms of the Austrian Land Tirol. The coronet on the eagle's head appeared for the first time on seals in 1416, the green wreath appeared on coins in 1567.

304. The 'small' arms of imperial Austria, 1915. See fig. 312.

303. Falcon belled and jessed, the head hooded.

305. Eagle's leg conjoined to a sinister wing.

*Stephen Nemanya (1168-1196) established Serbia's independence from Byzantium and adopted her double-headed eagle, in silver instead of gold.

306 *left* and 307 *right.* The wings of the eagles are charged with Kleestengel (the literal translation is clover-stalks).
The inescutcheon in the arms of Brandenburg is the insigne of an arch-chamberlain (literal translation of Erzkämmerer) of the Holy Roman Empire. The bonnet on the head of the eagle refers to the dignity of Kurfürst (prince elector) of the Margrave of Brandenburg.

Arms of the Kingdom of Prussia and of the province of East Prussia up to the end of World War I.
The initials F R stand for Fridericus Rex (the first king of Prussia).

Arms of the province of Brandenburg of the Kingdom of Prussia up to the end of World War I.

308. Eagle with two additional heads on the wings, from c 1300. Arms of Reinmar von Zweter in the *Codex Manesse.*

310. Eagle of the Holy Roman Empire, from c 1300. *Codex Manesse.*

309. The 'small' arms of imperial Russia, 1857-1917. In this version the double-headed eagle acts as supporter for the arms of Moscow, which are in the centre surrounded by the collar of the Order of St Andrew. The arms of Kazan, Poland, Taurida and Kiev (with Novgorod and Vladimir) are on the dexter wing. The arms of Astrakhan, Siberia, Georgia and Finland are on the sinister wing. Tsar Ivan III, 1462-1505, married to Zoë (Sophia), niece of the last emperor of Constantinople, regarded himself as the heir to the Byzantine empire and took the Byzantine double-headed eagle as his device.

311. Arms of the Federal Republic of Germany (West Germany), 1950. The eagle's wings are inverted, but if the eagle is used without the shield they are elevated and displayed. This is a modernized form of the ancient imperial arms illustrated in the *Codex Manesse* from c 1300.

312. Arms of the Federal Republic of Austria, 1945. The mural crown stands for the burgher, the sickle for the farmer and the hammer for the workman. The broken chain was added in 1945 and distinguishes the arms from the ones of 1919.

Other Birds

313. A moor hen or moorfowl reguardant, the arms of Brande, Denmark, 1942.

314. A heron volant, in the arms of Dover, Denmark, 1950. The arms became obsolete in 1966 when Dover was fused with other communities (Ry).

315. A swallow volant, in the arms of Gladsaxe, Denmark, 1948.

316. Pelican, vulning its breast.

317. A cormorant, in the beak a branch of seaweed called laver, the arms of Liverpool, Lancashire, England, 1797.

318. A pelican in its piety (standing in its nest, wounding its breast to feed its young).

319. A swan rising or rousant, wings displayed and inverted, in the allusive arms of Unterschwaningen, Bavaria, West Germany, 1860.

320. A crane rising or rousant, wings elevated and displayed, in the allusive arms of Kransberg, Hesse, West Germany, 1953.

321. A cock or dunghill cock, the arms of Seelze, Lower Saxony, West Germany, 1934.

322. An owl, in the arms of Planegg, Bavaria, West Germany, 1951.

Swans, herons, cranes, ducks, geese, etc., are not said to be armed like the eagle. If their beaks and legs are different in tincture from the rest of their bodies, they are blazoned as beaked and membered.
A cock is armed, crested and jelloped of a certain tincture (meaning his beak and spurs, his comb and his wattles).

The Fabulous Creatures of Heraldry

323. Griffin striking fire with steel and flint (belonging to the insignia of the Golden Fleece). Adaptation from a woodcut by Albrecht Dürer, 1515.
The griffin or griffon, a fabulous animal half eagle and half lion, is the monster that occurs most frequently in armory. Its ancestors can be found in the art of ancient Babylon, Syria and Greece, as symbols of divine power and as guardians of the divine.

324. The golden dragon was the symbol of the imperial family of China.

325. A Russian design for a dragon.

326. Male griffin segreant.

327. A griffin in the rampant position is said to be segreant. See fig. 551.

328. Heraldic tiger or tyger.

329. Wyvern with wings displayed. The wyvern of English heraldry is green, the rolls of armour on its chest and tail and the inside of its wings are red.

330. Basilisk, in the arms of Kazan, Russia, 1781, based on a seal from the late 16th century.

331. Dragon rampant (or segreant). The red dragon of Wales is passant. Dragons appear statant and sometimes displayed although this is rare.

332. Heraldic panther, in the arms of Graz, Styria, Austria, 13th century.

333. Cockatrice.

334. Heraldic panther, in the arms of Ingolstadt, Bavaria, West Germany, 14th century.

335. Wyvern.

336. A Lindwurm (in German heraldry, a dragon quite often without wings), in the arms of Murnau, Bavaria, West Germany. Known from a seal of the 14th century.

In the mythology of ancient Greece and the northern countries, the dragon was a guardian of oracle founts, virgins and treasure. As a military emblem it was used by nearly all the nations of antiquity. In heraldry the dragon is used as a charge, as a crest and as a supporter.

337. Dragon, in the arms of Lindenhardt, Bavaria, West Germany, 1567.

338. An enfield rampant gules appears as a charge and a supporter in the achievement of the London borough of Enfield.

339. An opinicus appears as crest (an opinicus statant Or) of the Worshipful Company of Barbers of the City of London.

340. The troll of northern mythology is known in this form from scandinavian heraldry. See fig. 836.

341. Sea-lion. See figs. 362 and 690.

342. Heraldic antelope or ibex.

343. The yale appears for the first time in heraldry as a supporter of the arms of John, Duke of Bedford and Earl of Kendal, 1389-1435. His earldom of Kendal and the dukedom of Somerset were granted in 1443 to Sir John Beaufort who took the eagle and Bedford yale as supporters. The Beaufort yale was white, semé of bezants, maned, unguled and armed Or.

The English heralds have contributed several extremely imaginative monsters to the menagerie of heraldry. These include the enfield, the opinicus, the yale, the pantheon and the bagwyn. There are others not given here. These beasts are not known in continental heraldry.

344.

345.

The salamander (spirit of fire) was the famous badge of King Francis I of France, 1515-1547, and appears as a charge in the arms of Le Havre and Fontainebleau. In heraldry it is often tinctured vert but can be of any other colour or metal. (The salamander of nature resembles a lizard but is scaleless and has a soft moist skin which in the case of the Feuersalamander (German, Feuer — fire) is black with irregular bright yellow spots.)

346. In heraldry the legendary phoenix resembles an eagle (sometimes with one or more long feathers on its head) rising from flames.

347. Pegasus forcené. The pegasus is a creature of Greek mythology, a symbol of poetic inspiration. It has been used as an emblem of air-transport in modern times.

348. Unicorn salient, in the arms of Saint-Lo, France.

349. A unicorn rampant. The unicorn often appears in paintings, prints and tapestries as a symbol of virginity, and it was mentioned by Aristotle and Plinius.

350. A sea-horse should have webbed feet in English heraldry.

351. Lion with the head of a king (German).

352. An eagle with the head of a goat was the heraldic device of the Counts von Ziegenhain. It appears today in the arms of the Hessian towns of Neukirchen, Schwarzenborn and Treysa, West Germany.

There are several other hybrids in heraldry, not illustrated here. These include the were-wolf or man-wolf (a man's head on a wolf's body), winged monkeys, winged stags, sea-dogs, sea-cats and many others.

353. The pantheon, as illustrated in Prince Arthur's Book, 16th century, supporting a banner of Sir William Paulet (Marquess of Winchester in 1551). The pantheon's tincture is purple, powdered with golden stars (estoiles). It has golden hooves and a gold crown about its neck.

354. A cock with the head of a goat, the arms of Ziegenhain, Hesse, West Germany, early 16th century. Ziege is German for goat.

355. The bagwyn, as illustrated in Prince Arthur's Book, supporting a banner of the arms of the Earl of Arundel (died 1580). This animal is black, but the horns and the long hair of the lower part of the tail are golden.

Figs. 353 and 355 are adaptations from drawings by A. C. Cole.

356. The triton or merman is sometimes depicted holding a trident, sometimes blowing a murex (shell).

357. A mermaid with two fishtails, the arms of Isen, Bavaria, West Germany, 1548.

358. The mermaid is often depicted holding a mirror and combing her hair.

359. There is a crowned harpy like this one, but with golden legs and talons, in the arms of Liechtenstein, where it represents East Frisia in changed tinctures. See figs. 455 and 898.

360. A siren or mermaid, in the arms of Warsaw, Poland, 18th century (present form). Her body is flesh-coloured, the fishtail argent.

361. An eagle with a king's head, in the great arms of Nuremberg, Bavaria, West Germany, 1936, known since the 13th century from seals. During the 15th century it turned into a harpy but is now used as shown above.

362. A sea-lion should have webbed feet in English heraldry.

363. A harpy issuant, crowned, in the arms of Emden, Lower Saxony, West Germany, 1495. See harpy in fig. 455.

364. Lion-dragon.

In Greek fable the centaurs were a wild tribe living in the mountains of Thessaly.

365. Centaur, sometimes used as a symbol for the art of equitation.

366. A sagittarius is a centaur shooting with bow and arrow. According to Greek mythology, after his death, the learned centaur Chiron (a great teacher in the art of healing) was placed amongst the stars at the order of Zeus, and his constellation was called Sagittarius.

367. A half man and half lion sagittarius is one of the arms attributed to King Stephen of England, c 1097-1154.*

368.

369.

The chimera was a she-monster originating from Greek mythology. According to Homer it is a mixture of lion, goat and serpent. According to some heraldists it is depicted with the head and the breast of a woman, the forepaws of a lion, the body of a goat, the hind legs of a griffin and the tail of a serpent. Others illustrate it as a goat with a lion's head and a dragon's tail. There seem to be several versions, even winged ones.

370. A sphinx couchant with wings, could also be depicted with the headgear of an Egyptian sphinx. The sphinx appears not only as charge but also as crest or supporter.

371. Greek sphinx.

372. Egyptian sphinx.

373. Assyrian sphinx.

*Adapted from *The Royal Heraldry of England* by J. H. and R. V. Pinches, Heraldry Today, 1974.

Sun, Moon and Stars

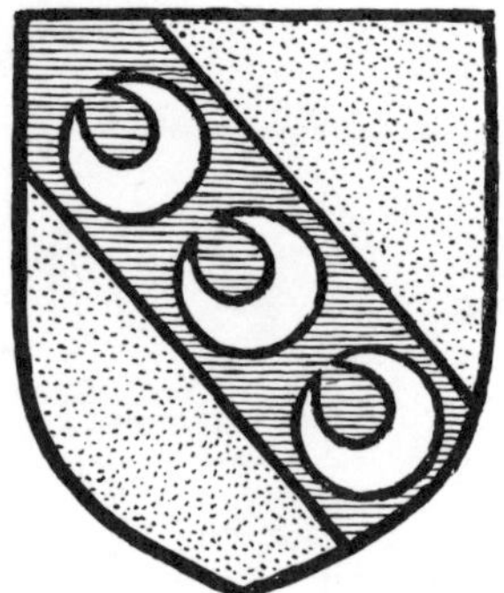

374. On a bend three crescents, in the arms of Lunéville, Lorraine, France.

375. A crescent increscent and a star of five points within its horns, in the arms of Nykøbing S, Denmark, derived from a 14th century seal.

376. A crescent between two six-pointed stars, one in chief and one in base, in the arms of Halle an der Saale, East Germany.

377. Sun in his splendour, in the arms of Banbury, Oxfordshire, England, 1951.

378. A five-pointed star (here stella maris), in the arms of the Dutch city of Maastricht, approved in 1819.

379. Crescent ensigned by an estoile of eight points, in the arms of Portsmouth, Hampshire, England, recorded at the visitation of 1686.

380. The estoile is a star of six wavy rays. If there are more than six rays, the number should be mentioned in the blazon.

381. Crescent decrescent.

382. Sun in his splendour (or in his glory). This is also depicted without a human face.

383. Molet or mullet, derived from molette, a spur-rowel. In Europe and Scotland the molet is a star of five points. In Scotland a pierced molet is a spur-rowel.

384. A star of six points is called a molet of six points in England.

Flowers, Trees, Plants and Leaves

385. Rose of the German princely house of Lippe. The tincture of a rose must be mentioned in the blazon since a rose proper is a natural and not a stylized one. See fig. 621.

386. The Luther rose. In 1530 Martin Luther stayed in Coburg and Prince John Frederick had a signet ring made for him engraved with this rose, which Luther called the badge of his theology.

387. The Tudor rose. The supporters of Lancaster used a red rose as their badge, those of York used a white rose. The two roses were united into the Tudor rose by Henry VII. See page 216.

388. A fleur-de-lis, in the canting arms of Lille, France, 1199.

389. From an early date the fleur-de-lis has been used as a charge all over Europe. It is a symbol of the Holy Virgin, and became particularly famous through the arms of the kings of France.

390. A conventional fleur-de-lis and three natural but stylized lilies in the arms of Eton College, Buckinghamshire, England.

391. A German fleur-de-lis from the 16th century. See fig. 623.

392. A fleur-de-lis, in the allusive arms of Florence, Italy.

393. An oak tree eradicated, in the arms of Hagen, North Rhine-Westphalia, West Germany, 1931, based on a grant of 1897.

394. On a triple mount in base three pine trees, the arms of Braunlage, Lower Saxony, West Germany, 1935.

395. On a mount in base a conventionalized linden tree, the arms of Homburg, Saarland, West Germany, 1937.

396. A stylized beech tree eradicated, the arms of Hagenbach, Rhineland-Palatinate, West Germany, based on a 13th century seal.

397. Three birch leaves pallwise, their stems conjoined in fesspoint, in the arms of Karislojo, Nylands län, Finland, 1965.

398. The thistle, famous in heraldry as the floral badge of Scotland.

399. An oak tree eradicated and fructed, in the arms of Offenbach am Main, Hesse, West Germany.

400. Three oak leaves pallwise between two acorns, the stems conjoined in fesspoint, the arms of Tammela, Tavastehus län, Finland, 1953.

401. The stock of a birch tree couped and eradicated sprouting therefrom two sprigs, each with three leaves, the arms of Karttula, Kuopio län, Finland, 1965.

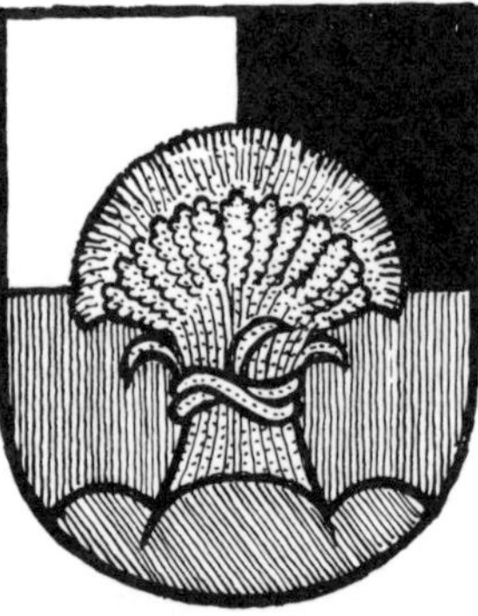

402. A garb of rye, in the arms of Röckingen, Bavaria, West Germany, based on arms from 1618.

403. Three ears of rye, in the arms of Rockenhausen, Rhineland-Palatinate, West Germany, 1844, based on older arms.

In both cases the rye, in German Roggen, is a play on the name of the town.

404. Three vine leaves sprouting from a branch couped, the arms of Stavanger, Norway, based on a seal from the late 16th century.

405. The 'still life' of three tulips in a vase, the arms of Dundee, Scotland, is a unique charge in civic arms.

406. Trefoil slipped.

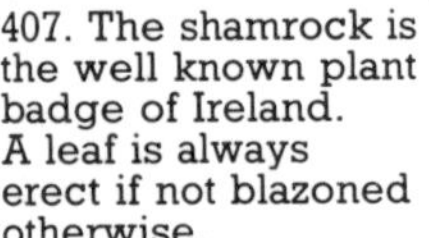

407. The shamrock is the well known plant badge of Ireland. A leaf is always erect if not blazoned otherwise.

408. Cinquefoil pierced.

409. A branch fesswise couped sprouting therefrom a twig embowed, bearing three linden leaves, the arms of Rotenburg a.d. Fulda, Hesse, West Germany, 1605.

Towers, Castles and Other Buildings

410. Tower.

411. Tower.

412. A stone wall embattled and arched.

413. Citadel.

Adaptations from the *European Armorial* (probably) by Jean le Fèvre, herald of the Order of the Golden Fleece, 15th century.

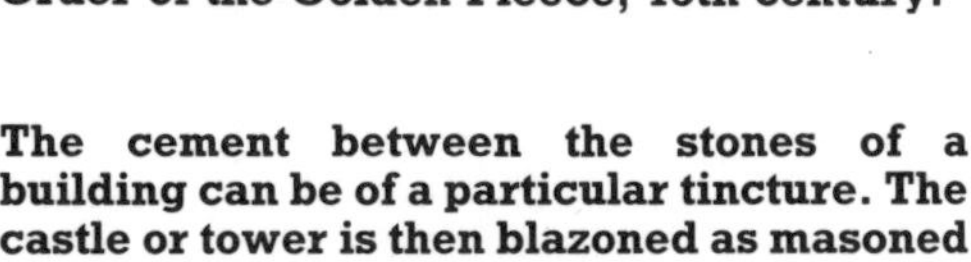

The cement between the stones of a building can be of a particular tincture. The castle or tower is then blazoned as masoned of such.

414. A castle triple-towered, folding doors open and portcullis raised.

415. A tower, in the arms of Épinal, Lorraine, France.

416. A tower triple-towered.

Ports and windows can be of a tincture different from that of the building.

417. A tower, in the arms of Vaucouleurs, Lorraine, France.

418. A tower senestrée d'un avant-mur.

419. When the term castle is used in British heraldry it usually signifies two round towers which are connected by a wall containing a port in which a portcullis may be shown. See fig. 427.

420. Castle, French style, château.
The port is coloured as the field.

421. Tower inflamed.

422. Arch on three steps, folding doors open.

423. Tent, ensigned with a pennon.

424. Windmill. Different types of windmills are used in heraldry. See fig. 1029.

425. A mill-stone charged with a mill-rind (mill iron or fer-de-moulin).

426. Different types of mill-rind.

427. Portcullis. The portcullis was a badge of the Beauforts, King Henry VII and Henry VIII, used this badge to show their Beaufort descent. See fig. 387 and page 216.

428. Padlock.

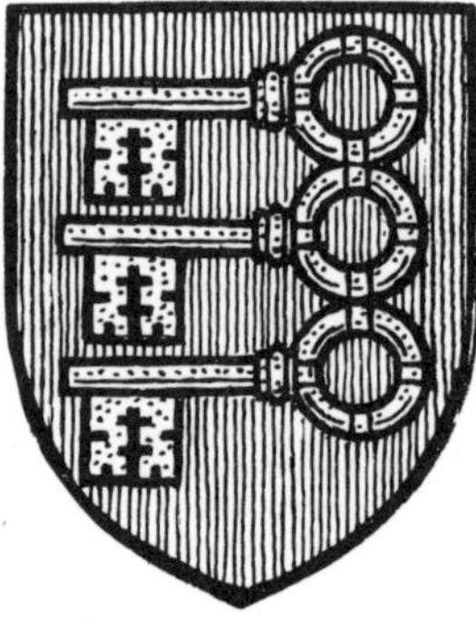

429. Three keys barwise in pale, the arms of Avignon, France, granted by Pope Clement VI in 1342. Two keys palewise, the wards upwards and outwards are said to be addorsed. See fig. 568.

430. Three keys, the arms of Oostende, Flanders, Belgium, 1831. The wards of those in chief are upwards and inwards. The key in base has its ward to the dexter.

431. Two keys crossed in saltire, the emblem of St Peter. In this position keys usually have the wards upwards and outwards. See fig. 1126.

432. A bridge of three arches connecting two towers, in the arms of Pont a Mousson, Lorraine, France. Canting arms as the French word pont means bridge.

433. A bridge of three arches, in the arms of Salamanca, Spain.

434. A bridge of one arch surmounted by three towers, in the arms of Cambridge, England, 1575.

Bridges are of various forms. The number of arches should be specified in the blazon.

435. Bridge of two arches triple-towered. French style, pont fortifié a deux arches.

436. Bridge of three arches embattled.

437. An arch and a double arch.

438. A church, in the arms of Slangerup, Denmark, derived from a 14th century seal.

439. Church.

440. Church, in the arms of Waldkirchen, Bavaria, West Germany, 1637.

In civic heraldry local castles, towers, churches and bridges sometimes appear as stylized charges.

441. Towergate with two alcoves, the arms of Vechta, Lower Saxony, West Germany, 1955, based on a 14th century seal.

442. Three houses, the arms of Dorfen, Bavaria, West Germany, derived from 14th century seals. The arms are canting since the German word Dorf means a village.

443. A wall without port, turreted with one tower, the arms of Schleswig, Schleswig-Holstein, West Germany, 1933, based on the first seal from 1299.

444. Wall turreted with three towers, arms of Oldenburg, 1927, based on a seal from the 15th century. The escutcheon in the port bears the arms of the house of Oldenburg.

445. The castle in the arms of Edinburgh, Scotland. (The colour of the mountain is of greyish rock). Registered 1732.

446. Three towers, the arms of Copenhagen, capital of Denmark, 1661. A tower with a cupola is said to be domed.

447. A castle, in the canting arms of Castile, Spain. This would be a tower triple-towered to a British heraldist. See fig. 556.

448. A castle, in the arms of Salzburg, Austria. Various conventionalized forms of castle appeared in town seals from the 13th century.

449. Three castles inflamed, in the arms of Dublin, Ireland.

Ships and Anchors

450. The hull of a ship with one mast, 15th century.

451. Ship with one mast in full sail, flag flying. A cog, from an early 15th century seal.

452. A boat, 15th century.

Figs. 450 and 452 are adaptations from the *European Armorial* (probably) by Jean le Fèvre, herald of the Golden Fleece, 15th century.

453. A sailing boat, in the arms of Geesthacht, Schleswig-Holstein, West Germany, 1915.

454. A boat with one oar, in the arms of Schifferstadt, Rhineland-Palatinate, West Germany, 1966, based on a seal from the 16th century.

455. Ship with three masts, each ensigned with a spur-rowel, hanging from the main mast an escutcheon*, the arms of Greetsiel, Lower Saxony, West Germany, 1963.

456. Anchor erect. The crossbeam, if of a different colour, is blazoned as timbered of such a tincture.

457. Anchor erect, the arms of Narvik, Norway.

458. Anchor erect and cabled. If the lower part with the barbs is of a different tincture, this is blazoned as fluked of such colour.

*Arms of the Cirksena, princes of East Frisia.

459. Galley or lymphad in full sail.

460. A Hansa cog in the arms of Bremerhaven, West Germany, 1947. The first sail bears the arms of Bremerhaven. The anchor and the fish are the devices of Geestemünde. The scythes belong to Lehe. The three towns were fused in 1947.

461. Galley or lymphad, sails furled, flag and pennants flying and oars in action.

462. Ship of French design (in full sail, pennant flying).

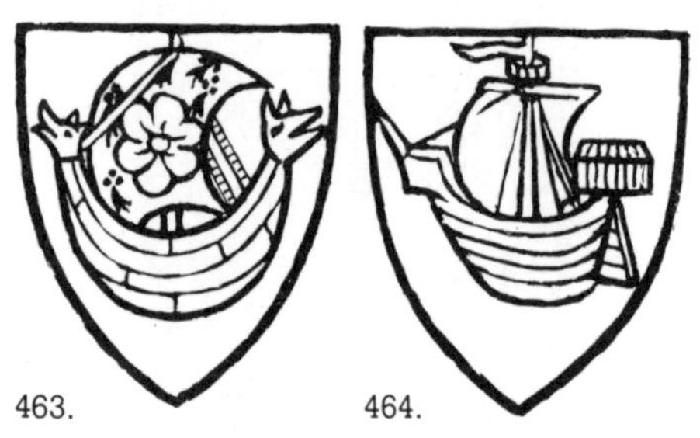

463. 464.

Two arms with ships in full sail, 15th century. Adaptations from the *European Armorial.*

465. Ship of Swedish design (sail furled, pennant and flags flying).

466. An early boat, in the arms of Helsinki, capital of Finland.

467. Portuguese design of a carrack in full sail, pennants flying.

468. Mediaeval ship in the arms of Helsingør, Denmark, derived from a 13th century seal.

469. Boat, in the arms of Kiel, Schleswig-Holstein, West Germany, 1901, derived from a 14th century seal. See fig. 504.

470. A two-masted ship in full sail, pennants flying, the arms of Spiekeroog, Lower Saxony, West Germany, 1968.

471. A three-masted ship in full sail, pennants flying, the arms of San Sebastián, Spain.

472. A three-masted ship in full sail, flag and pennants flying, the arms of La Rochelle, France, derived from the 13th century. See fig. 986.

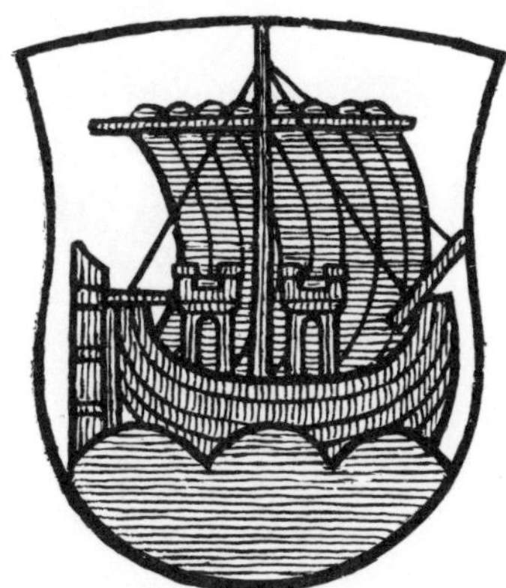

473. A 14th century warship, in the arms of Stubbekøbing, Denmark, derived from a 14th century seal.

474. A three-masted ship (galleon) in full sail, pennants flying, the arms of Nantes, France. The ermine in chief represents the arms of Bretagne.

475. Barquentine in full sail, flying at the foremast a flag, in the arms of Lower Hutt, New Zealand, English grant 1955.

476. Mediaeval ship, in the arms of Lisbon, capital of Portugal, derived from a stone sculpture from 1336.

477. Two merchant ships, in the arms of Marstal, Denmark, 1913.

Weapons

478. Two broad axes crossed in saltire, in the canting arms of Biel (Bienne) in Switzerland. The German word Beil means a hatchet.

479. A bow and arrow in full draught, in the arms of the Finnish province of Savolax, and for Kuopio län. The arrow is barbed and flighted, the bow is stringed (of a different tincture).

480. Two swords crossed in saltire, points upwards, in the arms of Abensberg, Bavaria, West Germany, 1809. The swords are hilted and pommelled (of a different tincture).

481. Two halberds crossed in saltire, the arms of Hallstadt, Bavaria, West Germany.

482. Scimitar fesswise, point to dexter, hilted and pommelled (of a different tincture), in the arms of Astrakhan, Russia, 1856.

483. Cannon, in the arms of Smolensk, Russia, 1780.

484. Spearhead, the arms of Trieste, Italy, version of 1919. The original arms, granted by Emperor Frederick III in 1466, were more elaborate. The spearhead is the symbol of St Sergius, patron of the city.

485. Sword palewise, in the arms of Alost (Aalst), Belgium. The sword is accompanied in chief by the arms of the Holy Roman Empire (dexter) and of Flanders (sinister).

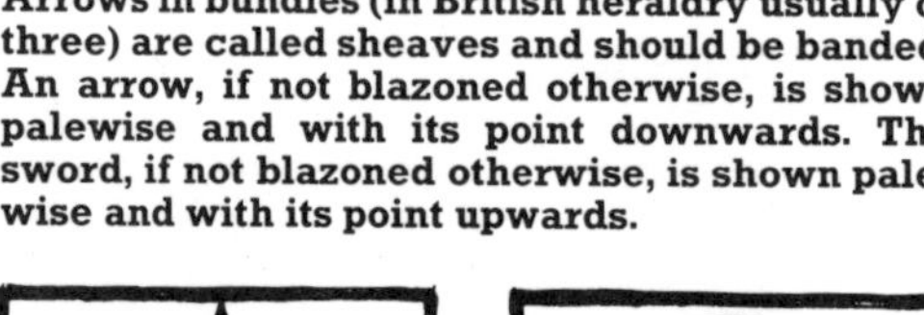

Arrows in bundles (in British heraldry usually of three) are called sheaves and should be banded. An arrow, if not blazoned otherwise, is shown palewise and with its point downwards. The sword, if not blazoned otherwise, is shown palewise and with its point upwards.

486. A battle-axe.

487. A crossbow.

488. Sword palewise, supporting with its point in chief a crown. The arms of Domremy, Lorraine, France. These are actually the arms of Jeanne d'Arc and her brothers, granted in 1429 by Charles VII, King of France.

THE HELM, CREST AND MANTLING

The collective term timbre describes the crest or the crested helm or other objects placed above the shield, such as crowns and mitres. The helm (helmet, heaume) with its crest and mantling is the most important appurtenance of an achievement (complete display of armorial bearings). During the early 13th century it gained such importance in Germany that it even appeared on seals without the shield.

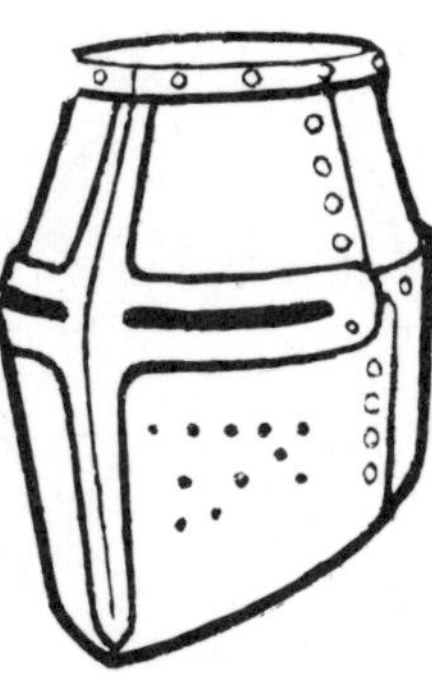

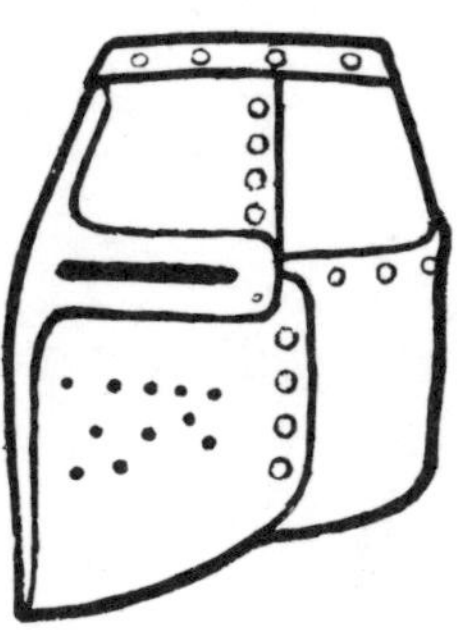

490. Pot helm from the first half of the 14th century. The pot helm was worn over a coif which was covered by a closely fitting hood of chain mail.

489. Knight of the early 14th century. His arms are displayed on the shield and on the horse's caparison, his crest is also placed on the horse's head. Adaptation from a seal of André II of Savoy.

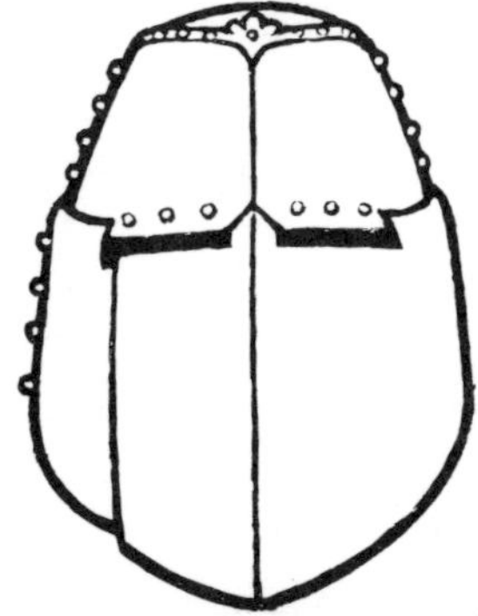

491. Pot helm from the second half of the 14th century. The left side is enforced (strengthened with a steel plate). The top is lined with leather.

492. Crested helm of Edward, Prince of Wales, called the Black Prince, 1330-1376, from his tomb at Canterbury. (The lion stands on a cap of maintenance, also called chapeau.)

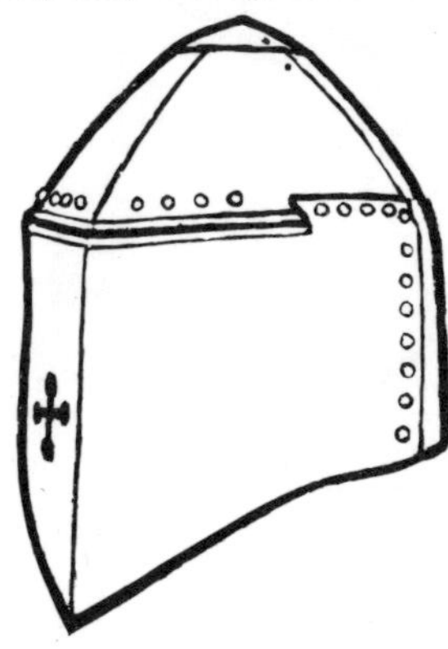

493. Barrel helm or great helm from the second half of the 14th century. This type of helm must be distinguished from the pot helm. It is not flat on top and its weight rested on the shoulders.

494. Knight of the second half of the 14th century. The crested great helm would be worn over the bassinet. Adaptation from an effigy of a member of the von Steinberg family in St Martin's Church, Hildesheim, West Germany.

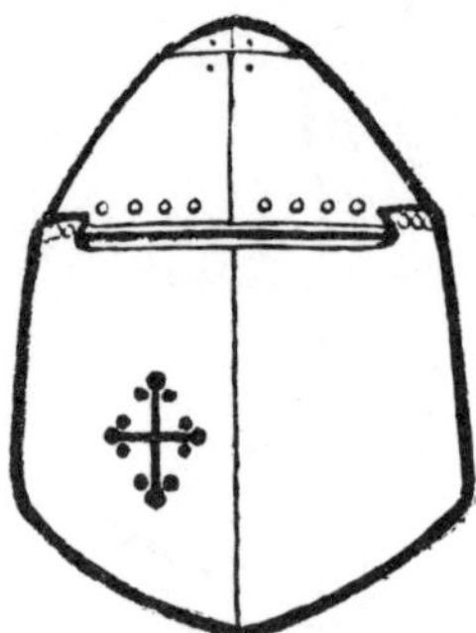

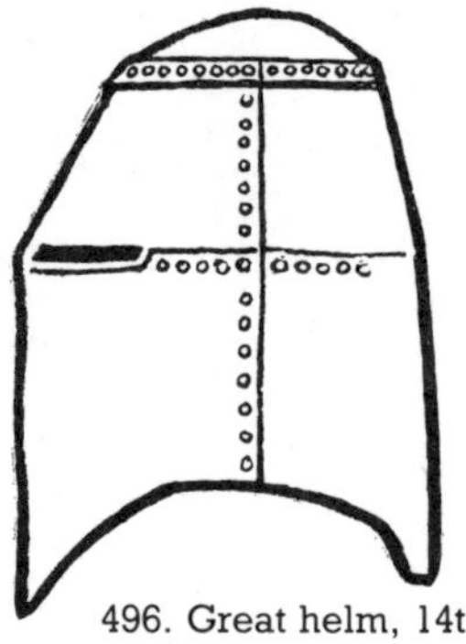

495. The same great helm as fig. 493 but en face. Second half of the 14th century. With the appearance of the great helm (end of the 13th century) the crest and mantling became normal accessories of the helm. It was easier to attach a three-dimensional crest-figure to a conical helm than to the pot helm which was flat on top.

496. Great helm, 14th century.

499. Flat fan-shaped crests, painted with the charges of the shield or parts thereof, were among the first ones to appear.

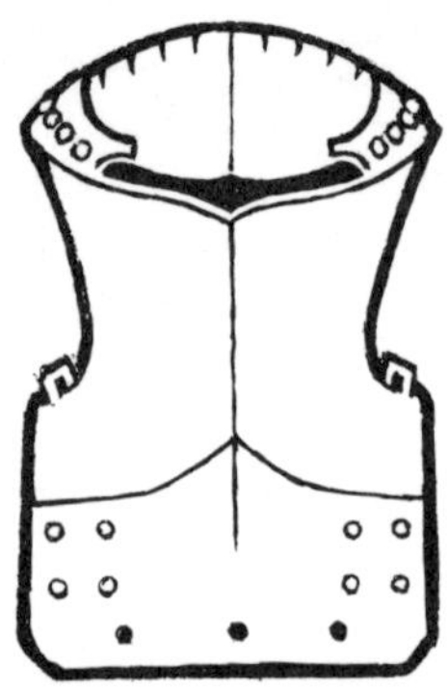

497. Tilting helm from the second half of the 15th century. This type of helm, evolved from the great helm, made its appearance at the end of the 14th century. It was used in the tilt or joust, at which combatants tried to unhorse each other.

498. Knight wearing a bassinet and square shields as protection for the shoulders. Fig. 499, drawn in correct proportion, shows the size of the helm in relation to the head. Adaptation from the *Loutrell Psalter*, c 1340.

500. Tilting helm, late 15th century.

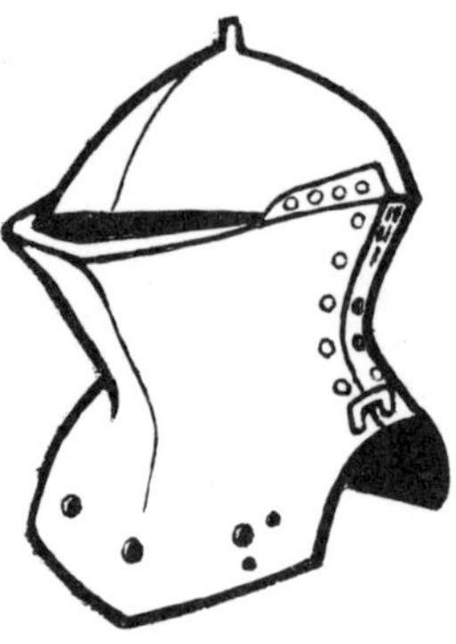

501. Tilting helm, late 15th century.

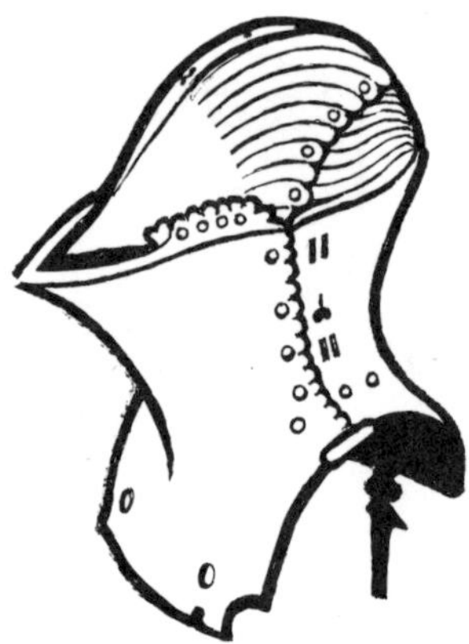

502. Tilting helm, early 16th century.

Figs. 490, 491, 493, 495, 497 and 502 are adapted from drawings by E. Doepler the Younger, from *Heraldisches Handbuch* by F. Warnecke, published by C. A. Starke, Görlitz, 1880.

The system of indicating tinctures by hatching and dots is used here for convenience only. It is anachronistic to employ it for armorial bearings which are designed in a style from before the middle of the 17th century.

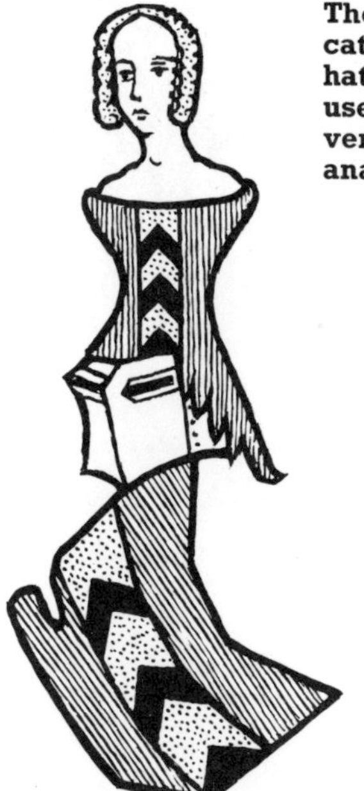

503. Arms of Count Rudolf of Nidau (Bern, Switzerland). The crest is placed on the helm like a cap, the mantling being an elongation in the back.

504. Arms of the Count of Holstein (Germany). Originally a crown on the helmet was a royal symbol, however, it was soon used by lesser princes and lords, and by the end of the 14th century it even adorned the helms of simple noblemen.

505. Arms of Thomas Beauchamp, Earl of Warwick (England). The crest-coronet is red. It may hint at the fact that the Earl was a great man, but it is definitely not a coronet of rank.

At the beginning of the 14th century helms were covered with tight-fitting caps. This was probably done to weaken the power of the sun as it shone on the closed steel helm. Gradually this cover became elongated at the back to protect the neck and the shoulders. See figs. 27-33. Originally the mantling could be of any colour and a lining was rarely shown. Today it is the custom to keep the outside as the main colour of the shield, while the inside is of its chief metal, however, there are many exceptions. Slowly the mantling became a decorative accessory to the coat of arms and was treated as such. It was depicted with jagged or scalloped edges, following the fashions in clothing of the day. In the 16th century the mantling was sometimes unrecognizable and was even looked upon as foliage. It is considered bad heraldry if a crested helm is displayed without mantling, or if a shield without helm is surrounded by lambrequins.

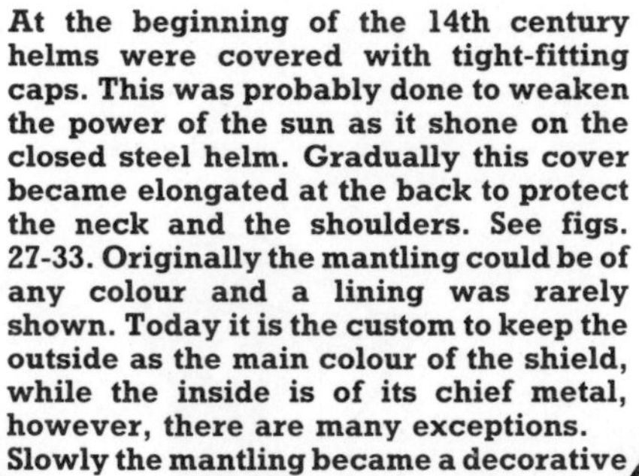

506. Arms of the Flemish knight, Jan Bode, Antwerp, 14th century.

507. Arms of a Burggraf of Nuremberg, Germany, from about 1380.

Figs. 503, 504 and 505 are copied from the *Armorial de Gelre,* second half of the 14th century. Fig. 507 is an adaptation from a stained-glass window in the church of St Kilian, Markt Erlbach, Bavaria, West Germany, in *Wappen in Bayern,* edited by R. M. Loos, Degener & Co., 1974. Fig. 506 is from *Inscriptions Funéraires et Monumentales de la Province d'Anvers,* Antwerp, Belgium, 1856 and 1863.

508. Arms of the King of Poland.

509. Arms of the Holy Roman Emperor.

510. Arms of the Duke of Savoy.

511. Arms of Humphrey, Earl of Stafford (Duke of Buckingham), 1402-1460. From his Garter stall-plate in Windsor, England. With the tilting helm the mantling became larger and twisted and showed its lining.

512. Adaptation from an engraving by Albrecht Dürer c 1512. The crest-wreath (torse) of twisted material not only held the mantling in place it also hid the unsightly spot where the crest was fastened to the helm.

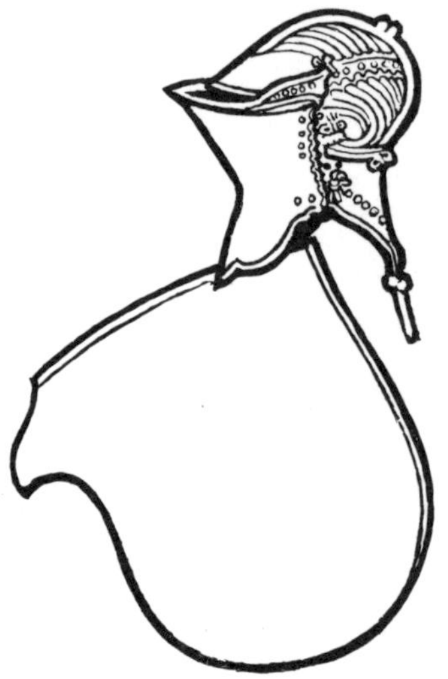

514. Adaptation from the famous engraving 'The Coat of Arms of Death' by Albrecht Dürer, 1503.

513. Arms of Henry Bourchier, Earl of Essex, 15th century. From his Garter stall-plate in Windsor, England. Devices of the shield were often repeated in the mantling. Note the size of the crest.

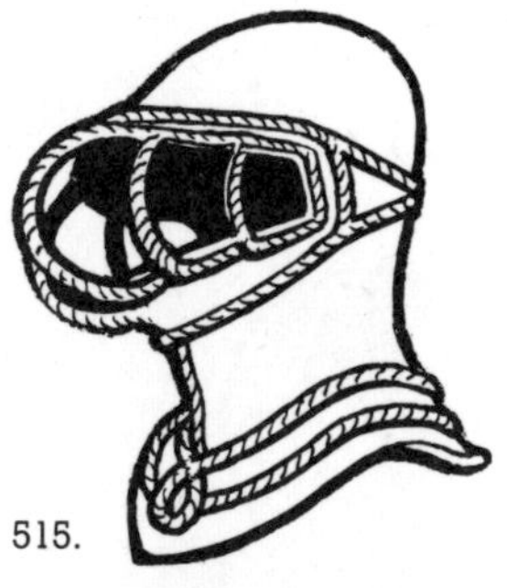

515.

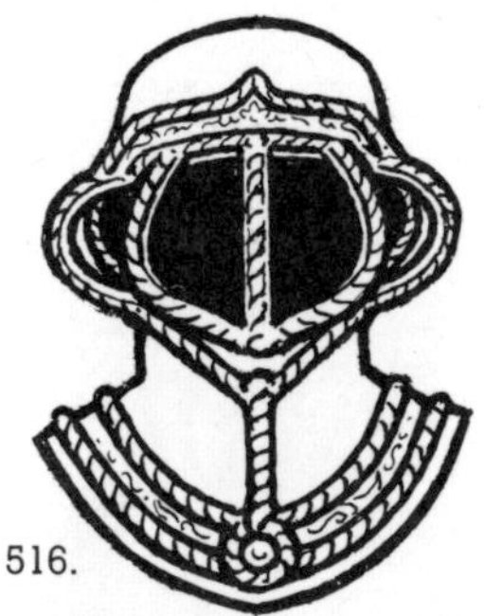

516.

Ceremonial helm with bars, made of leather. Barred helmets appeared during the middle of the 15th century. They were used for ceremonial purposes and for the display of the crests before a tournament. It is unlikely that they were worn in the melée, where sword or mace were the weapons. However, there were great helms in an earlier period which had bars across the slit.

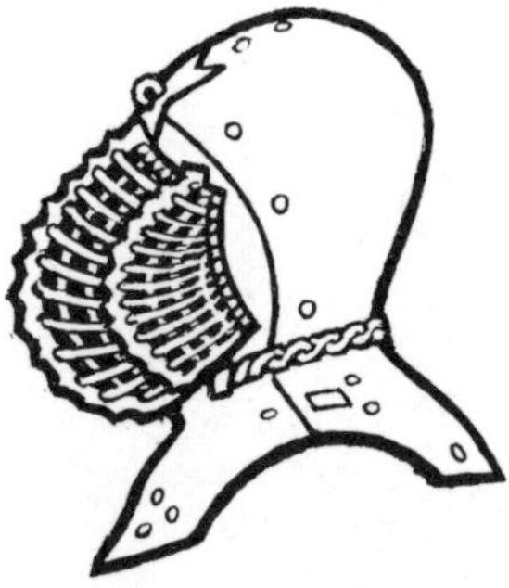

517. The opening before the face is protected by iron lattice. This type of helm from the 15th century was used in tournament with sword and mace.

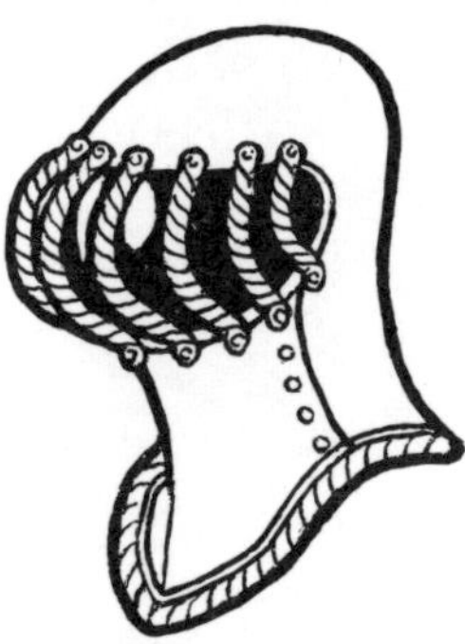

518. Ceremonial helm with bars, 15th century. Such helms are a normal part of an armorial achievement over tombs but never belong to the armour of a knight's effigy.

519. The Emperor Maximilian I wearing a vizored helm (armet) with crest and mantling. Adaptation from a woodcut by Hans Burgkmair, 1508.

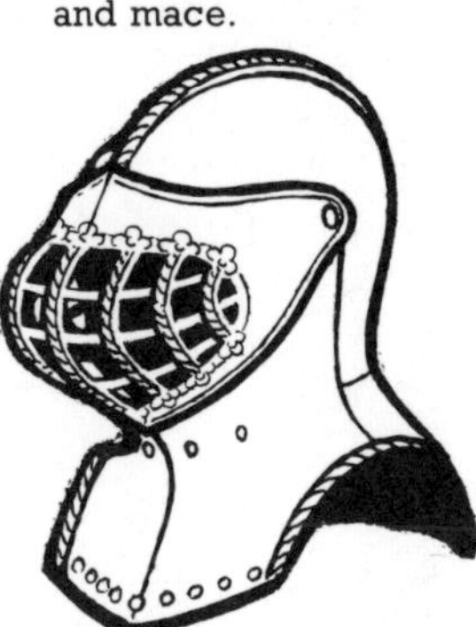

520. Ceremonial helm from the second half of the 16th century. Most of the ceremonial helms were made of leather. The bars were made of twisted rope that had been drenched in glue. The helm was then painted and gilded.

521. Armet with vizor closed.

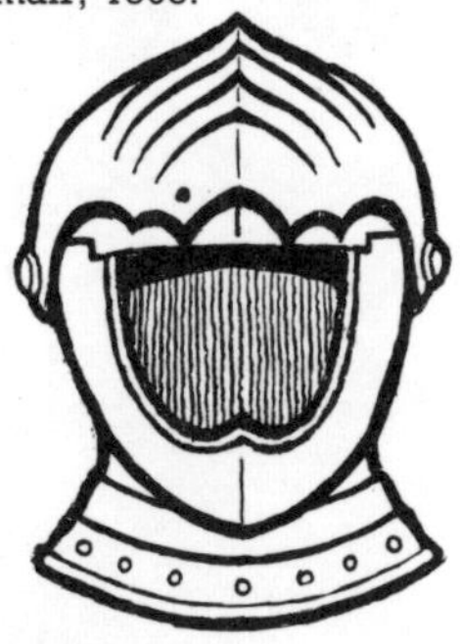

522. Armet en face with open vizor.

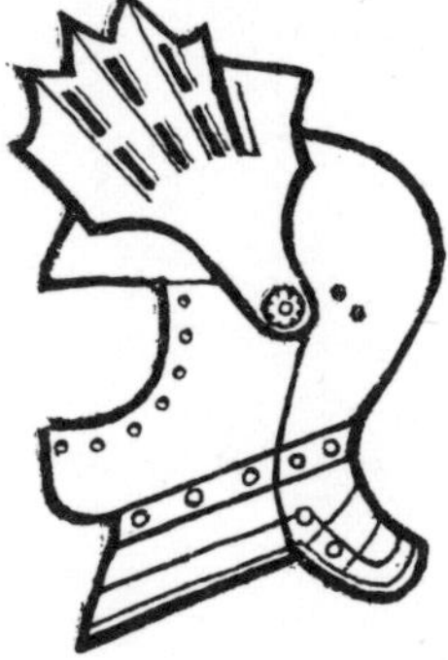

523. Armet with open vizor.

The armet became the favoured tournament helm of the 16th century. Originally it was decorated with an heraldic crest but this was soon replaced by ostrich plumes.
Vizored helms were the last ones to be introduced in heraldry. Gilded and affronté, the vizor open, became the helm for a king. It is used in this way in the royal arms of Belgium. Various heraldic versions (placed sideways, affronté, the vizor open or closed) can be found in today's heraldry of Great Britain and Italy. See figs. 608, 671, 709 and 820.

Figs. 508, 509 and 510 on the previous page are adaptations from the *Armorial Bergshammar* c 1450. The arms of this period were pleasantly simple, even those belonging to emperors, kings and princes, probably because shields and helms were still used in tournament and were not considered as mere emblems to be displayed on seals and paintings or in sculpture.
Figs. 515, 516, 520 and 522 are adaptations from drawings by E. Doepler the Younger.
Heraldisches Handbuch, F. Warnecke, G. A. Starke, 1880.

525. Barred helm from about 1520, an adaptation from a woodcut by Albrecht Dürer. Helms are normally lined in red but may be of any other colour.

524. Arms of the Herren* von Frankenstein, from the Armorial of Conrad Grünenberg, c 1480. The crest-wreath has never been compulsory in German heraldry. (*Herren pl the German word for seigneurs or lords. Today Herr is used like the English 'Mister'.)

526. Arms of the Herren von Zimmern und Messkirch, from the Armorial of Conrad Grünenberg, c 1480. Note the realistic drawing of the mantling.

527. Arms of the Rockox family of Antwerp, from a design of 1577. In the 16th century the mantling became more symmetrical, larger and much more elaborate. Note how the shield is suspended from the helm. Generally torse and mantling are of the principal colour and metal of the arms, unless they are blazoned otherwise. In the Romance countries especially, all the tinctures of the shield may be used.

529. A vizored 17th century helm, typical of the heraldic style of that period (English).

528. Arms of a member of the Fugger family, Antwerp, 1537.

530. The canting arms of the ancient patrician family de Draeck, Antwerp, 1538. The vizored helm has little in common with the armets actually used at that time. The shield is a typical 16th century creation. Like other arms on this page, the shield is suspended by a strap from the helm, a custom still popular in Belgian heraldry.

Figs. 527-528 and 530-531 are adaptations from *Inscriptions Funéraires et Monumentales de la Province d'Anvers,* Antwerp, Belgium, 1856 and 1863.

531. Arms of Jan Kesseleer, a merchant of Antwerp, who died in 1575.

BLAZON

Blazon is the technical language used to describe a coat of arms in such a way that a heraldic artist is able to visualize it and so paint it correctly. This means that the blazon has to be clear and accurate and easily understandable to avoid mistakes.

In describing a coat of arms the surface of the shield (the arms) comes first. Secondly, the crest is blazoned, and the mantling should follow. To assume that the mantling is always of the main colour and metal of the shield is wrong. This is proven by innumerable examples of armorial bearings in Europe. Also, the custom of using red mantlings with white lining for all arms, disregarding the different tinctures of the arms, which prevailed in Scotland for some time, was abandoned at the end of the last century. To describe the helm is not necessary. In countries where helms of rank are still in use, it would be enough to mention a helm befitting the degree of the armigerous person. The Belgian custom of including an elaborate description of the helm in the blazon makes little sense, as only the helm with bars is used in that country.

If the arms are ensigned with a coronet of rank, this is mentioned with the crest, for example, 'on a peer's helmet, within a viscount's coronet, on a wreath of the colours . . .'

If the arms have supporters, they are mentioned after crest and mantling, followed by the motto. If the shield is surrounded by the circlet or the collar of an Order of Chivalry, this is mentioned after the blazon of the shield. Finally the entire achievement is placed on a manteau in the case of European princely arms.

532. Kitchell. (English arms.)
Arms: azure, a falcon rising, belled and jessed Or, within a bordure of the last.
Crest: a demi-hawk Or.
Mantling: azure lined Or.

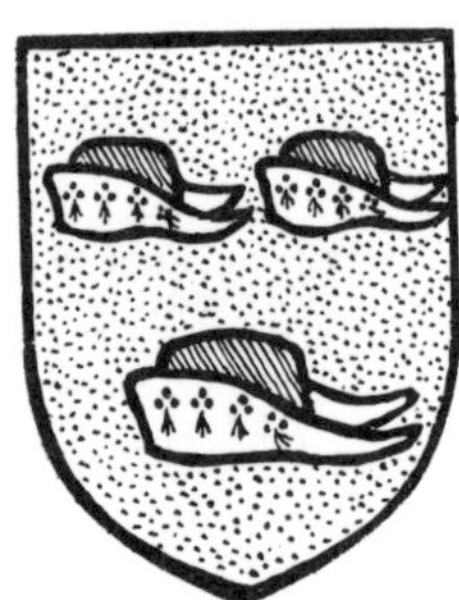

533. Sefton. Or, three chapeaux vert, turned up ermine.

534. De L'Isle and Dudley, Baron. Or, a pheon azure.

535. Earl of Dartmouth. Azure, a stag's head caboshed argent.

536. Granville. Gules, three clarions Or.

537. Ferrers. Gules, seven mascles conjoined Or (3, 3, 1).

The design on a shield is described by first naming its basic tincture (in the case of a divided field, such as per fess, per pale, per bend, etc., its tinctures). It can be scattered with small charges (semé of crosses crosslet or semé-de-lis), or it can be ermine or vair, etc. Secondly, the principal charge is mentioned (this can be a group of charges) occupying the most important space of the field.

Next are the secondary charges on the field. Then come objects placed on the charges which have been blazoned already, followed by charges such as chiefs, cantons and bordures (which do not occupy a position in or around the centre of the field) and the objects placed on them. If there are any marks of cadency they are the last thing to be mentioned.

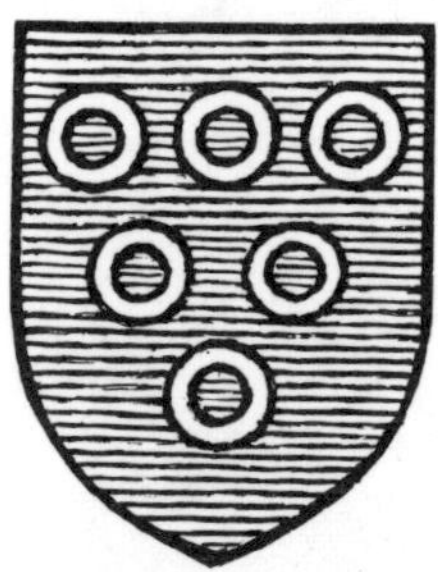

538. Musgrave. Azure, six annulets argent (3, 2, 1).

539. Conley. (Irish arms.)
Arms: argent, on a chevron gules between in chief two spurs and in base a battle-axe azure, shaft Or, a fleur-de-lis of the last between two crosses crosslet of the first.*
Crest: a bee erect proper.
Mantling: gules lined argent.

*For reasons of style, the repetition of words should be avoided in blazon as long as this does not make it more difficult or time-consuming to visualize the arms in question.

Blazon is the way armorial bearings are described according to the rules of heraldry. As this book is mainly concerned with the different forms and styles of coats of arms from all over Europe and not with the technical language of heraldry, blazon is, of necessity, covered briefly.

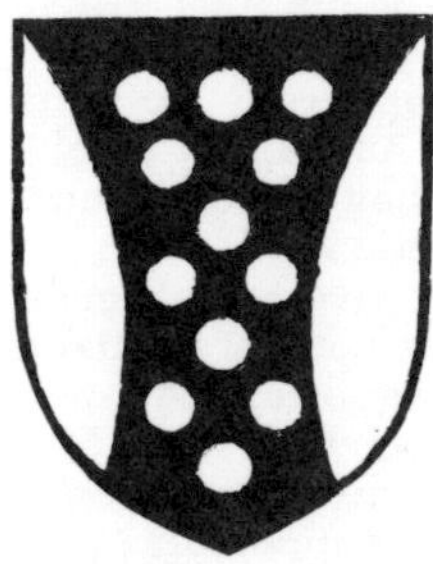

540. Spelman. Sable platy, two flaunches argent.

541. Geffrey. Or, ten billets sable, in chief a label of five points gules.

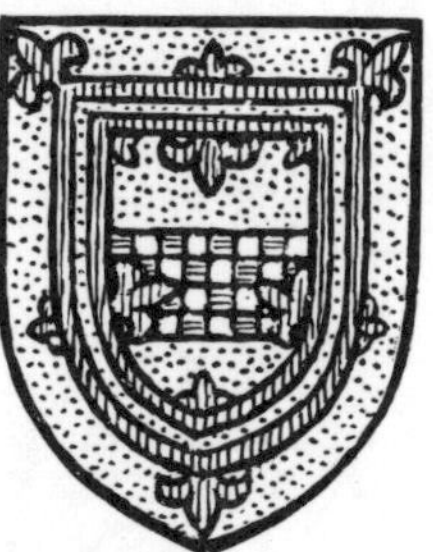

542. Stuart. Or, a fess checky azure and argent within a double tressure flory counter-flory gules.

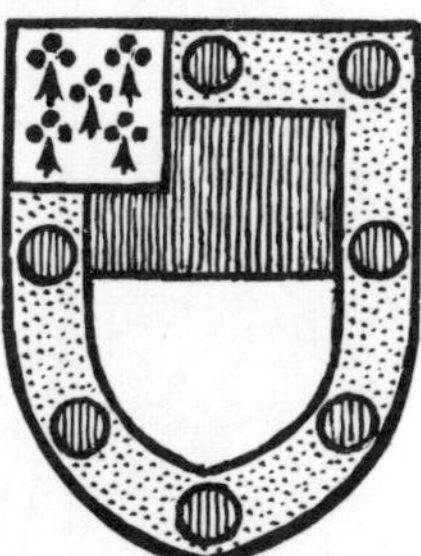

543. Woodfield. Per fess gules and argent, a bordure Or charged with eight torteaux, over all a canton ermine.

SUPPORTERS

Supporters are figures which hold or support the shield. They can be angels, human beings or semi-human beings such as tritons and mermaids. They can also be animals, such as lions, stags, horses, eagles, dolphins, or imaginary beasts, such as dragons, griffins, etc.
In the Romance languages, a difference is made between human and semi-human beings on the one hand and creatures of all kinds, natural or imaginary, on the other. The former are called tenants in French, the latter supports. If supporters are trees (a shield could hang by a strap from a branch) or inanimate objects, they are called soutiens.

544. *Right:* a lion and a stag were the supporters of the arms of the Kingdom of Württemberg (1817-1918). The antlers of Württemberg appeared for the first time on a seal of Count Conrad in 1228. The three lions represent the ancient duchy of Swabia. The motto means 'fearless and true'. See fig. 999.

Supporters probably originate from the decorative figures with which engravers filled the empty space between the arms in a seal and the text around its edge. Also, a knight on his equestrian seal was actually the supporter of his own arms. On other seals, the figure of a lady appeared, holding either her husband's shield or her husband's shield and her father's.
As parts of an armorial design, but not yet as fixed devices, supporters began to be used in the late 14th century. Sometimes badges served as supporters. For example Henry VII of England used a white greyhound and the red dragon of Wales both as supporters and as badges.

545. Landsknechte (mercenaries of the 16th century) as supporters. The size of the figures in relation to the shield is more realistic than in most modern drawings in which the supporters are too small.
Copied from a pen-drawing, 1517, by Hans Holbein the Younger.

For a long time supporters remained a matter of free choice. They were assumed, altered at will and perhaps dropped. In some cases they had a special meaning, in others they were purely decorative. Today they are restricted to certain ranks of the noblesse in some countries, while in other countries anybody can assume them. Nowhere else have supporters gained as much importance as in the heraldry of Great Britain.

546. Merely decorative supporters such as this stag were probably the forerunners of modern supporters which are charged on the shoulder with an armorial shield. Such figures are also used as charges in some civic arms, in Bavaria for example, where they either carry the arms of the state or of a former feudal lord of the region. See figs. 235, 244 and 997.

547. Arms of the Count of Flanders, copied from the *Armorial Bellenville,* second half of the 14th century. A supporter wearing the crested helm of an achievement must originally have been an artistic fancy, but it later became the rule in some cases. See fig. 900.

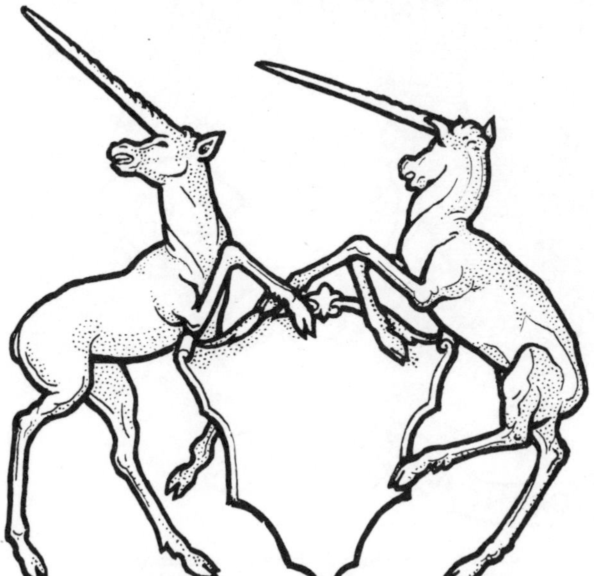

548. The two unicorns supporting a shield are copied from a pen-drawing by Hans Holbein the Younger c 1520. The realistic interpretation of the fabulous beasts is typical of the artistic spirit of the Renaissance. The shape of the shield shows Italian influence.

549. Lady as a decorative supporter. Adaptation from a woodcut by Albrecht Dürer(?), 1493.

550. Angel as supporter. An adaptation from a woodcut by Albrecht Dürer(?), 1493.

551. Griffin as supporter, copied from an heraldic illustration by H-G. Ströhl, 1915.

552. Many different supporters have been used by the kings of France. The angels are the best known and were used exclusively from Louis XIV onwards. They are also depicted as wearing dalmatics charged with the royal arms and holding royal banners. The collars below the shield are of the Orders of St Michael and the Holy Spirit.

In the time of Emperor Sigismund (1410-1437) the double-headed eagle became the heraldic device of the Holy Roman Empire and the emperor, while the ordinary eagle became the symbol of the German king. Some free imperial cities, owing allegiance only to the emperor, emphasized this by using the imperial eagle charged with their own arms. As a sign of favour the emperor granted certain princes of the empire the right to use the imperial eagle as supporter. See figs. 42 and 959.

553. The arms of Malta are supported by two dolphins on a compartment of 'water' (barry wavy azure and argent). The shield rests on a rock symbolizing the island. The cross of Malta is a memory of the time when it was ruled by the Chivalric Order of St John of Jerusalem (1530-1798). In World War 2 the island of Malta was awarded the George Cross. It is placed in dexter chief on the shield.

554. Double-headed eagle as supporter.

The savage or wild-man is widely used in European heraldry as a supporter. He is normally depicted with a wreath of leaves around the temples and waist, holding a heavy club. See fig. 993.

555. *Right:* arms of the Belgian family de la Boessiére-Thiennes. (The shield is ensigned with the coronet of a marquis, corresponding to their nobiliary degree.)

556. The arms of the kingdom of Spain are held by a single supporter — the eagle of St John, the badge of Aragon. In official illustrations the colour of the scroll for the motto is sometimes white and sometimes red. The two columns on each side of the eagle are the pillars of Hercules, badge of Charles I, King of Spain, who was Charles V as Holy Roman Emperor. The yoke is the badge of King Ferdinand I, the bundle of arrows the badge of Queen Isabella. The arms are quartered of: I and IV, quarterly, **1** and **4** Castile, **2** and **3** León, and II and III, per pale, **1** Aragon, **2** Navarre. The pomegranate of Granada is squeezed into the point of the shield.

557. The arms of the republic of Portugal are supported by an armillary sphere (an old astronomical instrument). It was granted as a badge to Prince Afonso by his father, King John II, who ruled from 1481 to 1495. It has been used as a badge for many centuries and appears in stone carvings, flags, tapestries and illuminated books.

Below: in former times angels were popular as supporters for the arms of clergymen. This illustration is adapted from a woodcut by Hans Burgkmair, 1499. It shows the arms of Hugo von Landenberg, Bishop of Constance. Supporters are no longer used by the clergy (and since Pope Paul VI, mitres and croziers have given way to hats and crosses).

AUGMENTATIONS

Augmentations are additions made by a sovereign prince, king or emperor to a coat of arms as a sign of princely favour or in recognition of meritorious acts and services rendered to the state or crown. They can take the form of a chief, a canton, an escutcheon or additional quarterings. They can also be crests or supporters. See fig. 567.
An augmentation can consist of the sovereign's own arms or parts thereof, his initials, a crown or the national colours etc.

558. Pierre Ryckmans, Governor-General of the Belgian Congo from 1934 to 1947, was posthumously ennobled with the title Count in 1962. His arms are augmented with a chief of Belgium.

559. Mathias Wolters, ennobled in 1847 by the King of the Belgians, received as an augmentation a chief of the colours of Belgium.

560. The painter Henri Leys, a member of the Royal Academy of Belgium, was honoured with the personal title Baron in 1865. His arms included as an augmentation, a canton of the Belgian colours charged with an inescutcheon of the painters.
The lion supporters are of natural colour. Note the banner-wings (banierylucht in Dutch, vol banneret in French). They are rare today but were fashionable in the Low Countries during the 14th and 15th century.

561. In 1465 King Louis XI of France granted to the Italian Piero de Medici the right to replace the topmost red roundel of his arms with a roundel of the arms of France.

563. The famous Flemish painter and diplomat Peter Paul Rubens was knighted by King Charles I in 1630 and granted as an augmentation to his paternal arms a canton charged with a lion of England.

562. Francois Dhanis was created a baron by King Leopold II of Belgium in 1894. The chief of his arms represents the flag of Congo, where Dhanis had been an inspecteur d'Etat.

564. Augmentations lacking artistic taste can ruin even the most beautiful coat of arms. The arms of Viscount Nelson of the Nile, are a famous example. The first augmentation was a chief, containing a landscape with a disabled ship, a battery in ruins and a palm-tree rising from the waters. The second augmentation would have ruined the arms completely had it not been omitted by Earl Nelson. It was a fess wavy azure, charged with the word TRAFALGAR in golden letters.

565. The canton of St George (argent, a cross gules) was granted to Sir Winston Churchill by Charles II of England for his services to Charles I. His son John Churchill, Duke of Marlborough, was honoured by the addition of an escutcheon of St George, charged with the arms of France, in memory of his victory at Blenheim in 1704.

566. Sir Frederick Treves, Bt., physician and surgeon to King Edward VII, was granted a lion of England in chief.

An augmentation sometimes serves as a sufficient difference (brisure).

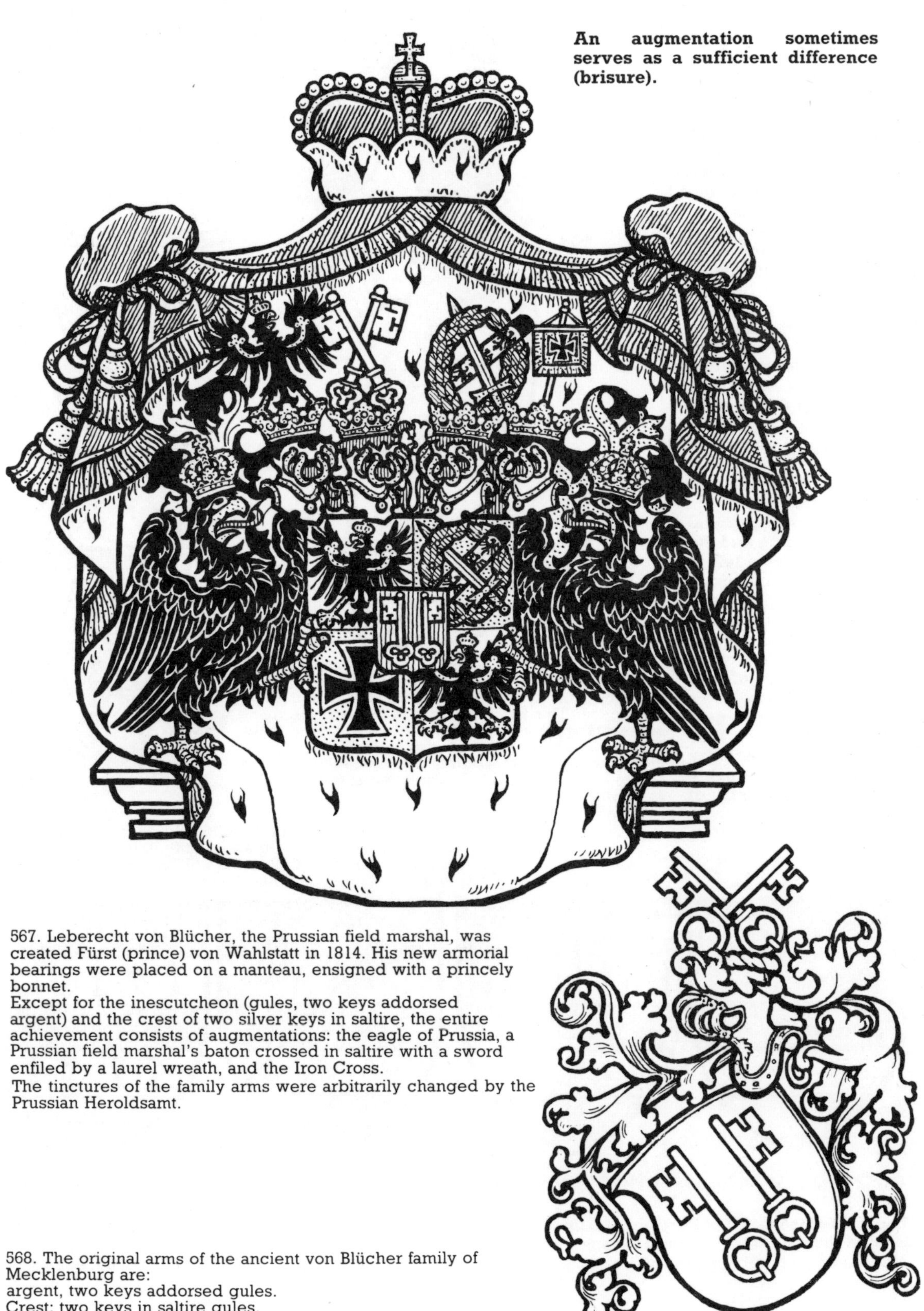

567. Leberecht von Blücher, the Prussian field marshal, was created Fürst (prince) von Wahlstatt in 1814. His new armorial bearings were placed on a manteau, ensigned with a princely bonnet.
Except for the inescutcheon (gules, two keys addorsed argent) and the crest of two silver keys in saltire, the entire achievement consists of augmentations: the eagle of Prussia, a Prussian field marshal's baton crossed in saltire with a sword enfiled by a laurel wreath, and the Iron Cross.
The tinctures of the family arms were arbitrarily changed by the Prussian Heroldsamt.

568. The original arms of the ancient von Blücher family of Mecklenburg are:
argent, two keys addorsed gules.
Crest: two keys in saltire gules.
Mantling: gules and argent.

DIFFERENCING AND CADENCY

Differencing in Shield and Crest

When heraldic shields were in practical use on the battlefield and in tournament, it became necessary to distinguish the head of a family from his sons and relatives, who also had to be distinguished from each other. It was generally understood that the only person entitled to the pure, unaltered family arms was the head of the house. Thus, marks of differencing, and cadency, called brisures in French, had to be added to the arms of everybody else. This became a generally accepted custom in Europe, at least so far as the princes and the higher noblesse were concerned.

There was no international system of differencing and the choice of brisures was left to the persons concerned. However, bendlets and batons sinister were internationally known as brisures of illegitimate sons, though they were not the only marks of difference for illegitimacy.

Although brisures have generally fallen from use, they are still found in the heraldry of some royal and princely houses and in the heraldry of Scotland.

In countries of the German language, brisures in the shield were never as popular as in France or Great Britain, and the adoption of different crests sometimes seemed sufficient to mark a difference.

569. Early coat of arms of the Counts of Habsburg (Habspurg). This family eventually became the ruling house of the Holy Roman Empire and died out in the male line with Emperor Charles VI in 1740.
In the modern version of this achievement the comb on the back of the crest-figure is red and the lions wear blue ducal coronets.

570. After the death of Count Rudolf II of Habsburg in 1232 the younger branch of Laufenburg adopted the crest of Rapperswil (marriage of Rudolf III with Elizabeth of Rapperswil), two swans' heads with golden rings in their beaks.

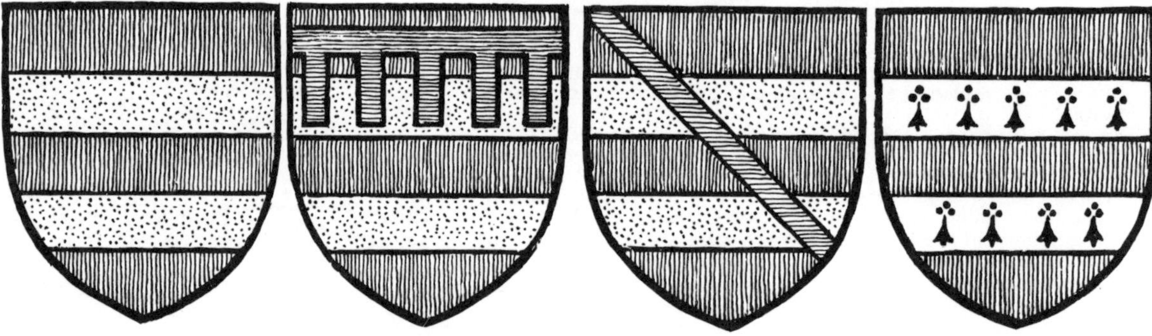

571. The Count of Harcourt.

572. Jehan de Harcourt.

573. Robert de Harcourt.

574. Robert de Harcourt.

The arms of the Count of Harcourt and three members of his family (Normandy, 15th century). The label and the bendlet could be easily recognized as marks of difference, but the change of tincture, one of the earliest modes of differencing, actually created new arms. (In the 13th century Richard de Harcourt used: Or, two bars gules.)

The Royal House of France

In mediaeval heraldry the label was used as a difference not only for the eldest son but also for other members of the family. The label could be differenced by various tinctures or by charging its points (the short pieces pendent from it) with small figures.
Bends, bendlets and cotices also served as differences. The Dukes of Bourbon differenced their arms with a bendlet or a cotice gules (fig. 577). Bendlets could also be diminished into batons, and bends could be charged with small figures.
Quartering is in itself a sufficient brisure if a son uses a quartering which the father does not bear (fig. 578).

575. The arms of the Kings of France ensigned with a French royal crown. The crown of the Dauphin is arched with golden dolphins. See fig. 552.

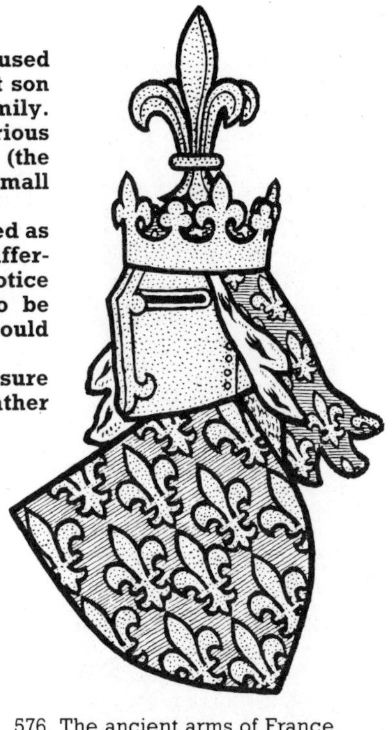

576. The ancient arms of France, probably first borne by King Louis VII in the middle of the 12th century, were: azure, semé-de-lis Or. In the second half of the 14th century Charles V reduced the number of fleurs-de-lis to three.

577. Arms of the Duke of Bourbon, first half of the 14th century. Differences were applied not only to the shield but also to the crest and the mantling.

578. The arms of the heir apparent, the Dauphin (dolphin), are differenced by quartering. In 1349 the last of the Dauphins de Viennois bequeathed his possessions to the King of France under the condition that the eldest son of a French king should always bear the title and the arms of the Dauphins.

579. Coronet of a bâtard, a recognized illegitimate child of a French king. (Two leaves between three fleurs-de-lis.)

580. The arms of the Dukes of Orleans are differenced by a white label of three points. The coronet is the one of the members of the royal house: children of the King and of the Dauphin (fils de France and spouses, and filles de France), and princes and princesses du sang.

Capetians and Plantagenets

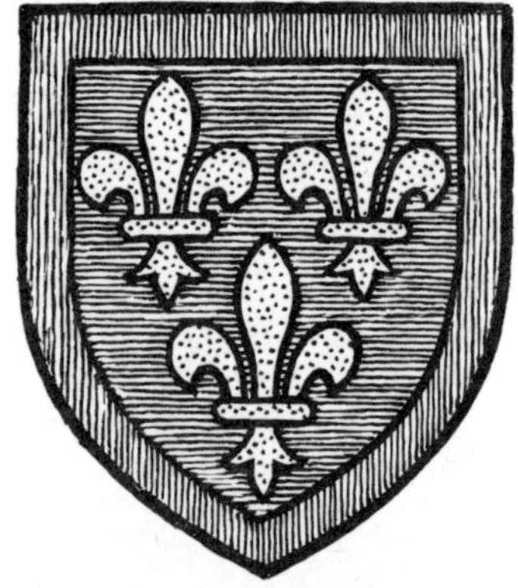

581. An escutcheon of France within a red bordure appears in the arms of the Duke of Calabria and other descendants of King Philip V of Spain, 1683-1746.

In mediaeval heraldry the bordure was mostly borne as a brisure. It was well suited for that purpose, as the arms borne within were not altered and the consanguinity between relatives was clearly expressed. Furthermore, the bordure could be of various tinctures, could have an ornamental outline (invected, engrailed, etc.) and be parted, checky, gobony, etc. In addition it could be charged with other figures. See figs. 594 and 596-601.

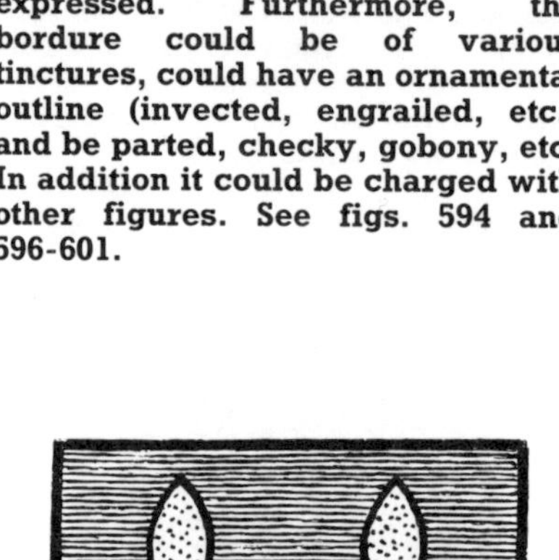

582. In the arms of the Dukes of Parma, also descendants of Philip V of Spain, the bordure is differenced with white escallops.

583. Small arms of the King of Spain. He is a descendant of King Philip V and a cadet of the house of Bourbon. See figs. 556 and 447.

584. Henri, Duke of Orleans, known as the Count of Paris, uses the plain arms of France, without the white label of Orleans, since he is the pretender to the crown of France.

585. France impaling Spain, borne by Alfonse, Duke of Anjou and Cadiz, head of the house of Bourbon. The red bordure is left out.

586. Arms of Edward III, King of England, 1327-1377, before his accession to the throne. Sometimes the label had five points.

587. Gules, three lions passant guardant in pale Or. The arms of England, known since Richard I and borne alone until Edward III quartered France ancient with England in 1340.

588. Edmund, first earl of Lancaster, Edward I's brother, differenced his arms with a label of France.

Royal House of Great Britain. Marks of Illegitimacy. Differencing of Noble Arms in Portugal.

589. Edmund, Earl of Kent, 1301-1329, a younger son of Edward I, bore England within a silver bordure.

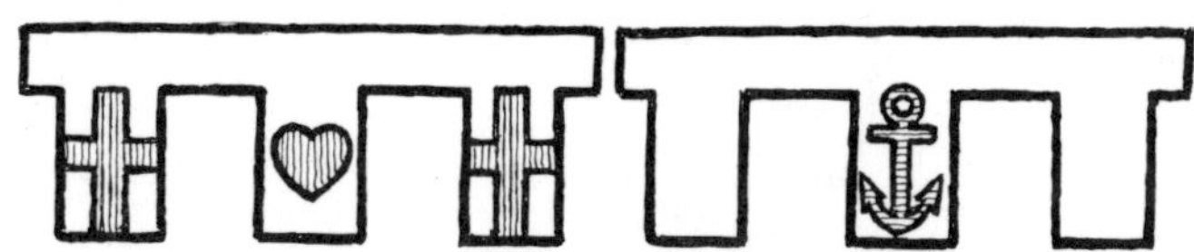

Label of Princess Anne, 1950. Label of Prince Andrew, 1960.

590. In the heraldry of the royal house of Britain labels are the only differences now used. The labels have three or five points which can be charged with red crosses, roses, lions, hearts, or with blue anchors, fleurs-de-lis or natural thistles. Labels are also applied to crests and supporters. The Prince of Wales bears a plain label argent. See figs. 960-966.

A
Sir Roger Clarendon

B
Don Pedro de Trastamara

C
Jean, Count of Dunois

D
Philip of Brabant, Seigneur of Crubeque.

E
Duke of Richmond

591. Differencing for illegitimacy.

Arms of illegitimate children have been differenced in many ways. It seems unlikely that there ever was a rule that was generally accepted. Some would bear their father's arms on a chevron, a canton (D), a bend (A) or a fess on an otherwise uncharged shield, others used different bordures (E). In early times, however, the bend sinister (also the bendlet sinister) seems to have been the brisure most generally adopted. Later the bendlet sinister was often diminished into a cotise sinister (C) which still later was shortened at both ends into a cotise sinister couped, called a baton sinister.

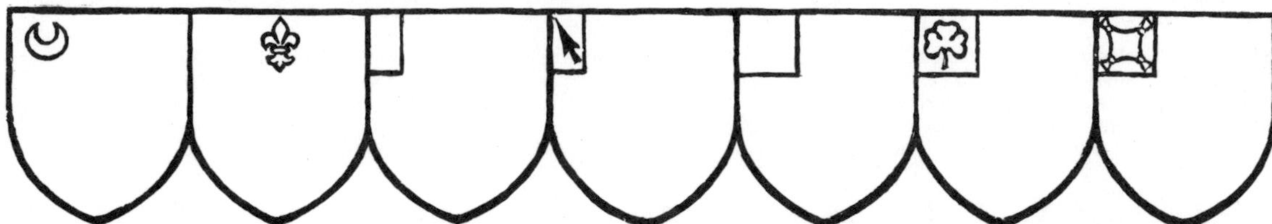

From father's or paternal grandfather's side of the genealogical table.

From the side of the paternal grandmother.

From mother's side. If from the maternal grandmother the canton is charged with a cushion. If from the mother of the maternal grandmother the cushion is charged with an annulet. Otherwise the figures used for differencing were chosen at random.

592. The Portuguese system of differencing has its origin in the regulations of King Manuel I, who ruled Portugal from 1495 to 1521. It is unlike any other system. It is true that the brisure personalizes the arms, however, since the Portuguese have an arbitrary choice of surnames, they may select any family name from father's or mother's side of their genealogical table and a coat of arms, which does not have to coincide with it. Thus, the system of differencing only serves to show from which ancestral line the arms are derived. The head of a lineage uses its arms without a difference, but should he be the head of more than one family, the arms are combined by quartering. The heir apparent to the arms of the head of a lineage never uses a mark of difference.

Scotland, England, Ireland

593. *Right:* the label, a temporary mark of cadency in England, Scotland and Ireland, is borne by the eldest son during his father's lifetime. It may be of any tincture but argent, which is reserved for cadets of the royal house, and the rule against placing colour on colour and metal on metal should be observed.

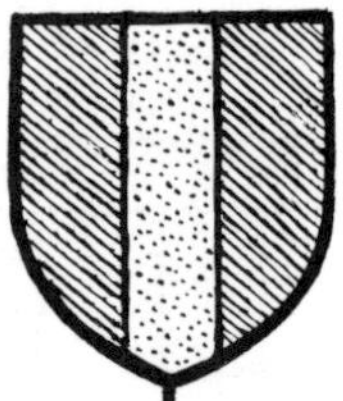

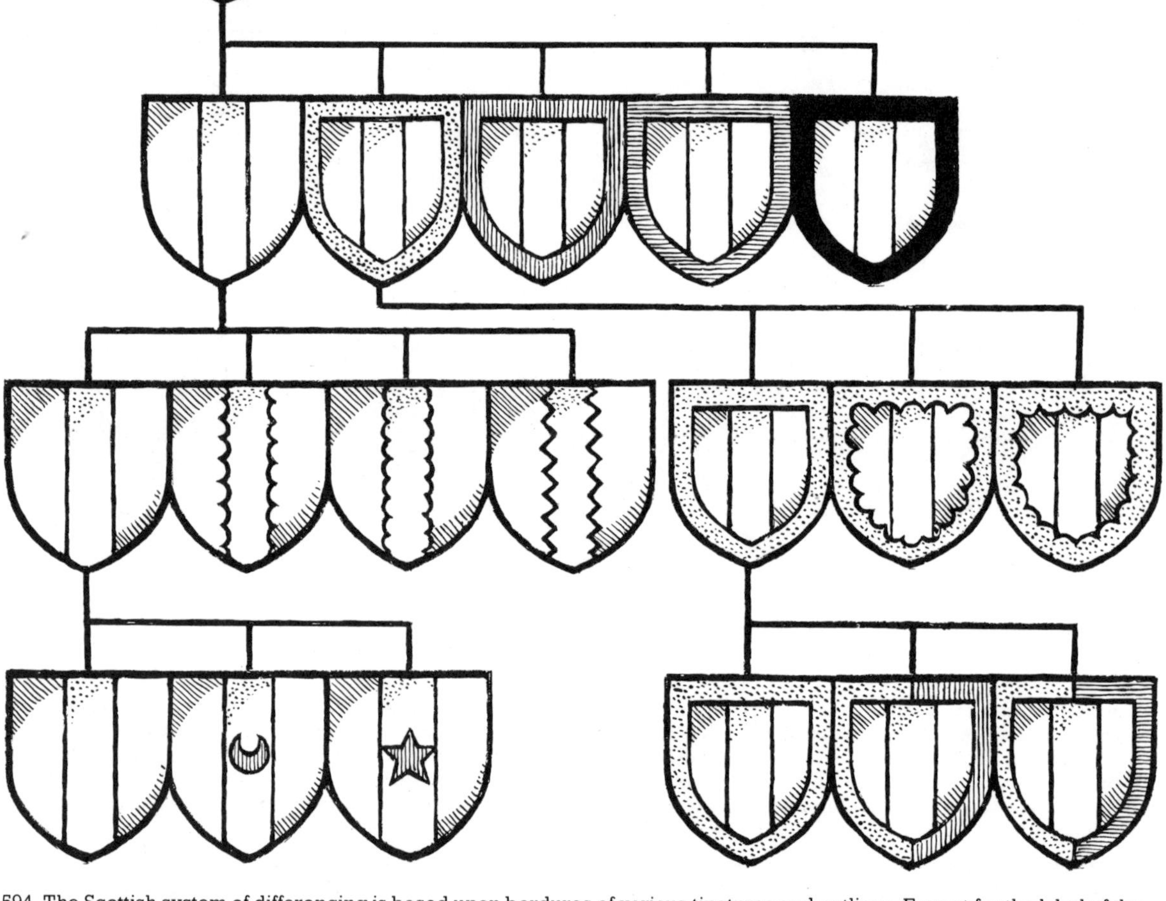

594. The Scottish system of differencing is based upon bordures of various tinctures and outlines. Except for the label of the eldest son all these changes are permanent, actually creating new arms which themselves become subjected to differencing by following generations. The second son of the first armiger will normally have a bordure of the same tincture as the main charge of his shield. The bordures of his younger brothers will be of varying tinctures. However, the system does not seem too strict, since a certain freedom of choice is retained if other brisures would be more appropriate.

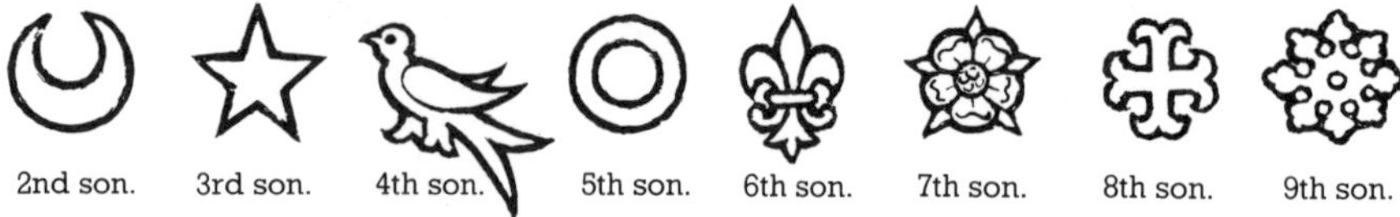

595. Marks of cadency in England and Ireland, based on a method originating in the late 15th century. This system seems to be on its way out but it is still used to distinguish junior branches of a family. These marks of cadency may be of any colour or metal as long as the rule against placing colour on colour or metal on metal is not violated. They are usually placed in the chief of the arms, but should be placed in the centre if the shield is quartered, unless they belong to one of the quartered arms in particular. The following generation would charge their father's mark of cadency with their own.

596. Arms of Malcolm James Irving of Gribton, 14th chieftain. Matriculated: Court of the Lord Lyon, 1972.

597. Arms of Edward Irving of Bonshaw, clan chief in the 16th century. The arms were recorded by his heir-male in the New Lyon Register c 1672. The basic arms of the clan.

The six achievements taken at random from a family-tree illustrate the effect of differencing on armorial bearings in Scotland. In each case the original arms are preserved well enough to show the consanguinity of the armigers.

598. Arms of Sir Stanley Gordon Irving, K.B.E., C.M.G. Adaptation from his matriculation, Court of the Lord Lyon, 1969.
The crescents in the bordure stand for a second son.

599. Arms of Edward James Bruges Irving in Kirkintilloch (1907-1976). Matriculated: Court of the Lord Lyon, 1958. The brisure is of a second son of a third son of a second son.

600. Arms of John Bell Irving in Kirkbride (born 1912). Matriculated: Court of the Lord Lyon, 1959. The bordure is the same as in his older brother's arms but the sinister part is charged with five gouttes sable (blobs of ink) in respect of his profession as a master printer.

601. Arms of Alastair Michael Tirvey Maxwell-Irving (born 1935), only son of Barbara Annie Bell Irving and Reginald Tirvey. He assumed his mother's surname of Irving jointly with Maxwell from which family she also descends. She is the sister of Edward James Bruges Irving and of John Bell Irving. The 'canton gules charged of a bendlet gemel wavy Or' is a brisure since she is not an heiress and has only a derivative right in her brothers' arms. The second quarter of the shield stands for Maxwell, the third for Herries. Matriculated: Court of the Lord Lyon, 1961.

The Saxon States before World War I

602. The Duchy of Saxe-Altenburg.
1 Altenburg, **2** Eisenberg, **3** Orlamünde, **4** Pleissen; over all an inescutcheon of the arms of the house of Saxony ensigned with the crown of a reigning duke in the German empire.

603. Arms of the house of Saxony.
The crancelin or chaplet was generally enarched in former times, and the shield was sometimes barry of Or and sable, as it was used in the arms of the Prussian province of Saxony.

604. The Duchy of Saxe-Coburg and Gotha.
1 Thuringia, **2** Meissen, **3** Henneberg*, **4** Coburg; over all an inescutcheon of the house of Saxony.
*Canting arms since the German words Henne and Berg mean hen and mountain.

605. The Duchy of Saxe-Meiningen.
1 Thuringia, **2** Henneberg, **3** Römhild, **4** Meissen; over all an inescutcheon of the house of Saxony ensigned with the crown of a reigning duke in the German empire.

606. The Kingdom of Saxony, 1889.
1 Meissen, **2** Thuringia, **3** Palatinate Thuringia, **4** Palatinate Saxony, **5** and **6** the arms of the house of Saxony, royally crowned, **7** Pleissen, **8** Vogtland, **9** Orlamünde, **10** Landsberg, **11** per fess and per pale, Oberlausitz, Altenburg and Henneberg, **12** Eisenberg. The shield is ensigned with the royal crown.

607. The Grand Duchy of Saxe-Weimar.
1 Thuringia, **2** Meissen, **3** per pale, Henneberg and Neustadt-Arnshaugk, **4** per pale, Blankenhain and Tautenburg; over all an inescutcheon of the house of Saxony ensigned with the crown of a reigning grand duke in the German empire.

These are the simplified arms (mittlere Wappen) of the former Kingdom of Saxony and the Saxon duchies. All the shields were normally ensigned with their respective crowns. The reigning dukes actually used the crown of a grand duke, the grand dukes used a royal crown. See figs. 901, 903 and 978.

The Royal House of Belgium

608. Arms of the King of the Belgians. The shield 'sable, a lion rampant Or, armed and langued gules' is identical to the arms of the former duchy (now province) of Brabant.
It is encircled by the collar of the Order of Leopold.
Behind the shield two sceptres are crossed in saltire, the one topped by a hand of justice, the other with a Belgian lion.
Placed above the shield is a vizored helm of gold, affronté, the vizor raised, crowned with the royal crown. The mantling is gold and lined with black. The supporters are two lions rampant guardant in natural colour, each supporting a national banner (per pale, sable Or and gules). The motto L'union fait la force in golden letters on a red scroll, edged black, is placed below the shield.
This achievement is displayed on a manteau of purpure (now often red), fringed gold and lined with ermine, which is ensigned with the royal crown.
Princes of the royal house have the same basic armorial bearings, however, the helm is placed sideways and the sceptres as well as the collar of the Order of Leopold are left out.

Note: before World War I the lion in the arms was charged on the shoulder with an escutcheon of Saxony 'barry of ten Or and sable, a crancelin in bend vert'.

The Royal Houses of Belgium (continued) and Italy

609. The arms of the heir apparent, the Duke of Brabant, are the same as the arms of the King of the Belgians but in a differenced achievement.

610. Arms of princes of Belgium descending from a duke of Brabant but not having this title themselves. These arms are now used by Prince Albert, Prince of Liège, his sons Philip and Laurent and by Prince Alexander.

611. Arms of princes of Belgium who are not descendants of a duke of Brabant and do not have that title themselves. Used only by Prince Charles, Count of Flanders, brother of King Leopold III.*

612. Ex-King Umberto.

613. The former Italian heir to the throne, Prince Victor Emmanuel.

614. The Duke of Aosta.

615. The Duke of Genoa.

Differencing in the former royal house of Italy.

*It is of interest to note that the Count of Flanders as a prince of Belgium does not bear the arms of Flanders 'Or, a lion rampant sable, armed and langued gules'.

The Royal House of the Netherlands

616. The royal arms of the Netherlands. 'Azure, semé of billets, a lion rampant crowned Or, armed and langued gules, holding in its dexter paw a sword, and in the sinister a bundle of arrows proper'. This is a modification of the ancient arms of Nassau 'azure, billetty and a lion rampant Or'. See fig. 1191.
The shield is ensigned with the royal crown and supported by two lions. The motto is Je maintiendrai.
The arms are displayed on a pavilion, an heraldic tent which is a more pompous version of the manteau and is normally reserved for sovereigns. In all probability pavilion and manteau have their origin in the seals of princes of the 14th and 15th century in which purely ornamental carpets are spread out behind armorial bearings, sometimes held by small human figures. The pavilion and manteau might also descend from the draperies around a throne or simply from tents. They became regular accessories of princely arms in Europe in the 17th century. Since the expression 'robe of estate' would be misleading in most cases, the French word manteau is used here (in German Wappenmantel – cloak of arms).

617. Arms of the children of Queen Beatrix and Prince Claus of the Netherlands. The shield is quartered of the arms of the Netherlands and Orange. The inescutcheon shows their paternal arms of von Amsberg.
All princes and princesses of the royal house use the royal crown.

618. The arms of Bernard Prince of the Netherlands are quartered of **1** and **4** royal arms of the Netherlands, **2** Lippe, **3** Swalenberg.

619. The arms of the sisters of the Queen are quartered of the arms of the Netherlands and Orange. The inescutcheon displays their father's arms of Lippe.

620. The arms of Prince Claus of the Netherlands are quartered of **1** and **4** royal arms of the Netherlands, **2** and **3** a modified version of the von Amsberg arms.

621. Small arms of Prince Bernard, before his marriage to Princess Juliana in 1937, as a Prince zur Lippe-Biesterfeld.

622. Arms of Prince Claus before his marriage to Princess Beatrix in 1966 as Claus von Amsberg.

MARSHALLING OF ARMS

Marital Arms, Arms of Women

623. Arms of Konrad Peutinger, of Augsburg, and his wife Margarete, née Welser. Adaptation from a bookplate (woodcut) by Hans Burgkmair, 1516.

624. Arms of Willibald Pirckheimer, of Nuremberg, and his wife Christina, née Rieter. Adaptation from a woodcut for a bookplate by Albrecht Dürer, c 1500.

In European heraldry the arms of a married couple are normally placed next to each other, the husband's shield to dexter. In Germany, Austria and Switzerland the shields generally lean towards each other and the charges on the husband's shield are turned around to face the arms of his wife's family, which is called heraldic courtoisie. Thus, the bend sinister in fig. 623 is actually a bend if the husband's arms are displayed alone. See fig. 625. Often the husband's helm is placed in the middle of the composition, resting on both shields. If it is placed on his shield, then helm and crest have to be turned to sinister to face his wife's arms.
The arms of noble families are often marshalled without helms but ensigned with a coronet of rank (fig. 626). In such a case the coronet of the husband is used.

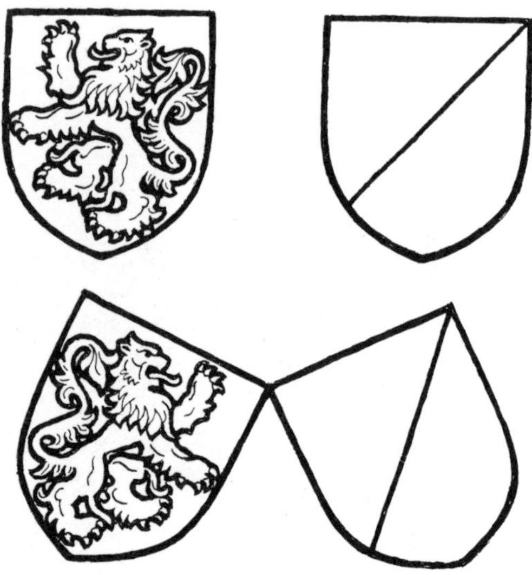

625. Heraldic courtoisie.

626. Arms of Nikolaus von Mach and his wife Marie-Hélène, née Baronesse von Stempel, 1958.

627. Arms of marriage of Jan van Ysschot and his wife Adriana, nee Bollaerts, from a tombstone, 1551, Antwerp. The basic composition, excepting the lozenge, shows the influence of German heraldry.

628. Arms of the knight Nicolas van de Werve, 1463, and his wife Dame Madeleine van Halmale, Antwerp. His complete achievement is placed above her shield on which her paternal arms are marshalled with those of her husband by impalement.

In the 16th century it became fashionable in Western Europe and Great Britain to use lozenge-shaped shields for the arms of women. For the purpose of displaying armorial bearings this is a very unpractical form which leads to unpleasant distortions of the design. Round or oval shields are a little more convenient. During the 17th and 18th century these were used for the arms of men, especially the clergy. Today the oval shield is sometimes preferred for the arms of married women.

629. Arms of a married woman between the shields of her husband and her father. Antwerp, 17th century.

The illustrations on this page are adaptations from *Inscriptions Funéraires et Monumentales de la Province d'Anvers,* Antwerp, 1856 and 1863.

630. Arms of Anne-Antoine-Desirée Domet de Mont (1746-1837), widow of Jean-Francois Bergeret, advocate at the parliament of Besançon, from her tombstone in Besançon.

631. Arms of Bernardine-Francoise Buson de Champdivers (died in 1878), wife of Adrien-Jacques-Marie-Joseph Puissant du Lédo, commisaire des guerres, from her tombstone in Besançon. The same arms as the husband's (dexter) are also used by the Duvernoy family (Franche-Comté).

Coronets of rank if they do not correspond to a title, should not be taken too seriously, since many of the French seem to use these as decorative additions to their arms.

632. Arms of alliance. Compositions like this, in which two complete achievements are placed side by side, the husband's arms turned to sinister, are typical in Germany, Austria, Switzerland and wherever German heraldry was of influence.
Arms of Carl-Alexander von Volborth and Emilie von Thal, married in Mogilev, Belorussia, in 1828.

Marshalling in Spain and Great Britain

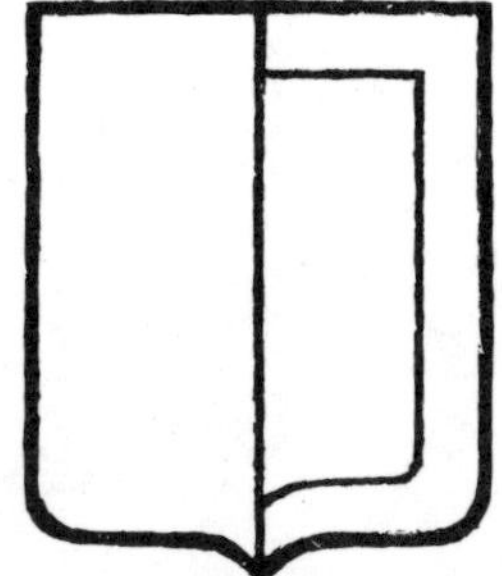

633. In Spanish and British heraldry the simplest way of marshalling the arms of a married couple is by impaling. The husband's arms are placed on the dexter side, the wife's paternal arms on the sinister side. Bordures and tressures of impaled arms are not shown complete; the side adjoining the line of impalement is omitted.

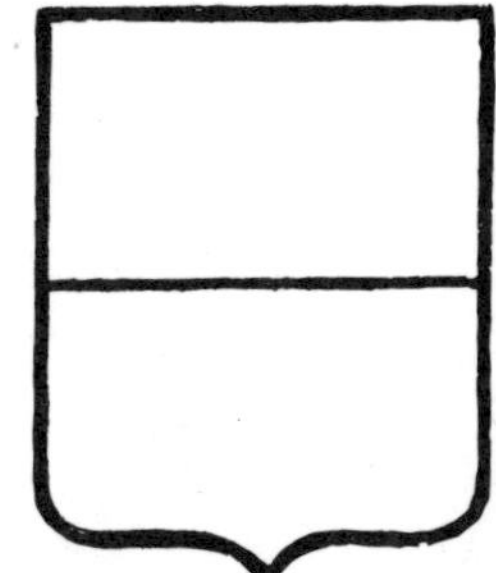

634. Matrimonial arms can also be marshalled by parting the shield fesswise. The husband's arms are placed in chief, his wife's paternal arms in base.

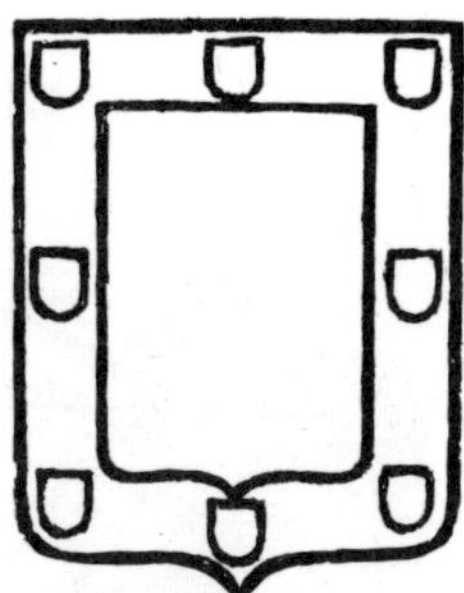

635. A typically Spanish feature, from the marshalling of earlier times, is for the husband to bear his arms within a bordure which is charged with figures or little escutcheons of his wife's arms.

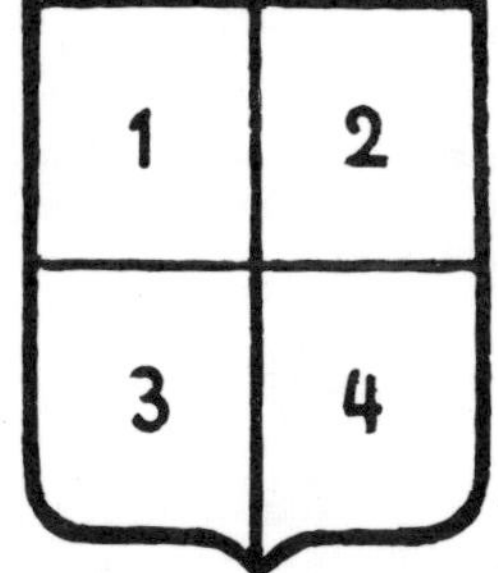

636.
1 Arms of the paternal grandfather.
2 Arms of the maternal grandfather.
3 Arms of the paternal grandmother.
4 Arms of the maternal grandmother.
Should one of the grandparents have no coat of arms, then the principal arms (1) can be repeated in the fourth quarter.

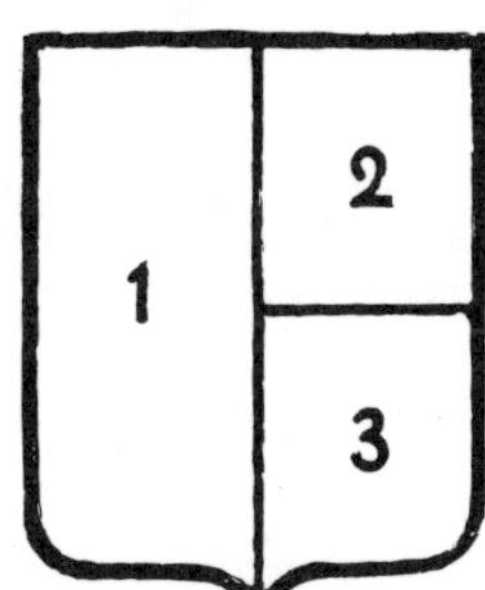

637. Or, if one of the grandparents is not armigerous, the remaining arms can be marshalled quarterly of three.

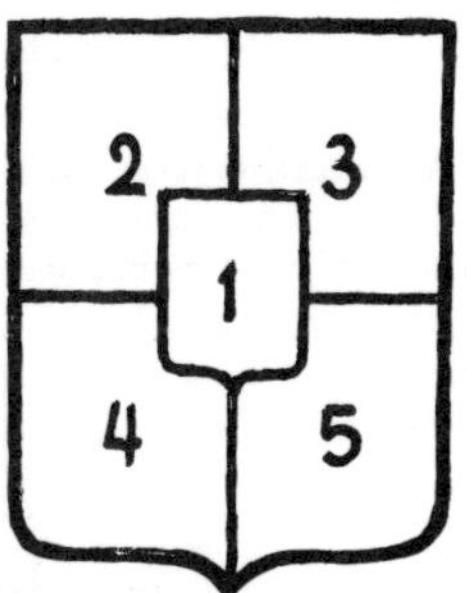

638. If there are five or seven arms to be marshalled, then the paternal arms are borne on an inescutcheon over all.

In Great Britain a daughter who is not an heraldic 'heiress' cannot transmit her father's arms to her children. In Spain any daughter of an armigerous father may transmit his coat to her children, provided her husband has a coat of arms with which to marshal it. Children marshal inherited arms by quartering.

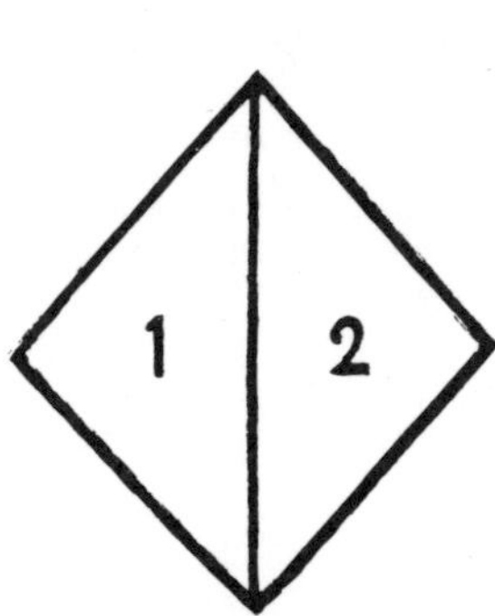

639. In Great Britain the arms of a widow are placed on a lozenge and no helm or crest are used. Her husband's arms are in the dexter half of the shield. See fig. 645.

640. The widow of a British peer may use her husband's coronet and supporters.

641. An English or Irish widow, being an heiress, uses her late husband's arms on a lozenge with her father's arms on an escutcheon of pretence. See fig. 646.

Marital Arms in Great Britain

642. Her father's coat of arms.

643. Arms of an unmarried woman.

644. Her fiancé's coat of arms.

An unmarried woman bears her father's arms on a lozenge. She does not add any mark of cadency for herself and does not use helm, crest or mantling. She may, however, use the motto on a scroll. For merely decorative reasons a bow of blue ribbon may be placed on top of the lozenge. (The arms on this page are imaginary.)

645. After she has married, her paternal arms are marshalled with her husband's arms. His are placed in the dexter half, hers in the sinister half of the shield. (Should the husband not be armigerous, then she cannot use her father's arms any more.)
The husband can use his own armorial bearings as before, without his wife's arms impaled. For her own purposes she could use the impaled shield ensigned with a bow of ribbon, to show that these are the arms of a woman.

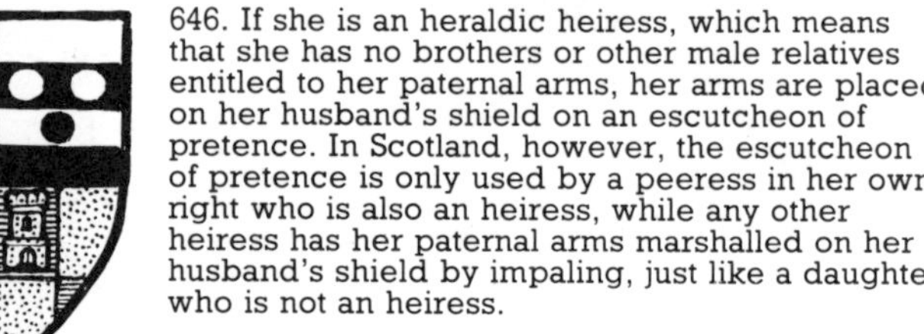

646. If she is an heraldic heiress, which means that she has no brothers or other male relatives entitled to her paternal arms, her arms are placed on her husband's shield on an escutcheon of pretence. In Scotland, however, the escutcheon of pretence is only used by a peeress in her own right who is also an heiress, while any other heiress has her paternal arms marshalled on her husband's shield by impaling, just like a daughter who is not an heiress.

647. In British heraldry children of an heiress may bear their parent's arms quartered (**1** and **4** the father's, **2** and **3** the mother's arms). The shield from then on stays permanently that way until one of the descendants marries another heiress.

648. *Right:* arms of a married knight and his wife. Since the wife of a knight does not share the emblems of his order, two shields are employed, the husband's on the dexter and the combined arms of husband and wife on the sinister. His shield is surrounded by the circlet of his order, while the other shield is surrounded by a decorative wreath, to keep the balance of the design. His crested helm is placed above the two shields. If there were supporters, they would stand on either side of the achievement. (The arms on this page are imaginary.)

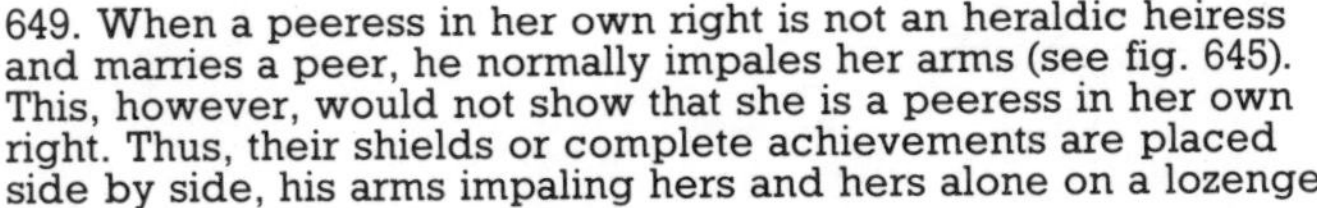

649. When a peeress in her own right is not an heraldic heiress and marries a peer, he normally impales her arms (see fig. 645). This, however, would not show that she is a peeress in her own right. Thus, their shields or complete achievements are placed side by side, his arms impaling hers and hers alone on a lozenge.

650. *Below:* when a peeress in her own right marries an armiger who is not a peer, he places her arms in pretence, ensigned with her coronet of rank, while her complete achievement is displayed to the sinister of his arms.
This arrangement is easy to understand but creates problems for the heraldic artist who has to make a pleasing design of it. It would help if the husband's helm and crest could be turned to show respect to the arms of his wife.

Arms of Women in Sweden

651. Queen Silvia of Sweden bears the royal arms of Sweden, but the inescutcheon of Wasa and Bernadotte is exchanged for her own arms: per pale gules and Or, a fleur-de-lis counterchanged. Copied from an official drawing (Riksarkivet, Heraldiska sektionen, Stockholm).

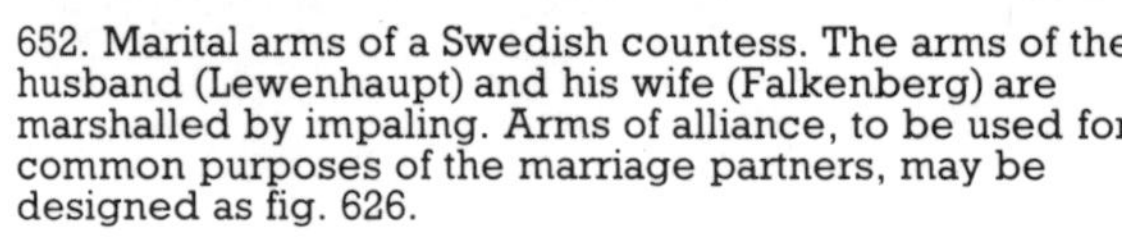

652. Marital arms of a Swedish countess. The arms of the husband (Lewenhaupt) and his wife (Falkenberg) are marshalled by impaling. Arms of alliance, to be used for common purposes of the marriage partners, may be designed as fig. 626.

653. Arms of an unmarried daughter of an untitled nobleman.

von Platen.

654. Arms of an unmarried daughter of a burgher family.

Boheman.

Figs. 652-654 are adapted from *Heraldisk Bilderbok* by Arvid Bergham, Stockholm, 1951.

Arms of Queens and Princesses of Belgium

655. Marital arms of Queen Elizabeth, wife of Albert I, King of the Belgians (grandparents of Baudouin I, the present King of the Belgians). See fig. 608. She was a Duchess in Bavaria by birth

656. Marital arms of Queen Fabiola, wife of Baudouin I, King of the Belgians. By birth she is Doña Fabiola de Mora y Aragon (her father is the Count of Mora and Marquis of Casa Riera). In this unofficial design (after R. Harmignies) her Spanish arms are placed on an oval shield. It is an artistic whim that the shields lean outwards.

657. Arms of princesses of Belgium are borne on a lozenge without any marks of cadency. The lozenge is ensigned with the royal crown.

BURGHER-ARMS

The seal, used extensively in the late Middle Ages to confirm and ratify all sorts of documents, was instrumental in spreading heraldry to the Church, governments of towns, the guilds and other institutions. The custom of the warrior-caste of using their arms on seals made this kind of pictorial identification fashionable and led to the adoption of arms by anybody using a seal. Armorial seals of noble women occurred in the 12th century. During the 13th century it became customary for burghers and artisans to adopt armorial bearings and in the 14th century some peasants took to using arms.

Examples of Swedish Burgher-Arms

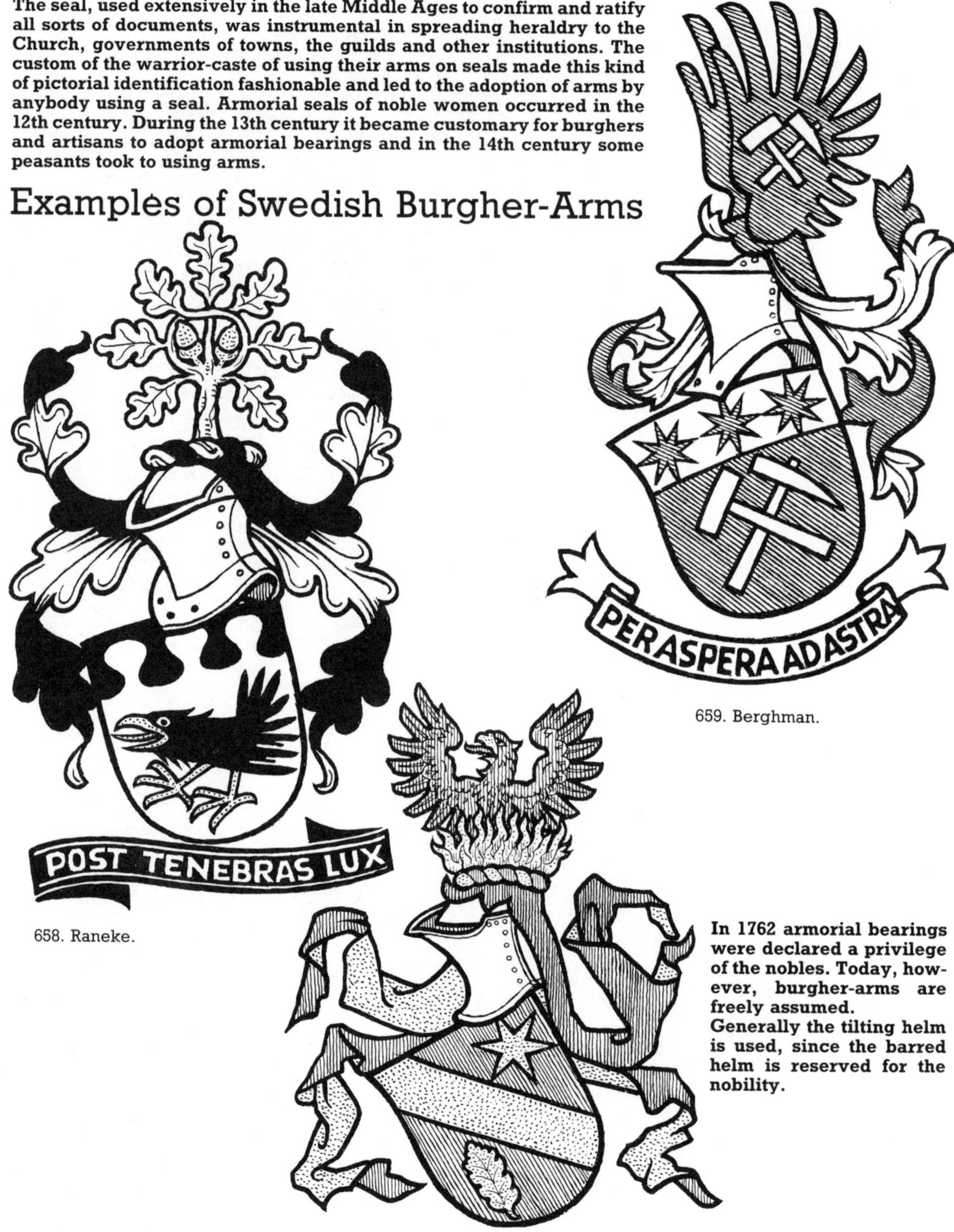

659. Berghman.

658. Raneke.

660. Ewerlöf.

**In 1762 armorial bearings were declared a privilege of the nobles. Today, however, burgher-arms are freely assumed.
Generally the tilting helm is used, since the barred helm is reserved for the nobility.**

It is possible that late mediaeval German burgher heraldry stimulated Swedish heraldry, especially in Stockholm where a large part of the population was German. However, unlike the noblesse, there are few cases where burgher-arms have been handed down through the generations.

Examples of Norwegian Burgher-Arms

Most of the Norwegian family arms used today date from the 17th and 18th centuries, and a great number of them came with immigrants from foreign countries. Since there was no authority denying anyone the right to use arms, they were freely assumed. Charges and crests of such arms often referred to the bearer's livelihood. Many Norwegian arms were used by one generation only, but the majority of them stayed with a family for generations, often slightly differenced. The arms of Smith, Kielland and Heyerdahl are more complex than the average arms in Norway, even for the 17th century. Realism, as in the arms of Smith, is quite common.

661. Kielland.

662. Cappelen.

663. Smith.

664. Heyerdahl.

Examples of German Burgher-Arms

665. Gerster. (Originating from Biberach a.d. Riss, Baden-Württemberg. Now in Miami, Florida, U.S.A.)

666. Grosser. (Originating from Silesia. Now in Munich, Bavaria.)

667. Fehleisen. (Swabian family, one branch was ennobled in Russia in 1825.)

Before the introduction of coronets and helms of rank there was no difference between the arms of nobles and burghers. However, Hausmarken which the latter frequently placed in their shields do not appear in the arms of the noblesse. Artisans often used the tools of their trade as charges.

669. Bilfinger. (Originating from Leonberg, Baden-Württemberg.)

668. Stapf. (Originating from Lieben near Füssen, Bavaria.)

In France burgher-arms are not supposed to have a helm. In Portugal the tinctures of their arms should not include metal (gold or silver).
Spanish heralds have granted armorial bearings to burghers (even to foreigners living in formerly Spanish territories) which are no different in style from the arms of untitled nobles.

670. Holbein. (Originating from Augsburg, Bavaria.)

The illustrations on this page are adaptations from coloured drawings by Gustav Adolf Closs, died 1938.

(See fig. 688 onwards for colour section for burgher-arms.)

GENTRY, UNTITLED CONTINENTAL NOBILITY, KNIGHTS AND BARONETS

Armigers (Esquires and Gentlemen) in Great Britain

Today an Englishman desiring a coat of arms can apply to the Earl Marshal through the College of Arms for a grant. A Scotsman can apply for a grant of arms to the Lord Lyon King of Arms.
After receiving his grant of arms the armiger ranks as gentleman, a designation of a noble degree which seems to have lost its original meaning in modern society.

The ancient landed gentry was a product of the feudal system; the political order effective in mediaeval Europe until the 15th century.
Gentlemen were either born of parents of rank or distinction, or gained the rank and also the right to bear arms by some outstanding achievement.
This description also befits the untitled nobility of Europe.
Until the 19th century esquires were the top layer of the gentry.

Some British heraldists defend the view that a modern grant of arms also confers a certain kind of nobility. This is difficult to accept for Europe where in certain countries non-noble arms easily outnumber the arms of aristocratic origin.
Also, there is a vast difference between honours bestowed by a sovereign in recognition of merit or service and an application for a grant of arms which may be made by anybody who wishes to do so. However, one cannot argue from country to country but has to consider the various political and sociological developments.
In Scotland armorial bearings are considered ensigns of nobility.

671. These arms were granted in 1596 to John Shakespeare of Stratford-on-Avon, father of William Shakespeare, 1564-1616.

672. John Milton, 1608-1674.

673. The arms of Henry Fielding, 1707-1745, bear for cadency a mullet within an annulet. He was the eldest son of the third son of the fifth son of George Fielding, Earl of Desmond. See fig. 595.

674. George Stephenson, 1781-1848.

675. Senhouse of Netherhall, Cumberland. (Visitation 1665.)

676. Law. These arms were granted in 1890 to the descendants of Edmund Law, D.D., Bishop of Carlisle, 1768-1787. See fig. 832.

677. Chesshyre of Canterbury, Kent.

Gentlemen or Esquires bear a steel-coloured tilting helm (figs. 500, 501, 502). In former times an armet was in use with its vizor closed, placed in profile as in fig. 671. See also figs. 521 and 529. In Scotland the barrel helmet is used for gentlemen (figs. 493-496), while feudal barons (not peers) and the heads of clans bear the tilting helmet.

In England the motto is not a necessary part of an achievement. It is generally placed below the shield. In Scotland it is considered an essential component and is usually set above the crest.

'HONORARY' ARMS, GRANTED TO AMERICANS BY THE COLLEGE OF ARMS IN LONDON

Americans of British and Irish descent can apply for officially granted and registered arms. Depending on which part of the British Isles they originally came from, they may contact the College of Arms in London, the Lord Lyon King of Arms in Edinburgh or the Chief Herald of Eire in Dublin.

678. The Reverend Hiram Kennedy Douglass of Florence, Alabama, U.S.A. The arms were granted in 1957 by the College of Arms, London.

679. Gilbert Merrill Titcomb, Sr. of Fort Fairfield, Maine, U.S.A. The arms were granted by the College of Arms in London, 1958.

680. Lorenzo Simmons Winslow of Pelham Manor, New York, U.S.A. The arms were granted by the College of Arms in London, 1958.

A well known example of a foreign grant is the coat of arms of John Fitzgerald Kennedy, 1917-1963, President of the United States, granted in 1961 by the Chief Herald of Ireland. Family heraldry does not concern the government of the United States and in theory any American citizen can assume a coat of arms.

Untitled Nobility in Belgium

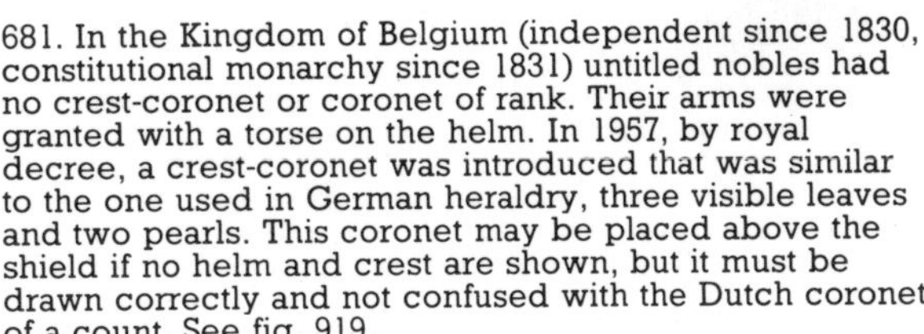

681. In the Kingdom of Belgium (independent since 1830, constitutional monarchy since 1831) untitled nobles had no crest-coronet or coronet of rank. Their arms were granted with a torse on the helm. In 1957, by royal decree, a crest-coronet was introduced that was similar to the one used in German heraldry, three visible leaves and two pearls. This coronet may be placed above the shield if no helm and crest are shown, but it must be drawn correctly and not confused with the Dutch coronet of a count. See fig. 919.

682. de Huldenberghe van der Borch de Flawinnes.

684. Bartholeyns.

683. Zaman. One branch of this family was ennobled by the Spanish King Charles II (as sovereign of the Spanish Netherlands) in 1694, another by Emperor Charles VI (as sovereign of the Austrian Netherlands) in 1722 and a third by Empress Maria Theresa in 1735. The last branch was ennobled by the King of the Belgians in 1858. Historical changes of the past 300 years are reflected in these grants. Only Napoleonic and Dutch grants are missing.

Helms should be shown placed sideways. Only barred helms are used. Pot helms had practically disappeared by the 15th century, and tilting helms are non-existent in the heraldry of the noblesse.
The shield is often shown hanging by a strap from the helm. This particular style is not confined to the Low Countries, it can also be found in Westphalia. See figs. 1066 and 1086.

Untitled noblemen use the French designation ecuyer behind their family names. In Dutch they can place the prefix jonkheer before their Christian name.

686. van Asten, ennobled by Empress Maria Theresa in 1755.

685. van Heurck.
This family is typical of several such families in Belgium. Their noble status antedates the Kingdom of Belgium but they failed to apply for recognition in the new Kingdom of the Netherlands, 1815, and in the Kingdom of Belgium, after 1831. They were ennobled by Archduchess Marie Elisabeth of Austria (Lieutenant Governor General of the Austrian Netherlands) in 1734, but they do not belong to the Belgian nobility.

687. de le Bidard, ennobled by Emperor Joseph II in 1786.

(Untitled nobility continued after colour section.)

(Burgher-arms continued from fig. 670.)

Arms of burghers and artisans were known in Germany by the close of the 13th century. Since Charles IV (1346-1378), emperors granted armorial bearings without raising the beneficiaries to nobiliary status, and in the 15th century they delegated their authority in heraldic matters to Pfalzgrafen (literally palace counts) who from then on also granted arms to burgher families. By the fall of the Holy Roman Empire in 1806 thousands of such arms had been granted.

689. Allmann. (Originating from Metz, now in Biberach a.d. Riss, Baden-Württemberg).

688. Schultz. (Hamburg.)

Despite the fact that arms could be granted, burghers continued to assume arms. Family heraldry is still very much alive in West Germany. The imperial chancellory and the palace counts prescribed the tilting helm for the arms of non-nobles, while they reserved the barred helm for the nobility. This rule was not always obeyed and many burgher families used the helm with bars and there were nobles who preferred to use the tilting helm.

690. Neubecker. (Originating from Hohensülzen, Rhineland-Palatinate).

Examples of Dutch Burgher-Arms

691. Schutte.

692. Anema.

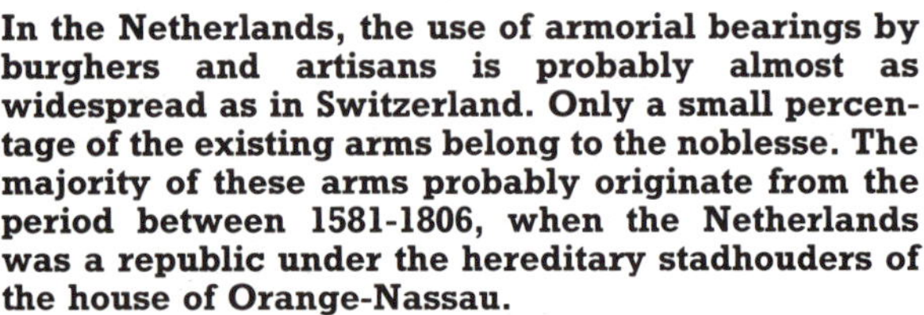

In the Netherlands, the use of armorial bearings by burghers and artisans is probably almost as widespread as in Switzerland. Only a small percentage of the existing arms belong to the noblesse. The majority of these arms probably originate from the period between 1581-1806, when the Netherlands was a republic under the hereditary stadhouders of the house of Orange-Nassau.
Anybody may use whichever type of helm he prefers, though it seems that the tilting helm is in little demand.
As far as supporters are concerned, they were probably once the privilege of the noblesse but today they can be assumed by anybody.

693. De Boo.

Examples of Belgian Burgher-Arms

694. Dugardyn.

695. Van Sevendonck.

The tilting helm is almost unknown in Belgian heraldry. In this respect the helm of the arms of Harmignies, which was adopted for aesthetic reasons, is not typical.

696. Harmignies.

697. Van Ackere. A branch of this family was ennobled in 1939.

Burgher heraldry is not popular in present day Belgium and the general idea seems to be that family heraldry belongs to the old bourgeoisie and the nobility. However, there are burgher families still using their ancient arms and new armorial bearings are adopted occasionally. There is ample evidence in the cities and towns that not only the patricians but also artisans, skippers (boat men), and others used coats of arms. It was normal for magistrates to bear arms.

Examples of Swiss Burgher-Arms

698. Schönauer.

699. Scheltner.

In Switzerland burghers and artisans used self-assumed armorial bearings as early as the 13th century. Many of these arms were based on the 12th century signs by which the houses of a town were identified, or on Hausmarken (German, pl, housemarks), which were used as signs of property. If they were placed in a shield and properly tinctured they turned into arms. See fig. 699. 14th century arms of farmers are known but they are rare and did not become numerous until the 17th century.

700 Schultheiss.

701. Hön. Burgher-arms do not necessarily have a crested helm.

702. Breitschwert.

703. Bachofen. (A number of these arms were canting. Backofen is the German word for baking oven.)

The heads and torsi of human beings, with or without arms, frequently appear as crests, as in the burgher heraldry of Germany.

Coronets of the nobility were frequently usurped especially during the 18th century. The coronet of a marquis must have been fashionable as it appeared above the shields of burgher-arms all over Switzerland.

The Tellenhut (broad-brimmed hat of Wilhelm Tell) was a symbol of liberty. It was used to decorate shields in the time of the French Revolution and the Helvetian Republic (1789-1803).

705. Wischack.

704. Finninger.

706. Thurneysen.

707. Zörnlin.

The arms on these pages were used by families in Basel during the 15th and 16th centuries. The style of armorial bearings in Switzerland was greatly influenced by the surrounding countries. In the 15th century, the German emperors and the dukes of Savoy began to grant arms to wealthy merchants. Other monarchs, including kings of France and England, followed this example.

Examples of Italian Burgher-Arms

In the Kingdom of Italy (until 1946), the arms of cittadini (burghers) were officially recognized if the family was of distinta civiltà (distinct civility) and could prove that the arms had been in use for at least a hundred years. There were about a hundred such armorial bearings.

708. Pezzi Siboni. (Russi-Pezzolo, e Milano.)

709. Alberotanza. (Mola di Bari-Bari.)

The helm of burgher-arms is of burnished steel with the vizor closed, placed in profile. In practice these helms are sometimes garnished with gold. Burgher-arms have no crest.

710. Rispoli. (Amalfi-Roma, Napoli, e Salerno.)

711. Portal. (Provenza-Palermo.)

712. Sanasi-Conti. (Torre Santa Susanna.)

Examples of Danish Burgher-Arms

Burgher-arms are known in Danish heraldry from early times, and the arms of farmers are preserved on seals from c 1300. During the reign of Christian V, King of Denmark (1670-1699) many burghers received grants of arms without being raised to nobiliary status, a practice which existed in the neighbouring German empire. However, arms of the middle class (men of learning, officials, officers, priests, pharmacists, wealthy merchants, etc.) continued to be self-assumed, as they are today.

714. Achen.

713. Bartholdy.

715. Fabricius.

Since the barred helm was regarded as a privilege of the noblesse, burghers generally used the tilting helm. Christian V granted certain 'royal functionaries' the right to use a barred helm in profile with four bars showing.

(Untitled nobility continued from fig. 687.)

Untitled Nobility in the Netherlands

716. Coronet of an untitled nobleman in the Netherlands (jonkheer). The same coronet is used by a knight (ridder).

718. Teding van Berkhout.

717. van Lennep.

719. van Valkenburg.

A Dutch nobleman can use any type of helm, in profile or affronté. There are no specific rules. The barred helm is the most popular.
The coronet of rank may be placed on the shield if no helm and crest are shown.
Supporters holding a banner are often found in the heraldry of the Low Countries. Originally supporters were undoubtedly the privilege of higher ranks than the untitled nobility. Now they may be used by burghers. Banners were used by banierheren (bannerets) but in many cases they were grants from a later time. A banierheer was a knight who led his men into battle under his own banner.

Untitled Nobility in France

The untitled French nobleman (gentilhomme) does not use a coronet. Theoretically the only difference between his arms and the arms of a bourgeois or roturier is that the latter is not supposed to use a helm. Crests are rare as they never played the important role in France that they played in Great Britain or Germany. The helm was even used without a crest to indicate nobiliary rank. Generally the mantling contains not only the first colour and the first metal mentioned in the blazon but all the tinctures of the shield. Supporters are used freely.

721. de Peyrusse.

720. de Bergevin.

The abstract simplicity of the majority of French arms, staying strictly within the limits of blazoning, is unique. Quartering is not overdone as in the arms of the German high nobility or in some British shields in which the arms of heraldic heiresses were collected. However, from the 17th century on, many of the great families of France used quarterings in imitation of the princes of Lorraine.

722. Espivent de la Villesboisnet.

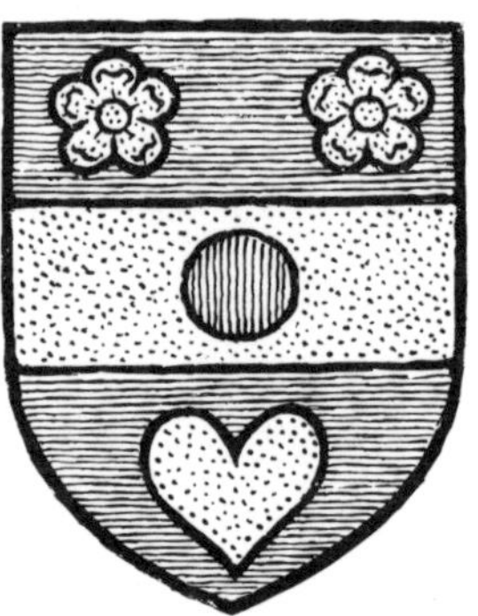

723. de Surirey de Saint-Rémy.

724. Dortet de Tessan.

725. de Choin du Double.

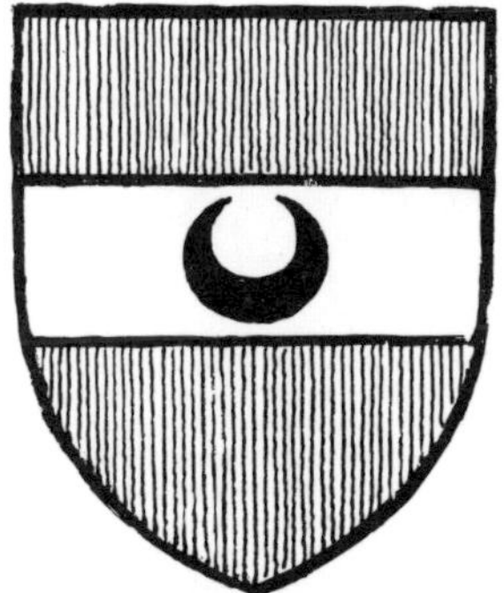

726. de Bonnault.

727. Jullien de Pommerol.

728. Doë de Maindreville.

729. Cazenave de Lacaussade.

730. de Cadoudal.

Untitled Nobility in Spain

The untitled Spanish nobleman (hidalgo) does not have a coronet of rank. Since crests are rare, his helm is usually adorned with ostrich feathers which are kept in the tinctures of the mantling. One typical feature of Spanish heraldry is the bordure which was once used for marshalling. See fig. 635. It may also be charged with a motto. See fig. 471.
In the 16th and 17th centuries supporters were quite common but nowadays they are rarely found despite the fact that everybody may use them.
As far as burghers are concerned, the situation resembles the one in France. In the Middle Ages the non-nobles could bear arms which were composed in the same way as the arms of nobles. At the end of the 15th century the right to bear arms became a privilege of the nobility. In modern Spain everybody has a right to arms but the unauthorized use of armorial bearings is illegal. A non-armigerous Spaniard may petition any of the heraldic officers for a grant of a new coat of arms, which will then be registered with the Ministry of Justice as the personal bearing of the grantee.

731. The arms of Faustino Menéndez Pidal de Navascués are parted per pale of Menéndez and Pidal.

732. The armorial bearings of the Cronista Rey de Armas, Vicente de Cadenas y Vicent. The helm is ensigned with the coronet of a king of arms. His shield is augmented with an inescutcheon of the royal arms of Spain, which is granted to each chronicler of arms as a symbol of office. The mantling is not attached to the top of the helm but to its inside, which is a slightly absurd custom but fairly popular in Spain.

733. Arms of Manuel Tamayo y Carrizosa.

Citizens of any former Spanish colony in America or the Philippines may petition the heraldic authorities in Spain for a new grant of non-noble arms. Ancient armorial bearings may be registered with the Spanish Ministry of Justice if the petitioner can present proof of descent from an armigerous ancestor in Spain.

734. *Right:* the coat of arms of Ignatius de Loyola, 1491-1556, founder of the Societas Jesu.

735. The coat of arms of José de Ribera, Claramunt de Pallás, Claramunt y Espuny, composed of the arms of these four families. This is an example of marshalling of the arms of the paternal and maternal grandparents. This is the proof of nobility required of a mediaeval hidalgo. See fig. 636. The puig floré (a mount flory) in the first and fourth quarters is a characteristic charge of Catalonian heraldry.

736. *Right:* the arms of the ancient noble family of Salcedo. The modern design is an adaptation from a painting by M. Navarro.

Patricians and Untitled Nobility in Italy

737. Coronet for a patrician (patricio) of northern Italy.

738. Coronet for a patrician of all Italy.

739. Coronet for a patrician of central and southern Italy.

740. Coronets for an untitled Italian nobleman (nobile).

741. Coronet for an hereditary knight (cavaliere ereditario).

742. Arms of the family of Segni. Typical of patrician arms is the helmet with its open vizor. An Italian characteristic is the use of both crest-wreath and coronet on the helm.

743. Arms of an Italian noble family without title, the Montini (nobili romani). The mountain composed of several hillocks is a characteristic charge of Italian heraldry.

744. Pericoli. Arms of a patrician family.

746. Arms of the untitled noble family de Orchi. The golden chief charged with a black eagle is called a capo dell' impero (chief of the empire) and indicated allegiance to the Holy Roman Emperor.

745. *Below:* arms of a nobile of the family of Ajroldi di Robbiate. If a nobleman belongs to a family whose head bears a title higher than his own, his personal coronet is placed above the shield, while the rank of the chef de famille is shown by the coronet on the helmet (in this case a barone).

747. The arms of the family of Pacchioni, nobles of Bologna, contain a modified version of a capo d'angio (chief of Angevin or Anjou), a blue chief with three golden fleurs-de-lis beneath a red label. It indicated that the armiger was a supporter of the King of Naples and of Sicily.

Untitled Nobility of Hungary

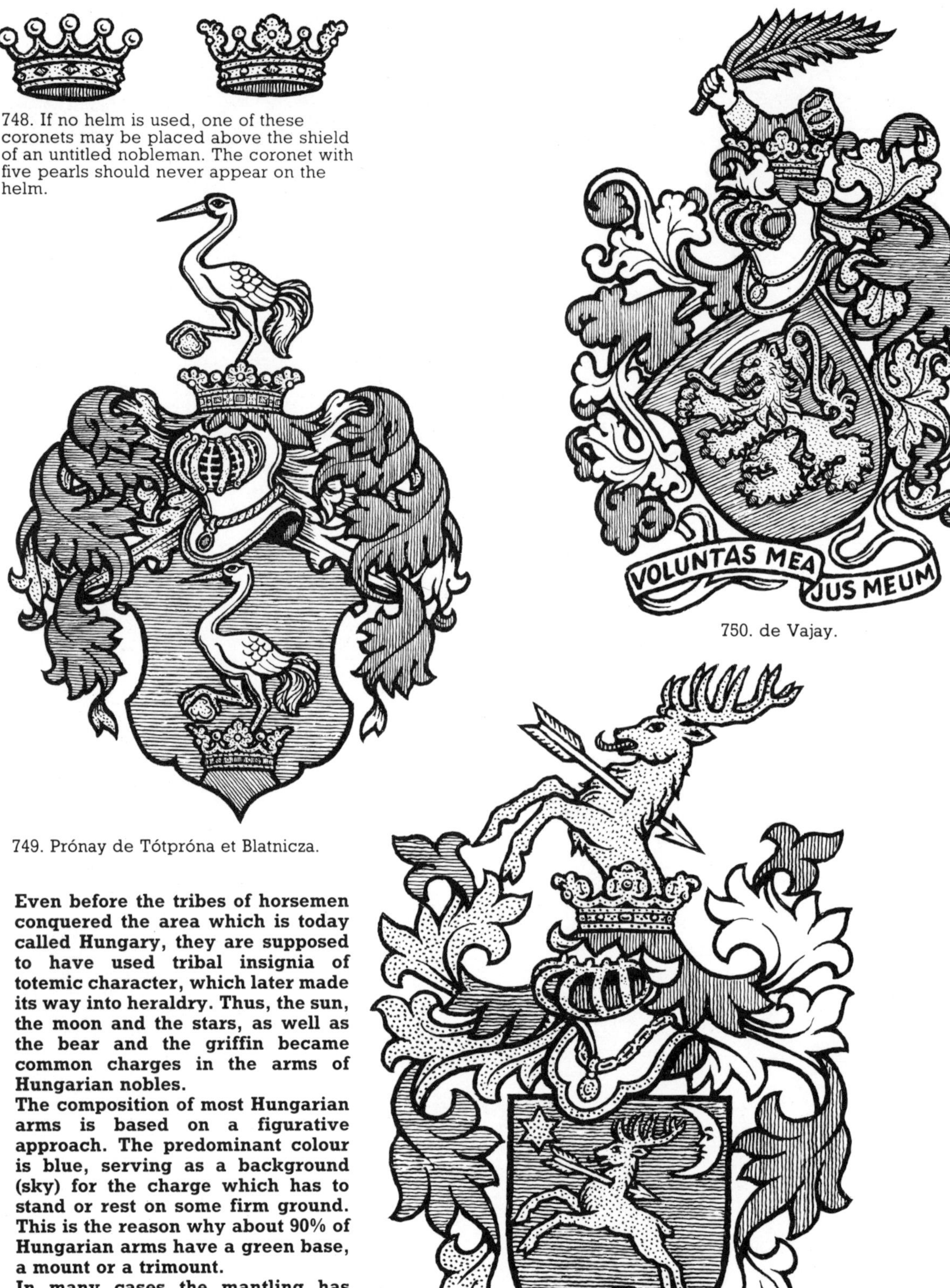

748. If no helm is used, one of these coronets may be placed above the shield of an untitled nobleman. The coronet with five pearls should never appear on the helm.

749. Prónay de Tótpróna et Blatnicza.

750. de Vajay.

751. Eördögh de Lászlófalva. One branch changed its name to Ábrányi.

Even before the tribes of horsemen conquered the area which is today called Hungary, they are supposed to have used tribal insignia of totemic character, which later made its way into heraldry. Thus, the sun, the moon and the stars, as well as the bear and the griffin became common charges in the arms of Hungarian nobles.

The composition of most Hungarian arms is based on a figurative approach. The predominant colour is blue, serving as a background (sky) for the charge which has to stand or rest on some firm ground. This is the reason why about 90% of Hungarian arms have a green base, a mount or a trimount.

In many cases the mantling has more than two tinctures, regardless of whether they are all contained in the shield or not. The usual combination is blue and gold on one side, and red and silver on the other.

752. Bedö de Kálnock et Hodgya.

The helm with bars is normally used but this is not a rule. Unless this type of helm is prescribed in the grant of arms, the tilting helm may be used instead. Crest-coronets are the rule, at least there are few Hungarian arms without one.

754. Tamáska de Baranch.

753. de Bartha.

Arms with simple divisions of the shield, or charged with ordinaries and subordinaries only, are extremely rare and mostly of foreign origin.

The constant fighting against the westward-pressing Turks during the 16th and 17th centuries left its mark on Hungarian heraldry. The chopped-off head of a Turk, with a long scalp lock and a drooping moustache, blood dripping from the neck, occurs in more than 15% of the arms. A reminder of the cruel and bloody wars against the invader. During the 150 years of Turkish occupation of the central part of Hungary, Transylvania stayed more or less independent. Grants of arms by her regents mark a distinct decline of heraldry. Most of these achievements have no crest and instead of heraldic designs, the shields sometimes contain paintings of battles between Turks and Hungarians.

Sometimes a whole garrison of 80 to 120 soldiers was raised to nobiliary rank, being granted one coat of arms for all of them to share. An extreme case is the collective grant of armorial bearings by Prince Stephen Bocskai to 9,254 mercenaries, ennobled in 1605. Some of them later received individual grants, while about 550 already had a coat of arms. About 2,000 of these families still exist today. Such generosity can only be explained by the great demand for soldiers during the wars against the Turks in the 16th and 17th centuries. Since the ennobled had to take part in the fighting at their own expense, the Prince would have saved himself a great deal of money. An arm in armour (or clothed) with a mace or sword in hand and resting on its elbow is not only a common charge but is also frequently used as a crest.

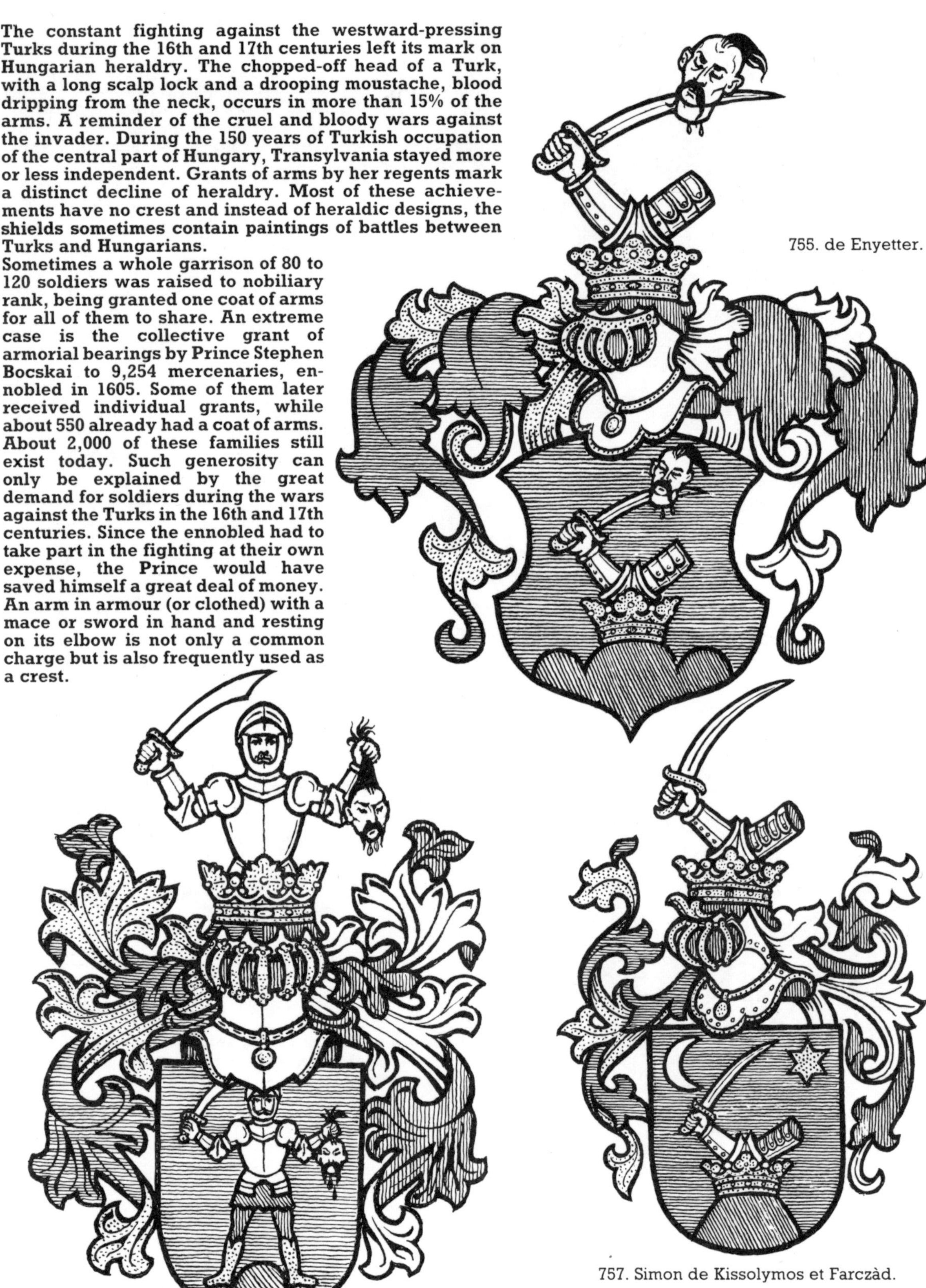

755. de Enyetter.

756. Harsányi de Sárospatak et Kisharsányi.

757. Simon de Kissolymos et Farczàd.

Untitled Nobility of Poland

758. Members of the Polish untitled nobility (Szlachta) normally place a crest-coronet on a barred helm, occasionally tilting helms are used. The coronet on the right should not be used on a helm.
If no helm and crest are shown, either one of the two coronets can be placed above the shield.

759. NAŁĘCZ (arms of inter alia Ostroróg, Raczyński, Rostworowski and Korzeniowski — the family of Joseph Conrad the novelist).

760. GRZYMALA (this version of the arms is used inter alia by Laguna, Przybyszewski and Ślaski).

The Polish system of heraldry is quite different from the systems of other countries. For instance, several noble families share the same coat of arms. These families can have different names and need not be related. In Polish such groups of families are called 'herby' and have names of their own, probably going back to ancient war-cries, which could have been used by clans, tribes or other family groups. This is the reason why their arms are called proclamatio-arms. The illustrations are of typical Polish arms with their proclamatio names.
Charges that are common in other European countries, for instance, bars, bends, chevrons and other ordinaries, as well as divisions of the shield, are very rare in Polish heraldry.

The colours are not always the same for all families within a group, and other modifications of charges or crests are quite common.

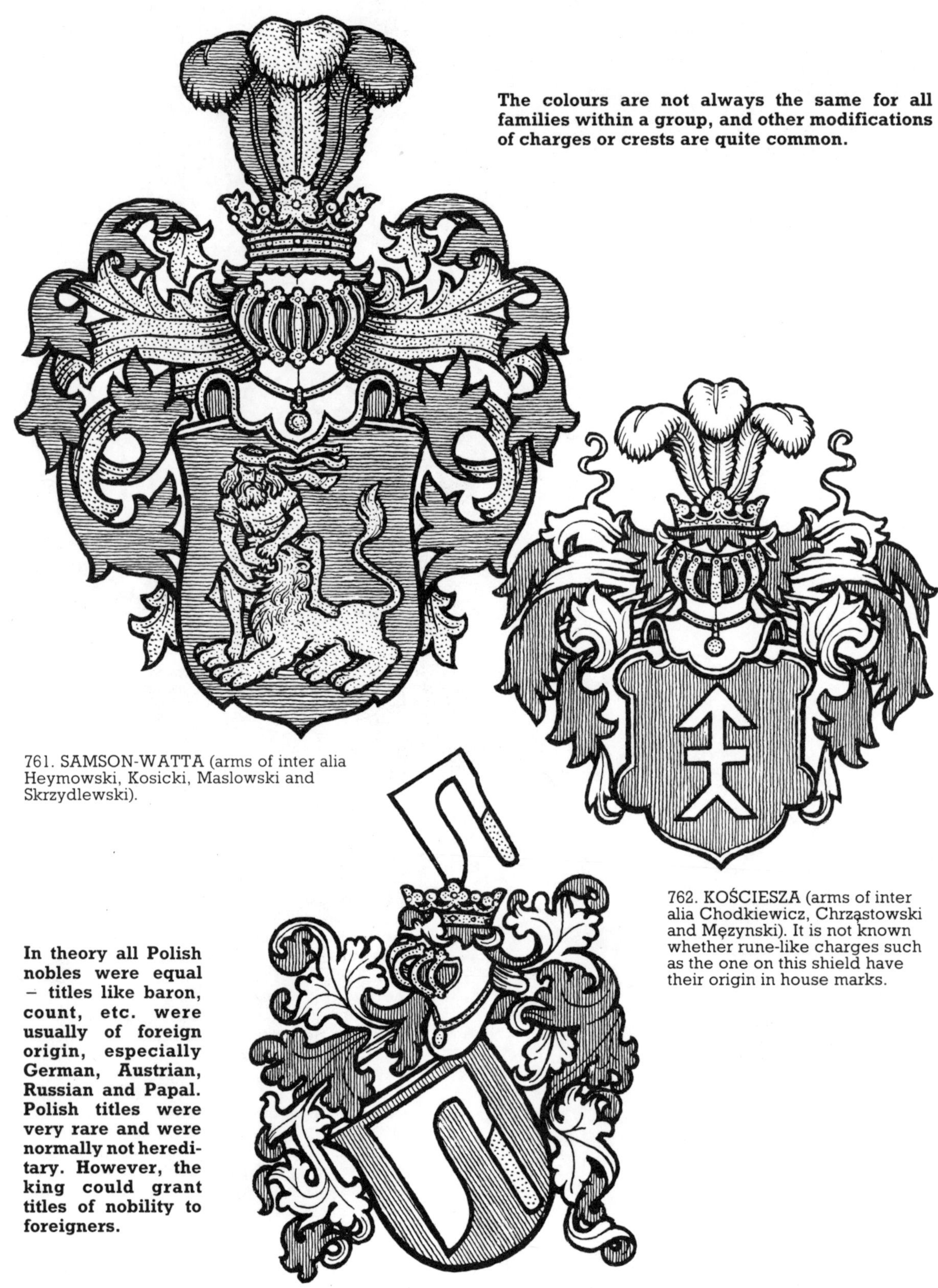

761. SAMSON-WATTA (arms of inter alia Heymowski, Kosicki, Maslowski and Skrzydlewski).

762. KOŚCIESZA (arms of inter alia Chodkiewicz, Chrząstowski and Męzynski). It is not known whether rune-like charges such as the one on this shield have their origin in house marks.

In theory all Polish nobles were equal – titles like baron, count, etc. were usually of foreign origin, especially German, Austrian, Russian and Papal. Polish titles were very rare and were normally not hereditary. However, the king could grant titles of nobility to foreigners.

763. TOPÓR-STARZA (arms of inter alia Ossoliński, Tarlo and Tęczyński).

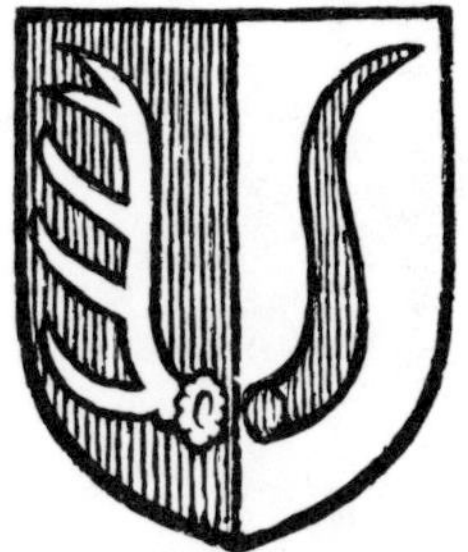
764. Rogala.
See fig. 813.

765. Leliwa.

766. Jastrzebiec-Bolesta (more than 550 families share these arms).

767. Sas.

768. LESZCZYC (arms of inter alia Dobrzycki, Radolin-Radolinski, Siemieński and Sumiński).

769. PILAWA (arms of inter alia Lachowsky-Lászloczky, Moskorzewski and Potocki).

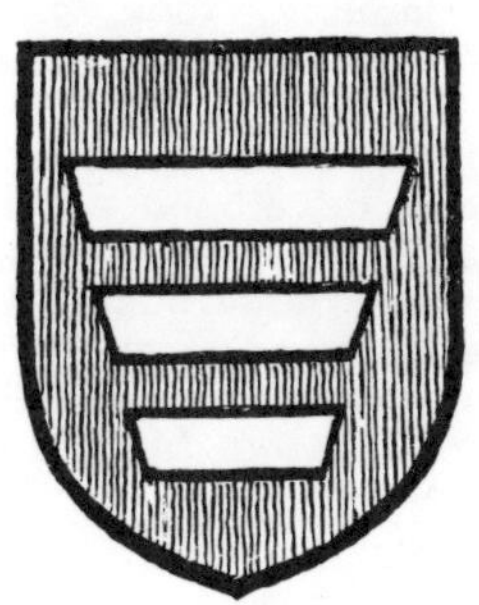
770. Korczak.

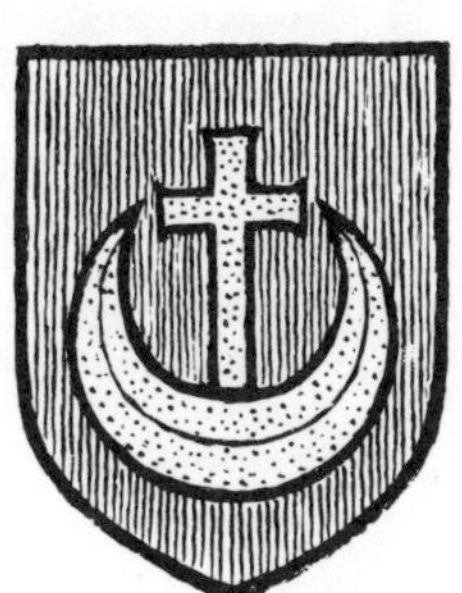
771. Szeliga.

772. Lis.

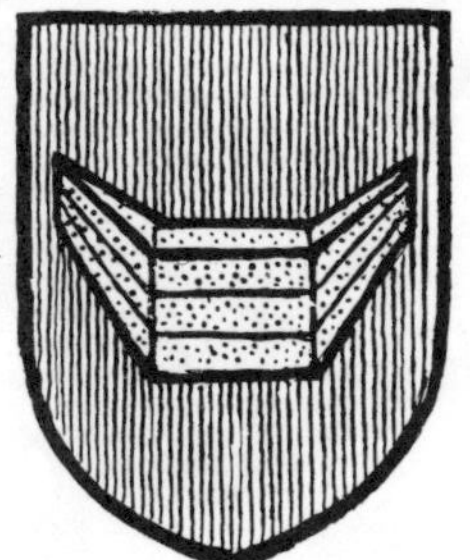
773. Lodzia.

Untitled Nobility of Russia

774. Coronet used by the untitled nobility of Russia.

In Russia heraldry developed rather late. From the 15th century onwards, Russian and Lithuanian nobles (mostly of princely rank) living in the western part of the country began, under Polish influence, to adopt armorial bearings. To the east, in what was then known as Moscovia, heraldic symbols were not used before c 1600. They first appeared on seals, and then, in imitation of the custom in Western Europe, they developed into regular coats of arms.

775. de Nabokov.

776. Pavlovitch.

A heart, pierced by an arrow or a sword, is a typical charge of Ukrainian arms.

Peter the Great, 1689-1725, trying to westernize his country, took great interest in heraldry and established an heraldic office in 1722, which was directed by a Heroldmeister (master of heraldry). Heraldry developed a foothold in Russia and armorial bearings were created for non-armigerous nobles and officers of the army and navy. By the end of the 18th century 355 new untitled nobles had been created by letters patent.

Old families were assigned a helm with bars which was placed affronté above the shield.

Despite the very strong influence of the heraldry of Western Europe, up until the end of the empire, 1917, there were attempts to make Russian arms more typically Russian. Some old families, with official sanction, began to use types of helm actually worn by Russian warriors of the 16th century and earlier.

777. Mordvinov.

Supporters were used by untitled as well as titled noblemen.

778. Melikov.

At the close of the 18th century Tsar Paul I ordered that all noble arms should be collected, registered and published in an armorial of the noble families of the Russian empire. The first volume appeared in 1797.

The six categories were:

1. Untitled nobility by imperial letters patent.
2. Noblesse d'epée, officers of the army who had reached the rank of colonel and officers of the navy who were captains of the first rank and above.
3. Noblesse du cap, government officials who had reached a rank equivalent to colonel.
4. Members of foreign nobility who had become naturalized Russians.
5. Titled nobility.
6. The old aristocracy, those families who were known as noble before 1685.

779. Lomikovsky.

The Leibkampanzi were members of the company of the Life Guards. Elizabeth, the youngest daughter of Tsar Peter the Great, was placed on the Russian throne by a military coup d'état in 1741. She rewarded the soldiers who had helped her by raising them to nobiliary rank, and they were given the honorary title of Leibkampanez and were granted armorial bearings. Their coats of arms were all of the same basic design. The shields were parted per pale, and the dexter half (sable, between three mullets argent a chevron Or, charged with three grenades fired proper) could be described as an augmentation which they all received. The sinister half contained their individual arms. They also all received the same (impossible) crest, a grenadier's cap, adorned with ostrich feathers and placed between two wings.

780. Zotov.

The charges selected for the arms of a new nobleman were supposed to symbolize his merits or allude to his name. His helm with raised vizor was set in profile.

781. Uluchkin.

Untitled Nobility in Sweden

782. Coronet used by untitled Swedish nobles. It may be placed above the shield if a helm is not used.

783. Gyllenbååt. Nobility by letters patent, early 18th century.

785. Scheffer.

784. von Samson-Himmelstjerna. Nobility by letters patent, 17th century.

Swedish heraldry has its origin in the Middle Ages and, in general, is not that different from the heraldry of Denmark. Both were greatly influenced by German heraldry. The history of the Scandinavian countries is very interlinked and so their heraldry developed its individuality rather late. Norway was united with Denmark by personal union from 1380-1814, and with Sweden from then on until 1905. In 1821 nobility in Norway was abolished by the Storting. Sweden was a partner of the Scandinavian union (with Denmark and Norway) from 1389-1523 (with intervals).

Untitled Nobility in Denmark

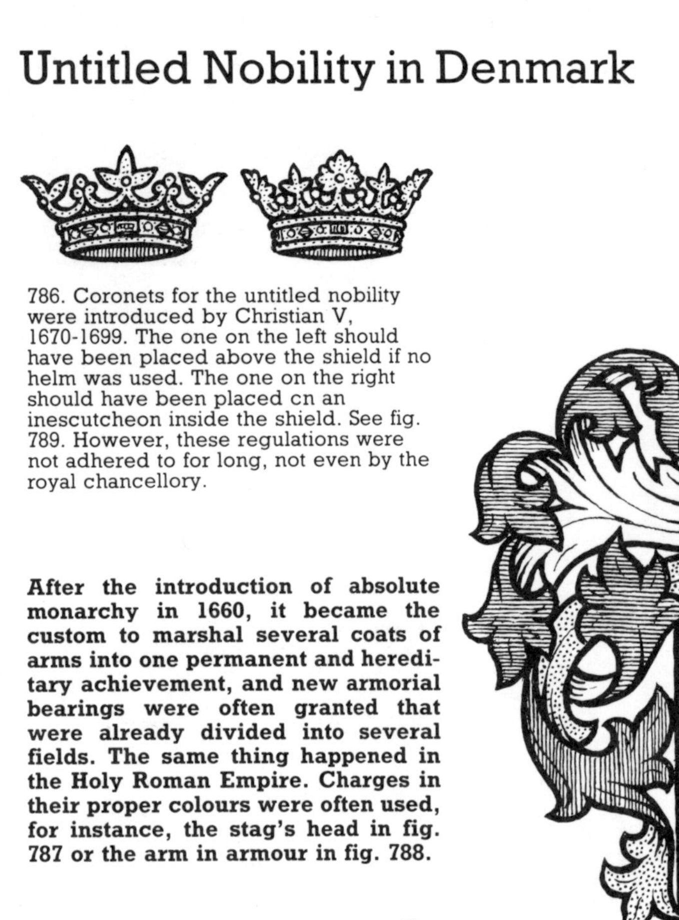

786. Coronets for the untitled nobility were introduced by Christian V, 1670-1699. The one on the left should have been placed above the shield if no helm was used. The one on the right should have been placed cn an inescutcheon inside the shield. See fig. 789. However, these regulations were not adhered to for long, not even by the royal chancellory.

After the introduction of absolute monarchy in 1660, it became the custom to marshal several coats of arms into one permanent and hereditary achievement, and new armorial bearings were often granted that were already divided into several fields. The same thing happened in the Holy Roman Empire. Charges in their proper colours were often used, for instance, the stag's head in fig. 787 or the arm in armour in fig. 788.

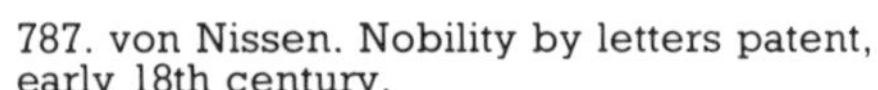

787. von Nissen. Nobility by letters patent, early 18th century.

788. von Rømer. Nobility by letters patent, 18th century.

789. Hegermann-Lindencrone. Nobility by letters patent, early 19th century.

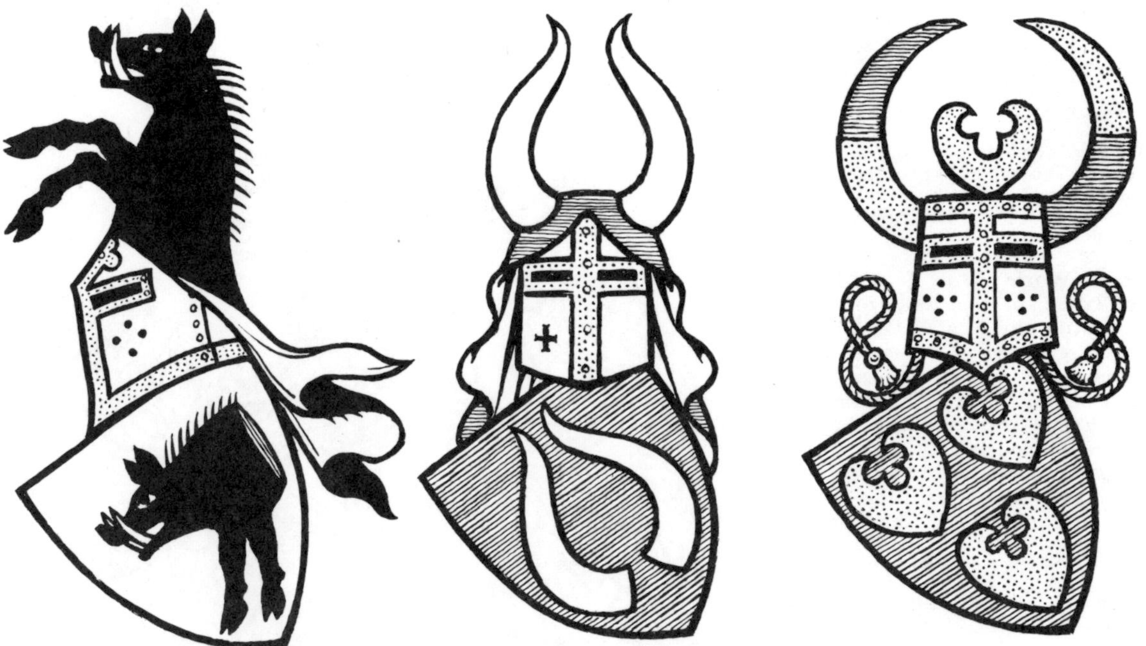

790. Høg. Extinct in 1478.

791. Todde. 1380, descendants unknown.

792. Ribbing. 1295, the family still exists in Sweden.

The earliest coats of arms of Danish noblemen are preserved on seals which date from the beginning of the 13th century. They were similar in style to the arms of the ancient noblesse in Germany. Unfortunately, as in most European countries, some of the old families that still exist have had their arms 'improved' at some time by quarterings and augmentations, especially from the 17th century onwards. In most cases this did not have a beneficial effect.

793. Drage. 1454, extinct 1536.

794. Lunge. 1268.

795. de Radestorp or Rastorp. 1281, extinct 1749.

Untitled Nobility in Germany

796. Two types of coronet for ordinary nobles. They may be placed above the shield if no helm and crest are used. The coronet with five pearls should never appear on the helm.

After World War I nobility was abolished in the new republics of Germany and Austria. In Austria the prefix von and the use of all noble titles were forbidden. In Germany they became part of the name.
In West Germany the reform of marriage and family laws from 1976 gives an example of the tendency to dissolve family tradition, stressing the importance of the individual.

797. von Mach. Arms of an ancient family of Polish origin.

Thus, a couple who are going to be married can choose between adopting the man's or the woman's surname, which any children then inherit. A man marrying the daughter of a nobleman might in agreement with his bride choose her family name. Since the former titles are now intrinsic parts of the family name, the republican law actually creates new members of the historic noblesse, at least in appearance. But the government is not concerned with family-heraldry, and it is questionable if a man who prefers his wife's name to his own is also entitled to the arms of her family.

798. von Hoffmann. Prussian nobility by letters patent, 19th century.

799. von Thal. Nobility by letters patent, Schwarzburg-Sondershausen, early 19th century.

UNTITLED GERMAN NOBILITY OF ANCIENT LINEAGE

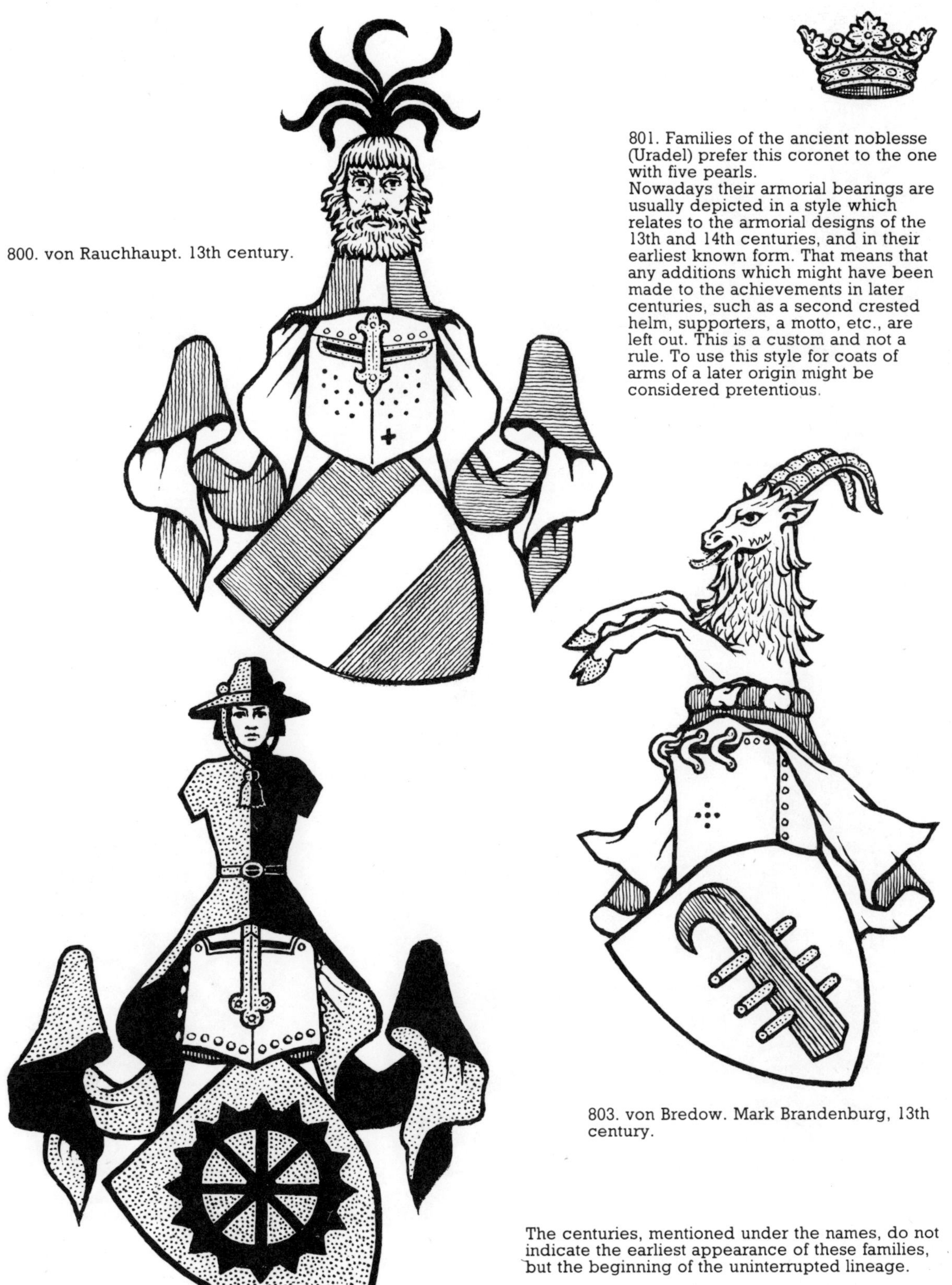

800. von Rauchhaupt. 13th century.

801. Families of the ancient noblesse (Uradel) prefer this coronet to the one with five pearls.
Nowadays their armorial bearings are usually depicted in a style which relates to the armorial designs of the 13th and 14th centuries, and in their earliest known form. That means that any additions which might have been made to the achievements in later centuries, such as a second crested helm, supporters, a motto, etc., are left out. This is a custom and not a rule. To use this style for coats of arms of a later origin might be considered pretentious.

803. von Bredow. Mark Brandenburg, 13th century.

The centuries, mentioned under the names, do not indicate the earliest appearance of these families, but the beginning of the uninterrupted lineage.

802. von Wedel. Pomerania, 13th century.

804. von Selchow.
Brandenburg, 13th century.

805. von Gersdorff. Silesia, 1301.

806. Schütz von Mossbach.
Thuringia, 14th century.

The crest-wreath is rare and a crest-coronet is only used if it appeared in the earliest version of an achievement. Quarterings and augmentations, being of later periods, are not used.

807. von Schönberg. Margraviate
Meissen, 13th century.

808. von Mallinckrodt.
Westphalia, 13th century.

809. von Trotha-Skopau.
Margraviate Meissen, 14th
century.

810. von Elterlein. Saxony, grant of arms by an imperial palace count in 1514.

811. von Hauff. Württemberg, nobility of the Holy Roman Empire by letters patent, 1604.

812. von Wolfersdorff. Vogtland, Saxony (Uradel).

813. Rogalla von Bieberstein. Ancient nobility originating from Bohemia. In Poland from the 12th century, Prussian in the 18th century. See fig. 764.

Untitled Nobility of German, Austrian and Bohemian Origin

814. *Right:* Edler von Frizberg. Austrian nobility by letters patent, 18th century.

815. von Römer. Saxony, nobility of the Holy Roman Empire by letters patent, 15th century.

816. *Right:* von Gerlach. Nobility of the Holy Roman Empire, 15th century.

The custom of quartering arms, which had its origin in the Spanish heraldry of the 13th century, spread all over Europe, excepting Poland and Hungary. In the 15th century a quartered shield became fashionable. Kings and princes quartered their family arms with the arms of the territories they ruled or claimed to have a right to possess. This caused politically less important people to quarter their arms to make their armorial bearings more impressive. Finally, new arms were granted which were already quartered.

817. *Right:* Edler von Remiz. Austrian nobility by letters patent, 18th century.

818. (von) Dreher. Württemberg, nobility of the Holy Roman Empire by letters patent, 16th century.

819. *Right:* von Sommerfeld. Bohemian nobility by letters patent, 17th century.

British Baronets and Knights Bachelor

Baronet is an hereditary rank below the peerage transmitted by primogeniture.
Baronets were instituted by King James I in 1611 in connection with the colonization of Ulster. This is the reason why baronets of England, Ireland and of the United Kingdom bear in their arms a small silver escutcheon charged with a red hand. This is a sinister hand, the arms of Ulster contain a dexter hand.
Since 1929 all baronets, excepting baronets of Scotland (or Nova Scotia), have a badge that contains this little shield. It may be shown with the arms of the holder, suspended by its ribbon below the shield.

821. Coat of arms of a baronet of the United Kingdom. Meredith of Montreal, Canada.

820. Coat of arms of a knight bachelor. Sir Peter Eade, Kt. 19th century.

822. Coat of arms of a baronet of Ireland. Cotter of Rockforest, County Cork.

In 1625 baronets of Scotland (or Nova Scotia) were instituted. They may bear a small canton or escutcheon of the arms of Nova Scotia in their shields. They are also entitled to a badge, bearing the arms of Nova Scotia, which is suspended by its ribbon below the shield.
Knight bachelor is a personal (not hereditary) rank, which represents ancient knighthood. Since 1926 a knight bachelor has had a badge which is placed below the holder's shield.
Barontes and knights have vizored helms of steel, placed above the shield affronté with the vizor raised. In practice these are often garnished with gold. The rule that this helm should face the spectator can create unpleasant effects if the crest must be turned to dexter. See figs. 821 and 822.

Hereditary Knights

823. Coronet for an hereditary knight in the Netherlands and in Belgium which was introduced by King William I in 1817 (Kingdom of the United Netherlands).
In the Netherlands this coronet is also used by the untitled nobility. See fig. 716. The (noble) title ridder, the Dutch word for knight, is also used in the Flemish speaking part of Belgium, while in the French speaking part chevalier is the correct designation.

824. de Van der Schueren. Arms of a Dutch hereditary knight in the style of the early 19th century. Nowadays, in a complete Dutch achievement, the coronet of rank above the shield is omitted.

In the Netherlands only six families have the title ridder, and in each case it is of foreign origin. In Belgium the title is usually transmitted by primogeniture but there are also knights who received the title ad personam.

825. de Decker.

Left: arms of a Belgian hereditary knight. The custom of placing the crested helm above a coronet of rank resting on the shield has its origin in the 17th century and is still adhered to in Belgium.

In Austria the title Ritter (knight) designated a rank below Freiherr (baron) and above Edler (noble). From the time of Emperor Charles VI, 1711-1740, until the fall of the monarchy in 1918, hundreds of hereditary knights were created. Nearly all of them were granted armorial bearings with two helms.

826. *Right:* arms of an Austrian hereditary knight.

von Liszt. Of Hungarian origin.

There is no difference between the arms of a French hereditary knight and the arms of an untitled noble. They should consist of shield, helm with torse and mantling. Since the Renaissance crests have been used sparingly.

827. *Below:* arms of a French hereditary knight (chevalier).

de Portier de Villeneuve. 17th century.

828. French pattern for the arms of a knight of the First Empire.
In Napoleonic heraldry helms and crests were abandoned and the coronets were replaced by a system of caps (toques) which indicated nobiliary rank. The shield of a chevalier d'empire contained a red pièce honorable (a fess, a bend, a chevron, etc.) charged with a simplified design of the badge of the Légion d'Honneur. Knights not of the Légion d'Honneur placed an annulet argent on the ordinary.

In the 19th century hereditary knights were created in the Kingdom of Bavaria. They ranked between the untitled nobility and the barons. There were also recipients of certain orders who were entitled to use Ritter von . . . before their surnames. In such cases the title was not hereditary.

829. *Right:* arms of a German (Holy Roman Empire and Bavaria) hereditary knight (Ritter).

von Molo.

The hereditary knight (cavaliere ereditario) is a rare title in Italy. It is found in Sardinia and Sicily and in the former Austrian provinces in the north of the country.

830. *Left:* the armorial bearings of an Italian hereditary knight.
Knights, invested with a knighthood from Austria or the Holy Roman Empire, would use their arms in the heraldic style from north of the Alps.

Prunas.

TITLED NOBILITY

British Barons (Lords)

Baron is the lowest degree of the English peerage. However, this title is never used, despite the fact that it is the legal term. A baron is always referred to as 'Lord'. In Scotland, where the legal term is lord, baron is used for the possessor of a feudal barony.

831. The coronet of a lord (baron). Coronets of peers are often depicted without the red cap.

832. Ellenborough. See fig. 704.

The achievement of a British peer is uniformly composed of shield, coronet of rank, crested helm with mantling, supporters and motto. Nowadays shield and supporters ought to stand on firm ground, a 'compartment'. Crest-coronets are very rare in comparison to the heraldry of central Europe, Hungary and Poland.

A very characteristic feature of British heraldry is that the helm may be left out of an achievement while the crest is placed 'on a wreath of the colours' or a crest-coronet is put above the shield, or, as in the case of a peer's achievement, it may float above the coronet of rank. See fig. 43.

833. Bagot.

Dutch and Danish Barons

The coronet for a Dutch baron is the same as for a Belgian or German baron. A coronet is no longer used on the shield if a helm and crest are used.

834. Huyssen van Kattendijke. Arms of a Dutch baron in the style of the early 19th century. The fleurs-de-lis are French augmentations, the rose is an English one. See fig. 1178.

The arms of these two Danish barons are characteristic grants of the 17th century. The inescutcheons, ensigned with baronial coronets, bear the ancient arms of these families (on the left from Kurland, on the right from Sweden). In both cases helm and crest are not used, but the arms of Wittinghof have two brown griffins as supporters, while the shield of Trolle is framed by two palm branches which are tied together below the shield by a bow of blue ribbon. See figs. 885 and 888.

835. af Wittinghof (Vietinghoff). Family of ancient nobility, friherre (baron) by letters patent, 17th century.

836. Trolle af Brahetrolleborg. Family of ancient nobility, friherre (baron) by letters patent, 17th century.

When a member of the untitled nobility was raised to a higher degree, such as baron or count, his arms were not always 'improved' by augmentations, supporters, additional crests, etc., but were sometimes left unchanged. Thus, the Baron af Hobe Geltingen (fig. 837) kept the arms of the ancient von Hobe family of Mecklenburg and placed the baronial coronet with seven pearls on the helm. This latter practice, typical of the decline of heraldry in the 17th and 18th centuries, is frowned upon by heraldists in Great Britain and central Europe, since these coronets, inventions of 'paper-heraldry', have never been used on real helms. However, in some countries, such as Sweden or Italy, coronets of rank on helms are the rule.

837. af Hobe Geltingen. Friherre by letters patent, early 19th century.

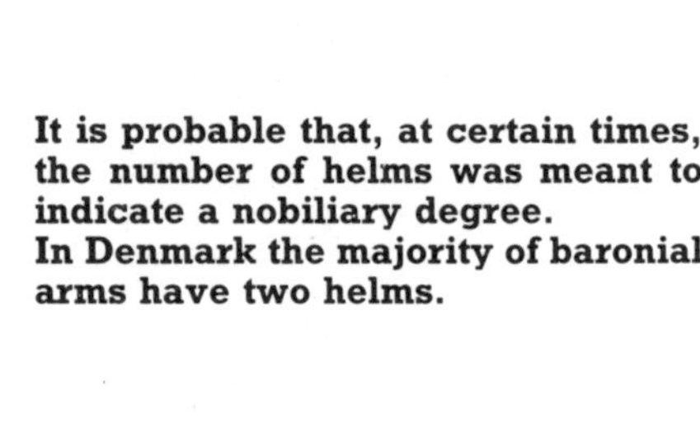

It is probable that, at certain times, the number of helms was meant to indicate a nobiliary degree.
In Denmark the majority of baronial arms have two helms.

838. af Stenglin.

Swedish Barons

839. Coronet for a Swedish friherre (baron), used on the helm as well as on the shield.

The coronet of eleven pearls is a distinctive feature of the arms of a Swedish baron.
There are usually two helms, both bearing this coronet, and a third coronet is placed above the shield. However, there are baronial achievements which have three helms or only one helm. Not every baron uses supporters.

840. von Wrangel, of the house of Ludenhof.

Both these families are of ancient noblesse and bear their original arms on an inescutcheon.
Below the shield of von Stackelberg hangs an odd augmentation, a Paukentuch which is the fabric round a cavalry drum.

841. von Stackelberg, of the house of Thomel.

German Barons

842. Older form of coronet for a Freiherr (baron), also used in Austria.

843. More recent form of coronet for a baron, also used in the Austro-Hungarian empire.

844. von Rotberg. Switzerland, 13th century.

845. von Gemmingen-Hornberg. Baden, 13th century.

846. von Gültlingen. Swabia, 12th century.

Families of the ancient noblesse (Uradel) often prefer to have their arms depicted in their earliest known form. See figs. 800-809.
If the shield alone is displayed, a coronet of rank may be placed above it. However, since different styles should not be mixed, a type of shield should be used that does not clash with a coronet of the 17th or 18th century.

847. von Stetten. Franconia, 13th century.

It is customary for two helms to face each other, but it would not be wrong if they were both turned to dexter. The arms of the titled nobility were often depicted with a coronet of rank set on the shield, with one or more helms above it. Nowadays these coronets are left out.

Mottoes have been used sparingly in German heraldry although they became more popular at the end of the 19th century.

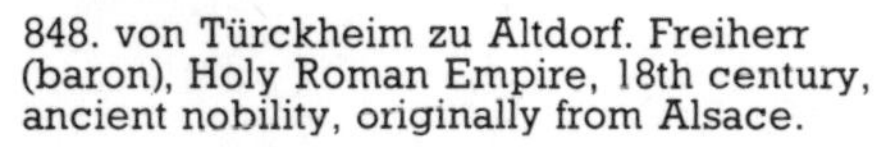

848. von Türckheim zu Altdorf. Freiherr (baron), Holy Roman Empire, 18th century, ancient nobility, originally from Alsace.

Many titled families have supporters for their achievements, but this does not apply to all of them. In Germany supporters never had the importance they have in British heraldry, and are not looked upon as a standard appurtenance of a titled nobleman's coat of arms.

849. Thumb von Neuburg. Hereditary marshals of the house of Württemberg. Ancient nobility of Swabia, 12th century.

French Barons

851. Pattern for the arms of a baron militaire of the Napoleonic empire. See fig. 828. The red sinister canton indicates a baron, the sword a soldier. The counter-vair pattern at the edge of the toque (cap), the silver clasp at the front and the three white ostrich feathers are also ensigns of a baron, and so are the two silver lambrequins.

850. A more recent form of coronet for barons.

852. Pattern for the arms of a baron évêque (baron bishop) in Napoleonic heraldry.

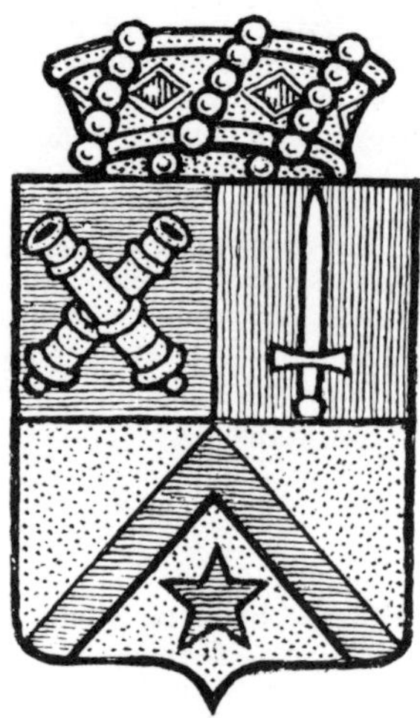

853. Boulart. After Napoleon's downfall the toques and lambrequins disappeared and holders of Napoleonic titles began to use the traditional coronets of rank. Only the particular style of composition and charges bring to mind the origin of such arms. See also figs. 854 and 857.

854. Pinoteau.

855. In the traditional heraldry of France the composition of armorial bearings is practically the same as in other countries. In the seventeenth century the helm was placed above the coronet of rank.

856. Nowadays the coronet of rank usually rests on the helm, however, as in former times, the helm is often discarded and the coronet rests on the shield. The French baronial coronet is called a tortil. It is also used in Russian heraldry.

857. Guiot de la Cour.

Belgian and Spanish Barons

858. Some Belgian barons use the couronne brabançonne (actually a cap) which was introduced under the rule of Austria.

859. Coronet of a Belgian baron.

The achievement of a baron created by a Belgian king is of the same type as fig. 825, but with supporters, and the coronet with seven pearls is placed above the shield.

860. Triest de Gits. Ancient noblesse of Flanders, 13th century, created barons by the Empress Maria Theresa in the 18th century.

861. Helm with coronet for a Spanish baron.

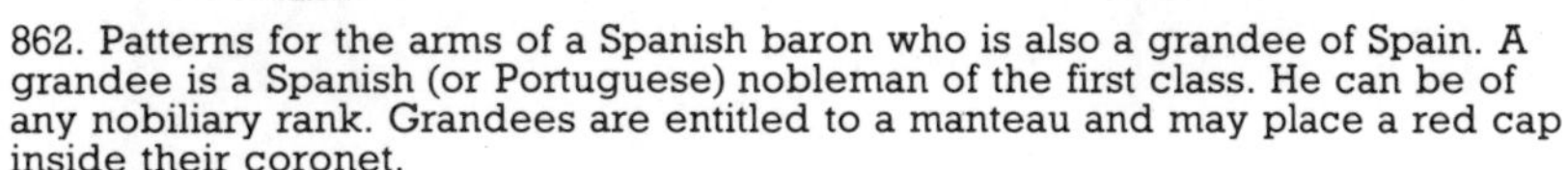

862. Patterns for the arms of a Spanish baron who is also a grandee of Spain. A grandee is a Spanish (or Portuguese) nobleman of the first class. He can be of any nobiliary rank. Grandees are entitled to a manteau and may place a red cap inside their coronet.

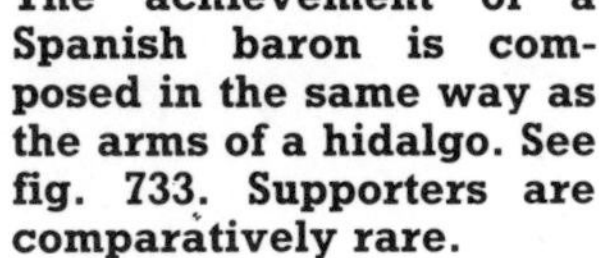

The achievement of a Spanish baron is composed in the same way as the arms of a hidalgo. See fig. 733. Supporters are comparatively rare.

Italian and Portuguese Barons

863. French style coronet for an Italian barone.

865. Monti della Corte. One coronet of rank is placed above the shield, another on the helm. To avoid repetition, two different coronets are used, both for the same rank.

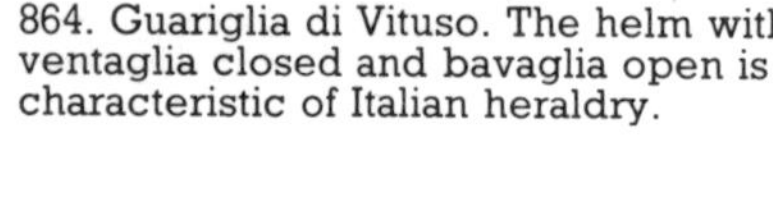

864. Guariglia di Vituso. The helm with ventaglia closed and bavaglia open is characteristic of Italian heraldry.

866. *Left:* this modern coronet for an untitled Portuguese nobleman was not used under the monarchy.

867. *Right:* pattern for the coat of arms of a Portuguese nobleman, here a baron. Coronets of rank may rest on the helm or on the shield.

Viscounts

868. Coronet of a Belgian vicomte (in Flemish burggraaf).

869. Dutch coronet of a burggraaf from the period when Belgium and the Netherlands were united, 1815-1830. No family in the Netherlands uses the title today, but the coronet is used by a few Belgian vicomtes.

870. Coronet of a British viscount.

871. Armorial bearings of the Belgian Viscounts de Vaernewyck.

872. Pattern for the arms of a British viscount. The red cap inside the coronet may be left out in an heraldic representation. In Scotland the motto is placed above the crested helm and the mantling of a peer is red and lined with ermine. (Naturally the supporters do not have to be lions.)

873. More recent form of a coronet for a French vicomte.

874. Older form of coronet for a French vicomte, which is also used by a Spanish vizconde.

875. Another type of coronet which is used by French and Portuguese viscounts.

876. Armorial bearings of Joseph Joachim Louis, Vicomte Laîné. A characteristic achievement of a pair de France at the time of the French restoration. The shield is encircled by the collar of the Order of the Holy Spirit and ensigned with the coronet of a viscount. Since he is a baron pair the manteau is topped with the coronet of a baron.

878. Arms of a Portuguese viscount, the 4th Visconde de São Sebastião.

877. Italian coronet for a visconte.

879. Other types of coronet used by viscounts in Italy.

The nobiliary rank of 'Viscount' did not exist in the empires of Russia, Austria-Hungary or Germany, nor in the kingdoms of Sweden, Norway or Denmark.

Russian, Swedish and Danish Counts

880. This comparatively modern coronet of a count is used in most European countries with the exception of Great Britain, the Scandinavian countries and the Netherlands. It was introduced into Russian heraldry where it was used above the shield and sometimes appeared on the helm.

881. Swedish counts use this type of coronet, with five visible leaves, which in many countries can be mistaken for the coronet of a duke. In a complete achievement it is placed on the helm. See figs. 924, 950 and 951.

882. The arms of the Russian Counts Tolstoi are composed according to western patterns. The original arms of the family are represented by the inescutcheon and the dexter crest.

883. The arms of the Swedish Counts Sparre af Sundby. At the end of the 17th century heraldic artists began to use manteaux instead of the normal mantling of the helms. This is now looked upon as bad heraldry. The arms are canting since the Swedish word sparre means chevron.

The coat of arms of a Swedish greve (count) normally has three helms, each bearing the coronet of his rank, and the shield is generally held by supporters. However, this does not apply in all cases.

Many of these arms have quarterings with an inescutcheon bearing the original arms of the family, a pattern which began in the 17th century.

The armorial bearings of the Counts Reenstjerna (see fig. 884) present a typical example.

884. Achievement of the Swedish Counts Reenstjerna, from the beginning of the 18th century.

By the middle of the 14th century kings had begun to place crowns above their heraldic shields. Crested helms began to lose much of their former importance when coronets of rank began to appear in the 17th century. In some countries, Denmark for example, these were prescribed in their particular forms. In France and Spain the titled noblesse preferred to have their arms ensigned by a crown or a coronet and helms were rarely used.
This fashion spread and armorial bearings without crested helms and mantling were granted to newly created counts and barons by the Danish kings.
The greatest number of these arms stem from the 17th century. They are usually composed of the shield, ensigned with a coronet. Some of them have supporters and some of them are framed by two palm branches tied together below the shield by a blue ribbon.
See figs. 835, 836, 885 and 888.

885. The arms of Counts Friis af Friisenborg are typical of Danish grants of the 17th century. The inescutcheon bears the original arms of the ancient noble family but turned to sinister.

886. Coronet for a Danish greve (count). It is used above the shield and also on the helm.

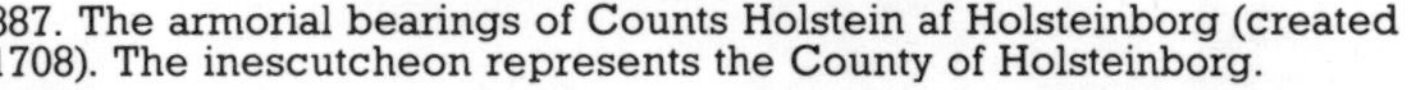

887. The armorial bearings of Counts Holstein af Holsteinborg (created 1708). The inescutcheon represents the County of Holsteinborg.

888. Arms of Counts Schack til Schackenborg. Hans Schack, created Count of Schackenborg in 1671, was a Danish field marshal.

At the end of the 17th century another international trend began to develop. No one wanted to renounce the new coronets, nor give up the crested helms, so the coronet of rank was set on the shield, and the helm was placed above it. This distortion of heraldic design could only have been invented by people who had no feeling for, nor knowledge of, the military equipment of the 13th or 14th century. Shields and helms should be depicted in their correct relationship, as far as size and style are concerned, and a coronet that can only fit a giant is out of place in an achievement. Some heraldic artists tried to lessen the discrepancy by reducing the coronet to the size of the crest-wreath or crest-coronet of the helm. It could then be placed between two helms, see figs. 840 and 841, if one helm was used the coronet could be placed by its side, resting on the shield.

In Denmark only a few coats of arms were granted with the coronet of rank set on the shield and the helms placed above it, and almost all of these are from the 18th and 19th centuries. This custom has now been abandoned in most countries, but is still practised in Great Britain, Belgium and Italy (see figs. 825, 832, 834, 864, 865).

French Counts and British Earls

889. Pattern for the arms of a comte militaire in Napoleonic heraldry. See fig. 851. The blue dexter canton indicates a count, the sword a soldier. The pattern of counter-ermine at the edge of the toque (cap), the clasp at the front and the five white ostrich feathers are also ensigns of a count, as are the four lambrequins (the two above are gold, the two below are silver).

890. Armorial bearings of Count de Montesquiou Fézensac. He was a member of the Collège électoral, which is indicated by the charge of the dexter canton in the shield. The blue manteau with its white lining indicates that he was a senator. The keys symbolize his office of grand chamberlain. See fig. 45.

891. Pattern for the arms of a comte archévêque (count archbishop). See fig. 852.

892. In the traditional heraldry of France the composition of armorial bearings does not differ from coats of arms in other countries. From the 17th century onwards titled noblemen would place a coronet of rank above the shield and set the helm with its appurtenances above it (if the latter was used at all). Today the coronet of rank may be placed on the helm.

893. The armorial bearings of General Leclerc de Hauteclocque, posthumously Marshal of France, 1902-1947. The shield is placed on the star of the Legion of Honour and encircled by the sash with the Order's badge pending from it. Behind the shield two batons of a maréchal de France are crossed in saltire. The crest figure is issuant from the coronet which is not considered good heraldry in most countries. A cri de guerre (battle cry) is placed above the crest, normally on a scroll.

(See fig. 913 onwards for colour section for titled nobility.)

PRINCES, DUKES, KINGS AND EMPERORS
Princes of the Holy Roman Empire, Austria and Germany

894. This type of hat was worn by a Kurfürst (prince elector) of the Holy Roman Empire in the 16th century.

895. Later type of hat for a prince elector, this was also used by Austrian dukes and princes.

896. Fürstenhut (hat of a prince), this was used by princes and dukes in the Holy Roman Empire.

897. More modern type of a princely crown.

898. Arms of the Princes of Liechtenstein.
1 Silesia, **2** Kuenringe (in contrast to the arms of Saxony, the field is barry of eight), **3** the Duchy of Troppau, **4** a modified version of the arms of the County of East Frisia, **5** in the point of the shield, the arms of the Duchy of Jägerndorf: over all an inescutcheon of the ancient arms of the princely house. See fig. 455 and 603.

Nowadays a manteau is often depicted as red, even if it is described as purple in the blazon.

899. Arms of the Belgian Princes de Ligne. Princes of the Holy Roman Empire, 1601. In Belgium a prince ranks before a duke. See fig. 47.

The German term Fürst (fem. Fürstin) describes members of the highest aristocracy of varying ranks and status. In this respect it corresponds to the English term 'Prince'.
As a specific title Fürst may mean a ruler of a principality or a titular prince, both ranking after a Herzog (duke) of their own category. The terms Prinz and Prinzessin denote sons and daughters of princely houses, of kings and of emperors.

900. The armorial bearings of Joseph Fürst zu Schwarzenberg, head of the house of Schwarzenberg. Austrian princes, princes of the Holy Roman Empire, 1670.
The shield is quartered of: **1** the ancient arms of the house of Schwarzenberg, **2** the ancient arms of the Counts zu Sulz, **3** the arms of the Seigneurs of Brandis, **4** an augmentation from 1599 for the victory over the Turks at Raab (Gyor, Hungary): over all an escutcheon of the arms of the former principality of Schwarzenberg. The chief of the Order of Malta indicates that the Prince is a knight grand cross of honour and devotion. The collar of the Order of the Golden Fleece encircles the shield.
The entire achievement could be placed on a manteau ensigned with the hat of a prince.
The tincture of the lion supporters is gold (not indicated in the illustration). Both lions wear helms (see fig. 547), the dexter one with the crest of Sulz, the sinister one with the crest of Brandis.

Dukes, Grand Dukes and Archdukes: Holy Roman Empire, Austria and Germany

901. Crown for a Herzog (duke) in the German empire, 1871-1918. This is actually a royal crown filled in with red or purple lining. It was also the crown for younger princes of a royal house.

902. The 'ducal hat' was originally adopted by prince electors to distinguish themselves from less important princes.

903. Crown for a Grossherzog (grand duke) or a royal crown prince. The crown is not completely filled with lining. At the turn of the century some grand dukes assumed royal crowns (i.e. without linings). Compare fig. 978.

904. Crown of a duke in Bavaria, and of Württemberg.

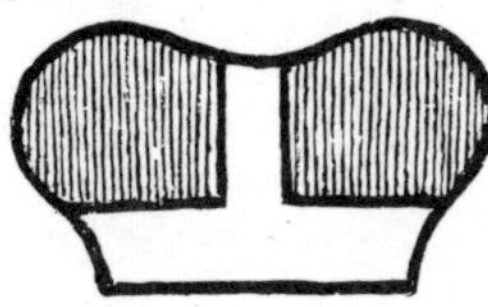

905. Hat of a duke of the Holy Roman Empire, 14th century. (Not used in heraldry.)

906. Crown of an heir to the throne of a ducal house in the German empire.

In the Holy Roman Empire, in Austria and in Germany, a Herzog ranked before a Fürst.

907. The shield of Austria ensigned with an archducal crown. From a woodcut by Albrecht Dürer, 1513.

908. Archducal hat.

909. Arms of the Archdukes of Austria (members of the imperial house of Habsburg-Lorraine), since 1896.
1 per pale, Hungary ancient, Hungary modern, **2** Bohemia, **3** per pale, Galicia, Lodomeria, **4** Lower Austria; over all the genealogical arms of the house of Austria: Habsburg, Austria and Lorraine. See figs. 569 and 570. The shield is placed on a manteau, topped by the royal crown of the archdukes (seven arches visible).

Dukes

910. Arthur Wellesley, Duke of Wellington, Knight of the Garter, 1769-1842.
The shield is quartered of Wesley or Wellesley and Colley or Cowley. The escutcheon in the chief point of the shield bearing the union badge of the United Kingdom of Great Britain and Ireland is an augmentation. The shield is encircled by the Garter and ensigned with a duke's coronet. The mullets on shield and crest are marks of cadency.

911. Coronet of a British duke. The tasselled cap, trimmed with ermine, is often omitted in heraldic representations.

912. Coronet of a French duke, after 1814. The tasselled cap, trimmed with ermine, indicates that he is a pair de France. In this form the coronet is used above a manteau. See fig. 950.

(Princes, dukes, kings and emperors continued after colour section.)

(Titled nobility continued from fig. 893.)

913. Coronet for a British earl. Like all the coronets of peers, it may be used without the red cap in an heraldic illustration.

914. Coronet for a French comte, older type.

915. The armorial bearings of the English Earl of Shrewsbury.

916. Arms of the French Comte de Ravel d'Esclapon.

917. Arms of the French Comte de Gérard du Barry.

Count is used in Great Britain to describe a nobiliary rank in foreign countries corresponding to a British earl. However, the wife of an earl is called 'Countess'.

Belgian Counts

919. Dutch coronet of a graaf (count).

Since French and Dutch (Flemish) are the two languages of Belgium both comte and graaf are used.

920. A 17th century coronet for counts.

LABORE ET CONSTANTIA

921. Coat of arms of the Counts Moretus Plantin, Belgian creation, 1906. The ancient arms are the same but without supporters or coronet of rank and crest-coronet, but with a crest-wreath.

922. Armorial bearings of the Belgian Counts de Brouchoven de Bergeyck, (created counts by Charles II, King of Spain, in 1679).

German Counts

923. Coronet for counts whose families belonged to the ruling families of the Holy Roman Empire (until 1806). Heads of a house have an orb surmounted by a cross instead of the ermine tail.

924. Coronet of a Graf (count), older form. A similar type of coronet is used by counts in Sweden. This would be looked upon as the coronet of a duke in several countries.

925. Coronet for a Graf, more recent form.

926. Coat of arms of Counts von Metternich, Holy Roman Empire, 1696, an extinct branch of the famous house. The imperial eagles are augmentations. The inescutcheon bears the original arms of the family.

927. The armorial bearings of Counts von Brandenstein-Zeppelin, Württemberg, 1909. The shield is quartered of: **1** and **4** von Zeppelin, **2** the dominion of Hengstfeld, **3** the dominion of Gaisberg; the inescutcheon bears the arms of von Brandenstein.

Italian Counts

928. Coronet for a conte palatino (palace count).

929. Coronet for an Italian conte (count).

931. Vimercati Sanseverino.

930. Mazzoti Biancinelli.

932. Pasquini.

In Italian heraldry titled noblemen usually use two coronets of rank in their achievements. These are often of two slightly different types. Also, a member of a titled family, not being the head of the house, places his own coronet above the shield as the coronet of the higher ranking head of house rests on the helm. See fig. 745. Supporters had to be granted or recognized by the Crown in former times, and are not used very often.

Italian and Spanish Marquises

933. Coronet for an Italian marchese (marquis).

934. Older form of a coronet for an Italian marchese which is also used in France and Spain.

935. Persichetti Ugolini.

936. Spreti.

According to the rules of the Italian Consulta Araldica (abolished by the republic), the helms of noblemen were supposed to be placed in profile or three-quarters profile. It seems, however, that from the rank of marquis upwards they were generally placed affronté. See also figs. 939 and 940.

937. *Right:* the arms of the Marqués de Aytona, Grandee of Spain, Knight of the Order of Calatrava. The batons of a capitán general are crossed in saltire behind the shield. The Marquis was believed (wrongly) to be entitled to the arms of the Prince Elector of Bavaria, on which was placed an inescutcheon bearing per pale Moncada and Aragon. Based on an 18th century design.

Spanish, French and Portuguese Marquises

In Spanish and French heraldry helms are placed affronté from the rank of marquis upwards.

939. The coat of arms of the Marqués de Castilleja del Campo, Knight of the Order of Santiago. Based on an 18th century design. He bore the arms of Ponce de León: per pale León and Aragón within a bordure charged with escutcheons of Vidaurre.

938. Arms of the French Marquis de Falvelly.

941. Arms of the Portuguese Marquis de Bellas.

940. Armorial bearings of the French Marquis de Paix de Coeur de Roumare.

British and Belgian Marquises

942. Coronet for a British Marquess. In an heraldic representation it may be used without the red cap.

943. Armorial bearings of the Scottish Marquess of Lothian. In Scotland peers have red mantlings lined with ermine but the crest-wreath is of the livery colours. The mottoes above the crest are characteristic of Scottish heraldry.

945. Coronet normally used by a Belgian marquis.

944. Arms of the Belgian Marquis van der Noot d'Assche. This ancient family of patrician origin (Brussels, 13th century) holds the title Marquis in primogeniture, created by William I, King of the Netherlands, in 1816. This is the reason for the use of the Dutch coronet for a marquis. No family in the Netherlands now bears the title Marquis.

947. Hat of a Russian knias (prince) as depicted in some Russian sources. In practice the same princely hat was used as was used in German or Austrian heraldry.

946. Gorchakov. The arms of Tshernigov.

948. Shakovskoy. The arms are quartered of Kiev and Smolensk. The inescutcheon bears the arms of Yaroslavl(?). See figs. 172 and 483.

The arms of the ancient princely families of Russia, descending from a common ancestor, were often shared by several houses. For instance, the Princes Bariatinski use the same arms as the Princes Volkonsky, since traditionally both descended from Sviatoslav II, Grand Prince of Kiev, originator of the Tshernigov branch of the house of Riurik. See figs. 172 and 483.

949. Bariatinski. The arms of Kiev and Tshernigov.

(Princes, dukes, kings and emperors continued from fig. 912.)

950. Coronet for a French duc of the ancien regime.

951. Coronet for an Italian duca. A red cap may be used inside. See fig. 958.

952. Coronet for a hertog in the Netherlands. However, there is no Dutch family bearing this title.

953. Arms of Michel Ney, Marshal of the Empire, created Duc d'Elchingen by Napoleon I in 1808. (He was created Prince of la Moskowa in 1812.)

In the French empire a duke ranked after a non-sovereign prince. In heraldry the titles shared the seven white ostrich feathers on the toque and the six golden lambrequins. The toque of a duke was edged with ermine and the blue manteau was lined with vair. A duke bore a red chief semy of silver stars (mullets) in his shield. In the achievement of Marshal Ney the badge of the Legion of Honour is displayed below the shield and two marshal's batons are placed in saltire behind the shield.

Dukes and Princes

954. *Right:* arms of a duque and grandee of Spain. These arms were granted to Christobal Colón (Christopher Columbus) after his discovery of America, which is referred to in the third and fourth quarterings (islands in the ocean and anchors). Between them, in the point of the shield, is the coat Columbus is supposed to have used before this one. The castle of Castile and the lion of León are augmentations. The anchors, crossed in saltire behind the shield, stand for the title 'Admiral of the Indias'.
The manteau and the coronet of rank belong to a later period and this design actually illustrates the arms of a duke of Veragua, which title was granted to Don Diego Colón, the oldest and only legitimate son of the explorer. See fig. 862.

955. Pattern for the arms of a prince and grand dignitaire of the Napoleonic empire. The chief of the shield and the manteau are semé of bees. In the hierarchy of the French empire, a prince ranked before a duke, which may be why this order of rank was continued, after the downfall of Napoleon I, in the Kingdom of the Netherlands and the Kingdom of Belgium.

956. Pattern for the arms of a sovereign prince of the Napoleonic empire. (Berthier for Neuchâtel, Bernadotte for Ponte-Corvo, Talleyrand for Benevent.)

(See figs. 946-949 of colour section for Russian princes.)

Italian Princes

958. Coronet for an Italian principe. In Italy a prince ranks before a duca (duke).

Left: the arms of an Italian prince are placed on a manteau which, according to the rules of the Consulta Araldica under the monarchy, is supposed to be purple with ermine lining (but without the black tails). In current practice, however, the manteau is red. It can be ensigned with the coronet of a prince, and also with the helm and its appurtenances, which is not done in other countries.
The tiara and the two keys indicate that a member of the family was a pope (Pius XII). The division of the shield is very unusual, but it was probably easier to depict the pontifical insignia in this way than in a chief.

957. Pacelli. Prince and Marquis Pacelli, created by the Pope in 1929, and by the King of Italy in 1941.

959. *Right:* the Princes Odescalchi use the hat of a prince and have their arms supported by a double-headed eagle because they were created princes of the Holy Roman Empire in 1689. Above the double-headed eagle is a papal insigne, the pavilion with the keys, also called ombrellino, which is borne by families who gave a pope to the Church or received it as an augmentation for outstanding services to the Church. The chief in the arms is the well known capo dell'impero. See fig. 746.

Odescalchi.

Styles of Coronet used by the Royal Family of Great Britain

960. Stylized version of the crown of the Sovereign.

961. Crown of the Prince of Wales, the heir-apparent. See. fig. 590.

964. The royal arms of the United Kingdom of Great Britain and Northern Ireland.
The arms are quartered of: **1** and **4** England, **2** Scotland, **3** Ireland. The shield is surrounded by the Garter. Plant badges adorn the compartment: roses for England, thistles for Scotland and shamrocks for Ireland.

962. Coronet of a son or daughter of the Sovereign, other than the heir-apparent.

965. Coronet of a son or daughter of a son or brother of the Sovereign, other than of the heir-apparent.

963. Coronet of a son or daughter of the heir-apparent.

966. Coronet of a grandchild of the Sovereign, who is issue of the Sovereign's daughters.

Kings and Princes

Princes of royal houses often receive the title 'Duke of . . .' (a province or a duchy of the realm). For instance, Prince Carl Wilhelm Louis of Sweden, brother of King Gustav VI, took the title Duke of Södermanland, while the eldest son of Gustav VI bore the title Duke of Västerbotten. Italian princes of the house of Savoy bear titles such as Duke of Aosta, Duke of Genoa, Duke of Bergamo, etc. Grand dukes of Russia and archdukes of Austria are imperial princes. See figs. 609 to 615.

967. The Danish royal arms, from 1948 to 1972, before they were simplified. Below the shield are the collars of the Order of the Dannebrog and the Order of the Elephant.

Some heads of formerly ruling houses use ancient titles. Thus, the great-grandson of the last ruling grand duke of Baden is the Markgraf von Baden. This title cannot be translated as 'Marquis', since a margrave was a ruling prince in the Holy Roman Empire while, in France and Italy for example, marquis and marchese are merely noble titles. The heir of the last King of Saxony is styled Markgraf von Meissen, while the head of the French royal house is the Comte de Paris.

968. The arms of Norway. The lion, already known from the 13th century, supports the axe of St Olav, the Patron Saint of Norway.

969. Coronet of the Swedish heir to the throne. The sheaf in the centre is taken from the arms of the house of Vasa which ruled in Sweden from 1523 to 1654.

970. Coronet for a prince or princess of the royal house of Sweden. Hertig and Hertiginne (duke and duchess).

971. The arms of Sweden. Albrecht of Mecklenburg, King of Sweden, introduced the three crowns as the territorial arms of Sweden in the 14th century. The shield is encircled by the collar of the Order of the Seraphim.

Royal Crowns and Imperial Crowns

972. The cap of Vladimir Monomakh, Prince of Kiev, was used for the first time by Ivan III in 1498.

973. Imperial crown of Russia, 1762. Crown of Catherine the Great.

974. This crown was created for Rudolf II, Emperor of the Holy Roman Empire, in 1602. The last emperor, Francis II, had already assumed the title of Francis I, Emperor of Austria in 1804 when the crown became the imperial crown of Austria.

975. The royal crown of Hungary, from the 11th century. Crown of St Stephen.

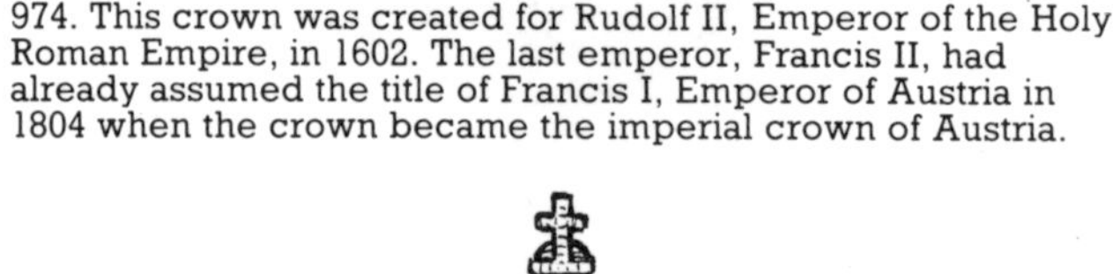

976. The royal crown of Bohemia from 1347. Crown of St Wenceslas.

977. The new imperial crown of Germany, 1871, modified in 1889. This heraldic crown existed only in drawings and sculpture.

978. The grand ducal arms of Luxembourg are ensigned with a royal crown.

979. French imperial crown. Napoleon I and Napoleon III, emperors of the French.

980. A royal crown with red lining rests on the shield of the Prince of Monaco.

CORPORATE ARMS

Great Britain

More than any other country in Europe, Great Britain uses the crested helm in civic arms.
The tilting helm is the normal helm used in the arms of a corporation. However, the crest of the arms of Edinburgh is borne on a knight's helmet.

Today any corporate body of sufficient status may be granted arms and crest in England. Supporters are reserved for the more important corporations.

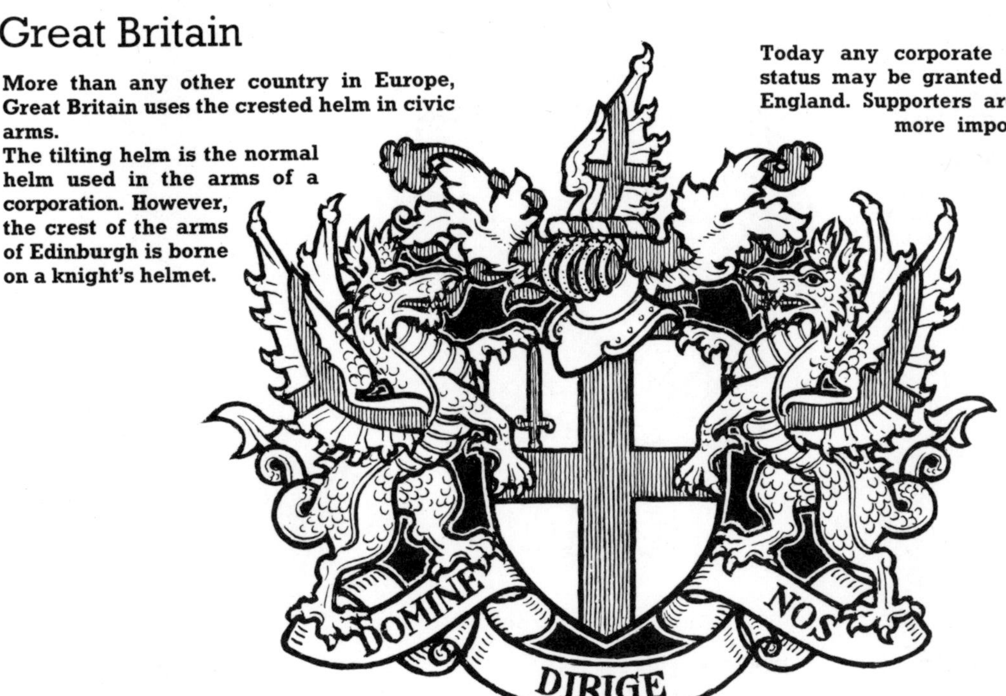

981. City of London, the ancient arms. The crest on a peer's helmet and the supporters were confirmed and granted in 1957.

982. Coronet for the arms of a Scottish district council. Scottish burghs are no longer granted crests, instead they use mural crowns of various tinctures, red for a burgh of barony, blue for a police burgh and natural (grey) stone for a royal burgh. A county council has a crown of two garbs between three points (visible) on a circlet.

983. City of Rochester, Kent, recorded at the visitations of 1574 and 1619.

984. Rothesay, Scotland, a royal burgh. The mural crown is of grey stone.

985. City of Salisbury, Wiltshire, recorded at the visitations of 1565 and 1623.

In British municipal arms the mural crown is used as a crest-coronet and also as a charge. It also appears occasionally as a crest-coronet in family arms.

Civic Arms in France, Belgium and Austria

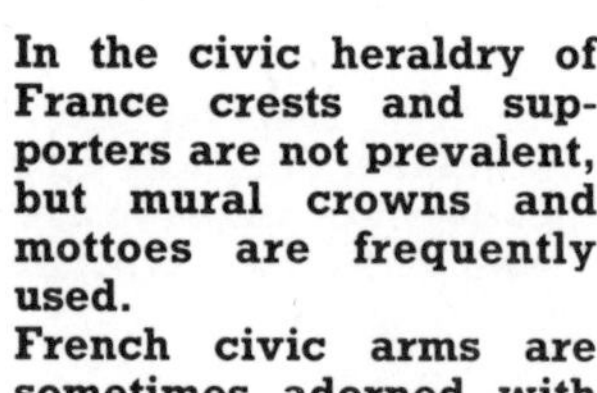

In the civic heraldry of France crests and supporters are not prevalent, but mural crowns and mottoes are frequently used.
French civic arms are sometimes adorned with decorations for bravery in wartime, which is unusual in other countries. See fig. 553.

987. Pattern for the arms of a town of the first order in Napoleonic heraldry.

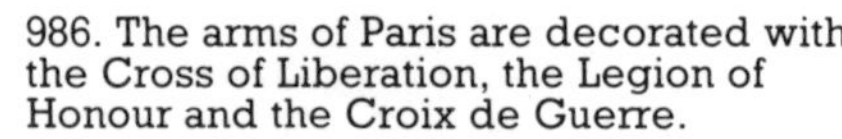

986. The arms of Paris are decorated with the Cross of Liberation, the Legion of Honour and the Croix de Guerre.

988. Pattern for the arms of a town of the second order in Napoleonic heraldry.

In France many city arms have a blue chief, either semé de lis or bearing three golden fleurs-de-lis, the badge of a 'good town of France'. In the heraldic system of the Napoleonic empire a town of top rank had a red chief charged with three golden bees. Towns of the second grade of importance received a blue canton in dexter, bearing the letter N in gold and above it a gold star. Towns of the third degree had a red canton in sinister, charged with the imperial N and a star in silver.

989. The arms of Brussels, capital of Belgium, show the archangel Michael defeating the devil in combat. The shield is ensigned with an ancient coronet of a count and supported by two lions carrying banners of Brabant and the city. Supporters carrying banners are frequently found in Belgian heraldry, mainly in the armorial bearings of titled noblemen.

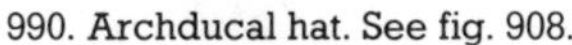

990. Archducal hat. See fig. 908.

991. The Styrian ducal hat. See fig. 332.

992. The princely hat of Salzburg. See fig. 896.

In the Federal Republic of Austria the provinces of Upper Austria ***(left)*****, Styria** ***(centre)*** **and Salzburg** ***(right)*** **still use princely bonnets above their ancient arms.**

993. The hand couped at the wrist was the original heraldic symbol of the Belgian city of Antwerp. It was the sole charge of the banners flying from the turrets of the oppidum in ancient seals. Eventually the banners disappeared, and a hand was placed in dexter, another in sinister, chief of the arms. The garland with six roses encircling the shield is probably an allusion to the landjuwelen (jewels of the land), a contest and an award for poetical and theatrical achievements in the Dutch language, originating in the 15th century. The (modern) coronet of a marquis probably refers to a period of history when Antwerp and environment formed a marquisate of the Holy Roman Empire. The couple of 'savages' holding the shield do not seem to have a particular meaning.

Civic Arms in the Netherlands and Germany

Helms and crests are not used, but many civic arms are ensigned with coronets and crowns, and supporters are common.

994. The three saltires in the arms of Amsterdam are symbols of justice, they also appear in the arms of Nieuwer-Amstel, Bergen-op-Zoom and other towns. The shield is ensigned with the imperial crown, which was granted by Maximilian I in 1488. Today this crown is fashioned after the imperial crown of Austria. See fig. 974. The lions supporting the shield are of natural colour. The motto, which was granted in 1946, means 'heroic, determined, compassionate'.

995. The arms of Belfeld, in the province of Limburg, confirmed 1926, have the figure of St Urban as a single supporter.

996. *Below:* the arms of Westerbork in the province of Drenthe, 1948.

997. *Left:* the three towns Buren, Beusichem and Zoelen were fused in 1977. The arms of the new Buren were granted in 1978. The dexter supporter is charged on the shoulder with the arms of Beusichem, the sinister with the arms of Zoelen. The shield is ensigned with a Dutch coronet of a marquis.

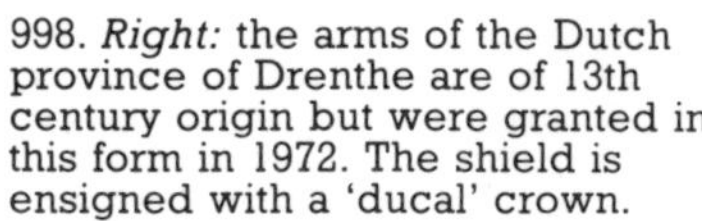

998. *Right:* the arms of the Dutch province of Drenthe are of 13th century origin but were granted in this form in 1972. The shield is ensigned with a 'ducal' crown.

999. *Left:* the arms adopted by the German federal state of Württemberg-Baden in 1954 are based on the ancient arms of the dukes of Swabia. The supporters, a stag and a griffin, symbolize the tradition of Württemberg and of Baden. The crown is a novelty in heraldry. It is composed of the arms of the old territories which are now located in the new state: Franconia, Hohenzollern, Baden, Württemberg, Palatinate and Swabian Austria. See fig. 544.

1000. A bear as the sole charge of the arms of Berlin appeared for the first time on a signet, known since 1618. These arms belong to West Berlin, a state of West Germany.

1001. The arms of Essen, North Rhine-Westphalia, are a shield charged with a sword. They have been known since c 1400. In 1623 the Emperor granted the city the right to use the imperial eagle. The ancient princely crown is an exception in German civic heraldry. Twin escutcheons are comparatively rare. They are also found in the arms of the cities of Nürnberg and Fulda.

1002. Red or stone-coloured mural crowns are used in German heraldry, but they are disappearing slowly. Before 1919, towns in which a German ruler resided were supposed to use a mural crown with five turrets. See fig. 37.

1004. The town of Köslin, Pomerania, was annexed by Poland after World War 2 and is now called Koszalin. The achievement is a comparatively rare example of civic arms with helm and crest.

1003. The arms of Tempelhof, a district of West Berlin, bear the cross of the Knights Templars, who were in possession of Tempelhof until 1312. All the districts of West Berlin use the red mural crown with the small escutcheon of Berlin. The arms are from 1957. See figs.1181-1192.

Civic Arms in Spain, Portugal and Italy

1006. Pattern for the arms of a small town in Portugal, according to the reform of official heraldry in 1930. The scroll is not meant to bear a motto, it is for the name of the town plus its status, for instance, 'Vila de Murao' or in the case of a city 'Cidade de Bragança'.

1005. The arms of Madrid, capital of Spain, have their origin in the 13th century. The bear is of natural colour. Two further fields were added, bearing a dragon and a wreath, but these are no longer used. See fig. 556.

1008. A Spanish mural crown.

1007. Pattern for the arms of a city in Portuguese heraldry, after the reform of 1930. The crown of Lisbon, capital of the country, is golden, as were the crowns of the Portuguese overseas provinces. See fig. 557.

1009. Italian mural crown for communes.

1010. The arms of Rome, capital of Italy, bear the letters SPQR for Senatus Populusque Romanorum, and a cross as symbol of the capital of the Catholic Church. The city was under papal rule, with only two interruptions, from the 5th century until 1870.

1011. Italian mural crown for larger cities.

Arms of Swiss, Dutch, Belgian and German Guilds

1012. Gardeners

1013. Boatmen and fishermen.

1014. Carpenters and masons.

1015. Blacksmiths.

Arms of some of the guilds of Basel, Switzerland, 1415.

1016. Butchers.

The arms of artisans were fairly common by the 14th century, and the arms of guilds are known from banners of the 13th and 14th centuries. However, the arms of guilds remained changeable until the 16th century. See the chapter on Burgher-Arms. Corporate arms were considered quite normal in some countries, for example, in Switzerland, while others, such as Denmark, seals were used but no true artisan heraldry was developed.

1017. Tailors and furriers.

1018. Glaziers, stainers and painters.

1019. Potters.

1020. Boatmen.

1021. Furriers.

1022. Tailors.

Arms of some of the guilds of Groningen in the Netherlands, 17th century(?).

1023. Arms of the Corporation of Furriers of Antwerp, Low Countries (now Belgium), 1550.

1024. Butchers (Antwerp).

1025. Boatmen of Antwerp.

1026. Butchers (Antwerp).

1027. Butchers of Antwerp. See fig. 993.

1028. Bakers of Antwerp.

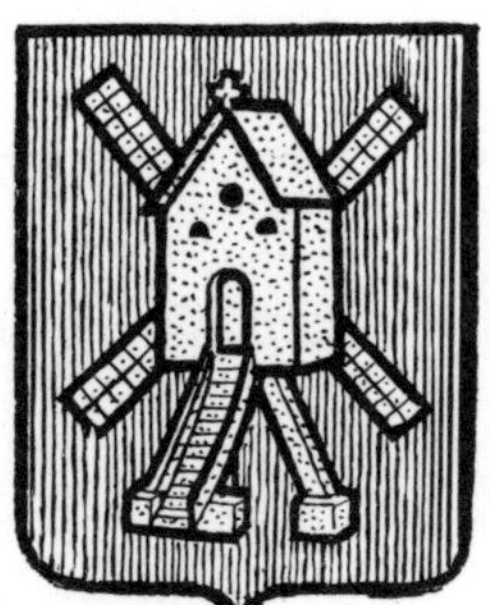

1029. Millers of Antwerp.

1030. Blacksmiths of Antwerp.

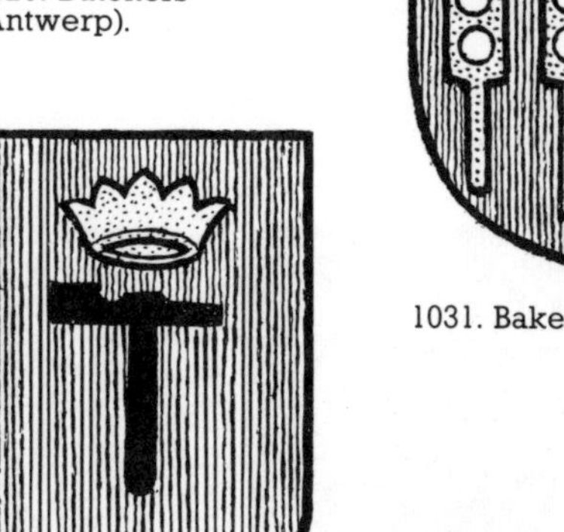

1031. Bakers of Ghent.

1032. Vintners of Ghent.

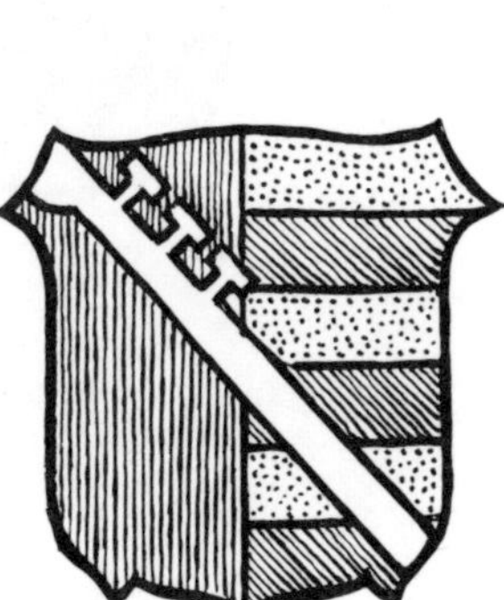

1033. Brewers of Ghent.

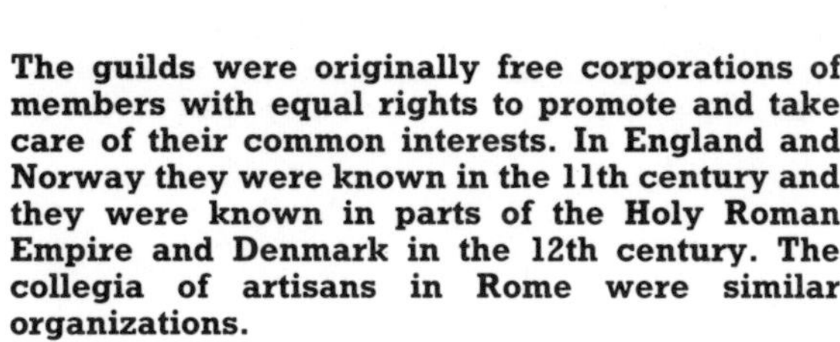

The guilds were originally free corporations of members with equal rights to promote and take care of their common interests. In England and Norway they were known in the 11th century and they were known in parts of the Holy Roman Empire and Denmark in the 12th century. The collegia of artisans in Rome were similar organizations.

The guilds, and other associations of merchants and craftsmen, used the tools or other symbols of their trade as charges for their arms. So it is not surprising to find similar, or even the same, arms used in different parts of Europe. Perhaps the best example is the arms of painters. See figs. 1050-1054 and compare figs. 1024 and 1037.

Arms of some of the guilds of Augsburg, Germany, 16th century.

1034. Fishermen.

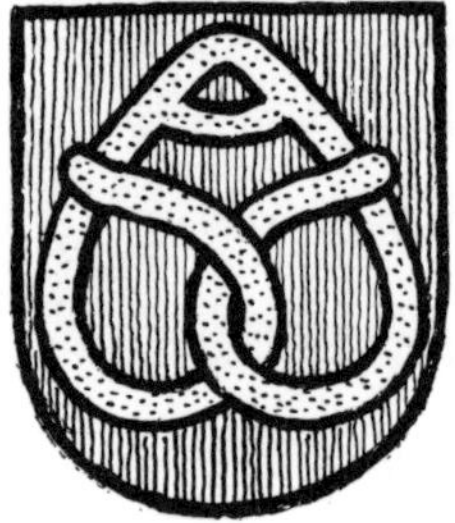

1035. Bakers.

1036. Shopkeepers.

1037. Butchers.

1038. Shoe-makers.

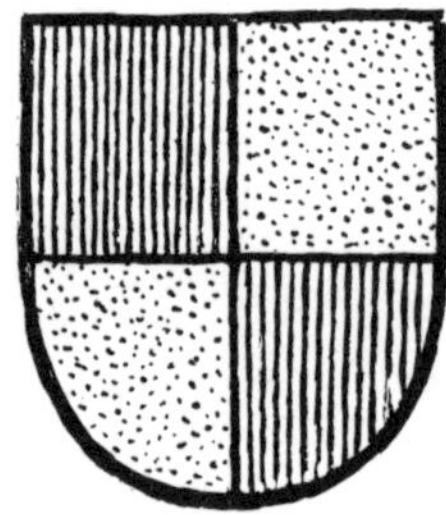

1039. Weavers.

1040. Tailors.

1041. Furriers.

1042. Blacksmiths.

1043. Brewers.

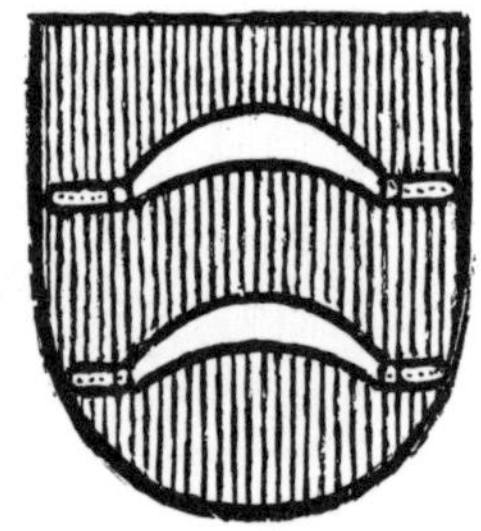

1044. Tanners.

1045. Carpenters.

In some German states and towns the guilds still functioned in the 19th century. In England they had lost their importance by the 18th century and in France they were abolished in 1791.

1046. Armorial bearings of the Worshipful Company of Painter-Stainers of the City of London. The original arms, which consisted of the chevron between three phoenix heads, and the crest (a phoenix proper) were granted in 1486. The latin of the motto makes little sense. The supporters are silver panthers, spotted with various colours. See fig. 346.

1047. Arms of the Worshipful Company of Carpenters of the City of London, 1466. The motto is: Honour God.

1048. Arms of the Worshipful Company of Feltmakers of the City of London, 1946.

1049. Arms of the Worshipful Company of Paviors of the City of London. A crest, supporters and motto were granted in 1929.

Corporate Arms and Personal Arms of Painters

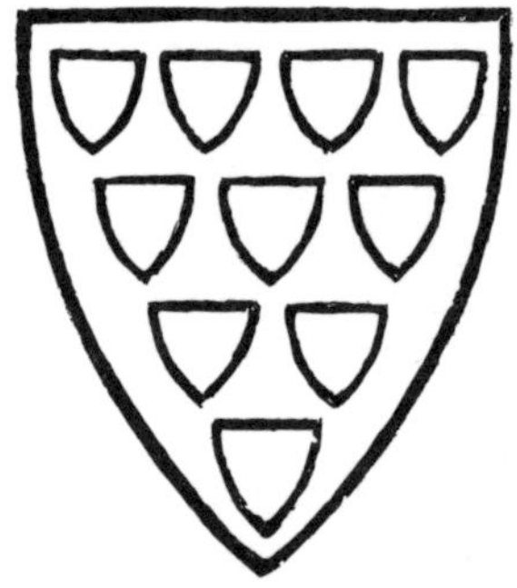

1050. The Guild of Painters of Cologne, Germany, 1396.

1051. The Guild of Painters of Freiburg, Germany, 14th century.

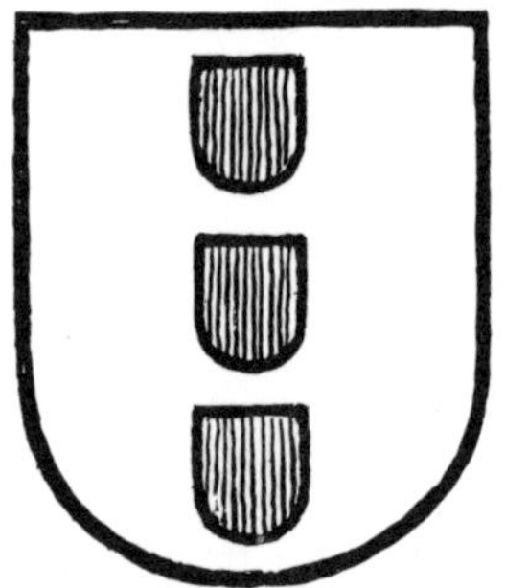

1052. In Basel, Switzerland, the tinctures were reversed and the escutcheons arranged in pale.

1053. In France and in the Netherlands the shield is blue and the escutcheons are silver, sometimes gold.

1054. Arms of the German painters (house-painters and artists).

The workshop of a mediaeval painter had little in common with the present-day workshop of a house-painter or the modern studio of an artist. The craft demanded a wide range of technical skills, from painting the walls of a house and its doors and shutters to more artistic and decorative work. Until the middle of the 14th century the making and painting of shields for war, tournament and ceremonial purposes, was one of his main sources of income. The painter of that period was called a Schilter in German. In modern Dutch a painter is still called a schilder, derived from schild (shield), thus the painters' arms are actually canting.

According to legend St Luke was not only a physician, he was also a painter. Painters adopted him as their patron saint and many of the guilds received his name. The winged bull, symbol of St Luke, often appears in connection with their arms. See fig. 177.

1055. Arms of the painter Steffel Prenner, 15th century.

1057. Arms of the painter Johann Moritz Riesenberger, died 1740, Hamburg, Germany.

1056. Arms of the painter Georg Fröschl, 15th century.

Painters often marshalled their family arms with the arms of their art, but they also assumed arms which contained elements thereof.

1058. Arms of the painter Niclas von Brune, Vienna, Austria, 1408.

Figs. 1055 and 1056 are from the books of the Fraternity of St Christopher, Arlberg, Austria, 15th century. Figs. 1050-1053 and 1059-1061 are adaptations from Siebmacher's *Grosses und allgemeines Wappenbuch.*

Corporate Arms of Book Printers, Stationers and Booksellers

1059. Arms of the Society of Book Printers, Leipzig, Saxony, 1720.

1060. Arms of the Society of Book Printers, from an etching of 1640, Leipzig, Saxony.

1061. Arms of the book printer Lorenz Kober of Leipzig, Saxony c 1615.

1062. Arms of the book printers of Germany, commonly accepted since 1883. Similar armorial bearings had been used before, based on the legend that they were granted to printers by Emperor Frederick III (1440-1493). The G in the shield stands for Gutenberg, the inventor of the art of bookprinting.

1063. Arms of the Stationers' Company, alias 'the Masters and Keepers or Wardens and Commonalty of the Mystery or Art of a Stationer and Newspapermaker of the City of London'. The arms were granted in 1557. A crest and supporters were granted in 1951.

1064. Arms of the Society of Book Printers of Jena, Saxony, 1657. (After Siebmacher.)

1065. Kretschmer. German burgher-arms of a family of printers and publishers.

1066. Arms of the Portuguese Corporation of Printing and of the Graphic Arts, 1963. These arms are probably no longer in use following the political changes in Portugal.

Since the start of the 17th century the griffin has appeared in so many of the arms of printers that it can be considered their heraldic beast.

1067. Arms of the book sellers of Leipzig, Saxony, 18th century. (After Siebmacher.)

Arms of the Medical Profession and Apothecaries

1068. The armorial bearings of the Royal College of Surgeons of England were granted in 1821. The drawing is in the rather elaborate style used at that time. The serpents and the lions couchant guardant in the shield are blazoned as proper. The supporters represent Machaon and Podaleirios (according to Greek myth the sons of Asklepios (Aesculapius)) who were physicians to the Greeks in the Trojan War.

1069. The rod of Aesculapius is the symbol of the medical profession. It should not be confused with a caduceus. See fig. 1081.

1070. Pestle and mortar, a symbol of the apothecaries.

1071. A pair of scales and a mortar with pestles as combined symbols of the apothecaries.

1072. Even an enema-syringe was used as an heraldic charge. In this case by the apothecaries guild of Saint-Lô, France, in the 17th century.

1073. Covered cups appeared in the arms of the apothecaries of Mayenne, France.

1074. The arms of the British Medical Association, 1955. The supporters, blazoned as proper, represent Hippocrates and William Harvey.

1075. Arms of the Bristol Royal Infirmary, England, 1967. The motto, borne on a scroll below the shield is 'Charity universal'. See fig. 177.

1076. Arms of the German Nobel prizewinner Dr Emil von Behring, 1901. A sword was used instead of a rod.

1077. Arms of the French physician Dufriche Desgenettes, an army doctor under Napoleon I. The sword, in bend sinister, in the sinister canton is the symbol of a baron, medical officer, in Napoleonic heraldry. Compare with fig. 851.

Medical Institutions (continued) and Symbols of Trade and Commerce

1078. The arms of the London Hospital, 1927.

1079. The English College of Physicians. The hand feeling the pulse of an arm is a very appropriate charge.

1080. The arms of the Guild of Surgeons of Gouda, the Netherlands, 1710. The pentacle or pentagram is a symbol of health. See fig. 1087.

1081. Caduceus or rod of Mercury. This is a symbol of trade and commerce. Compare with fig. 1069.

1082. A caduceus and a horn of plenty crossed in saltire, used in the arms of Kharkov, Ukraine, granted in 1781.

1083. The caduceus and the hammer in the arms of Tampere, Finland, stand for commerce and industry.

1084. The arms of Lloyd's Register of Shipping, 1957. The book in the arms is ensigned with a mercantile crown.

Corporate Arms of Music, Theatre and Dance

1085. Arms of the Worshipful Company of Musicians of the City of London, 1604.

1086. Portuguese arms of the theatre arts, 1961. See comment on fig. 1066.

1087. Arms of the Royal Academy of Dancing, 1937. Everything in this design seems to dance. The crest-figure represents Terpsichore, muse of dance. The does with golden wings are of natural colour.

1088. *Right:* arms of the Performing Right Society Limited, 1947, England.

Corporate Arms of Universities and Colleges

Many universities in Europe use symbolic designs on their seals. These are sometimes combined with heraldic elements. Other colleges have heraldic shields which may contain the arms of the state and/or the town in which they are located or parts thereof. Books, opened or closed, are often used as charges.
In Great Britain it is normal for universities and colleges to use armorial bearings. Most of these consist of shield and motto only, although a number use a crest and a few, for instance, the universities of Kent and Sussex, use supporters.

1089. *Right:* the arms of the University of Southampton, Hampshire, England, were originally granted to the Hartley University College in 1948.

1090. The arms of Queen's College, Oxford University were recorded in 1574.

1091. The arms of the London School of Economics and Political Science, granted 1922. The beaver is of natural colour.

1092. The arms of Balliol College, Oxford University were recorded in 1574.

RELIGIOUS ORDERS OF CHIVALRY

1093. Arms of the Order of the Knights Templars (Militia Christi). It was founded in 1118 and abolished by Pope Clement V in 1312.

1094. Badge of the Order of the Knights Templars.

1095. Arms of the Hospitallers of Saint Lazarus, a military and religious Order, founded in Jerusalem in the early 12th century.

1096. Badge of the Military and Hospitaller Order of Saint Lazarus of Jerusalem.

1097. The armorial bearings of Francis, Cardinal Spellman, Archbishop of New York (died 1967). The design is made in the old style (with mitre and crozier which are no longer used by cardinals, archbishops or bishops). The dexter half of the shield contains the arms of the Archdiocese of New York, the sinister half contains the personal arms of the Cardinal with a chief of the Order of Malta. The cross of the Order is placed behind the shield.

Only professed members of the Order of Malta have the right to place the Order's cross behind the shield. However, the concession to cardinals is an exception which the Prince Grand Master can grant to other prelates. It is forbidden to use any secular symbol of dignity or decoration in the heraldry of the Roman Catholic Church, excepting the crosses of the Order of Malta and of the Order of the Holy Sepulchre.

The Teutonic Order

1098. The ancient arms of the Hochmeister (high master), later Hoch- und Deutschmeister (high and German master).

1099. Arms of the Teutonic Order (Orden der Ritter des Hospitals St. Marien des Deutschen Hauses zu Jerusalem), founded in 1190 and converted into a religious Order of Chivalry in 1198. In 1928 the Order was changed into a clerical order by Pope Pius XI. The Teutonic Order is now called Brüder des Deutschen Ordens St. Mariens zu Jerusalem and consists of priests, lay brothers and lay sisters. Honorary knights and Marians are affiliated as familiares. Mission and parochial work are the main tasks of the brothers, while the sisters are engaged in Caritas and teaching the young.

1100. Later form of the arms of the Hoch-und Deutschmeister.

1101. Breast cross of the Teutonic Knights. Now used as a badge by the priests and brothers of the Order. The badge of the brothers is smaller than that of the priests. Priests, brothers and sisters wear a slender form of this cross on a black cord placed around the neck.

1102. The badge of an honorary knight is still worn by familiares of the clerical Order who receive this honour.
The badge of a Marian (the same cross but without the helm) is worn on a black and silver-white necklet.

1103. The arms of Archduke Eugen of Austria, the last of the Habsburg Hoch-und Deutschmeister, who abdicated in 1923. The 'genealogical' arms, Habsburg, Austria, Lorraine, are placed on the eagle's breast. Compare fig. 909. The Hochmeister of the clerical Order uses the ancient arms (fig. 1098). The marshalling of family or personal arms with the arms or insignia of the Order has not been permitted since 1929.

The Teutonic Order in the Netherlands

1104. Arms of a Baron van Nagell, marshalled by quartering with the arms of the Order.

1105. Arms of a Count van Rechteren.

1106. Arms of a Baron van Pallandt, marshalled by impalement with the arms of the Order.

Only a knight commander has the right to marshal his arms with the arms of the Order or place the Cross of the Order behind his shield.

1107. The Chivalric Teutonic Order, Bailiwick of Utrecht (De Ridderlijke Duitsche Orde, Balye van Utrecht) is the only part of the ancient Teutonic Order which still exists as an Order of Chivalry. It had become almost independent by the 15th century. The first Protestant Land-Commandeur was Jasper van Lijnden (1619), and under Hendrik Casimir, Count of Nassau, the knights were permitted to marry (1637) and the bailiwick separated from the main Order. Today the bailiwick is an Order for Protestant noblemen in the Netherlands, engaged in works of charity.

1108. Breast cross of a Commandeur (knight commander).

1109. Cross of a Kapittel-Ridder (chapter-knight) which is also worn by a knight commander.

The Order of the Holy Sepulchre

The Equestrian Order of the Holy Sepulchre of Jerusalem (Ordo Equestris Sancti Sepulcri Hierosolymitani) grew from the custom of European knights conferring knighthood on members of their class at the Holy Sepulchre. From 1500 onwards the guardian of the Franciscan monastery on Mount Sion performed this rite and from 1847 it was performed by the Latin Patriarch of Jerusalem. In 1868 Pope Pius IX united the knights in the Equestrian Order of the Holy Sepulchre.
The present Grand Master is Maximilian Cardinal de Fürstenberg.
The Order promotes projects in the Holy Land, such as the building and maintenance of churches, monasteries, universities, schools etc. It also sponsors the education of future pastors and teachers.

1110. Arms of the Equestrian Order of the Holy Sepulchre. In former times the crown of thorns was placed on the helm like a crest-wreath but now it is used as a crest. In the statutes of the Order, from 1950, the shield is blazoned as 'argent, the cross of Jerusalem Or'. However, in practice it is shown as red.

1111. Arms of Eugène Cardinal Tisserant, former Grand Master of the Order of the Holy Sepulchre (died 1972). Grand masters quarter their arms with the arms of the Order. Others place the cross of the Order behind their shields, or put the cross somewhere next to the achievement wherever it best fits the design. They may also, in a very conventional way, display their badge suspended from a black ribbon below the shield.

The Order of Malta

The Sovereign Military Order of Malta (Ordo Equitum Hospitaliorum Sancti Johannis Hierosolymitani) was formally recognized by the Pope in 1113. After the loss of the Holy Land, the Order first withdrew to Rhodes and later to Malta, of which it was the sovereign from 1530 to 1798. This is why the Order was called 'of Rhodes' and is still called 'of Malta'. In former times the knights were also called Knights of St John, after St John the Baptist who was patron saint of their first hospital in Jerusalem, from which they took their name. Today their headquarters are in Rome, from where the Order controls its extensive hospital and charitable work.

1112. The flag of the Order carries the Order's arms.

1114. The flag of the institutions of the Order carries the Order's badge.

1113. Arms of the Sovereign Military Order of Malta. The black manteau and the rosary encircling the shield symbolize the religious character of the Order.

1115. Arms of Grand Master Guillaume de Villaret, Provence, 1296-1304.

1116. Arms of Grand Master Giovanni Battista Orsini, Italy, 1467-1476.

1117. Arms of Grand Master Pierre Cardinal d'Aubusson, Auvergne, 1476-1503. He was the first grand master to quarter the Order's arms with his own.

1118. Cross of the Order.

1119. Arms of the first Prince Grand Master Alof de Wignacourt, France, 1601-1622.

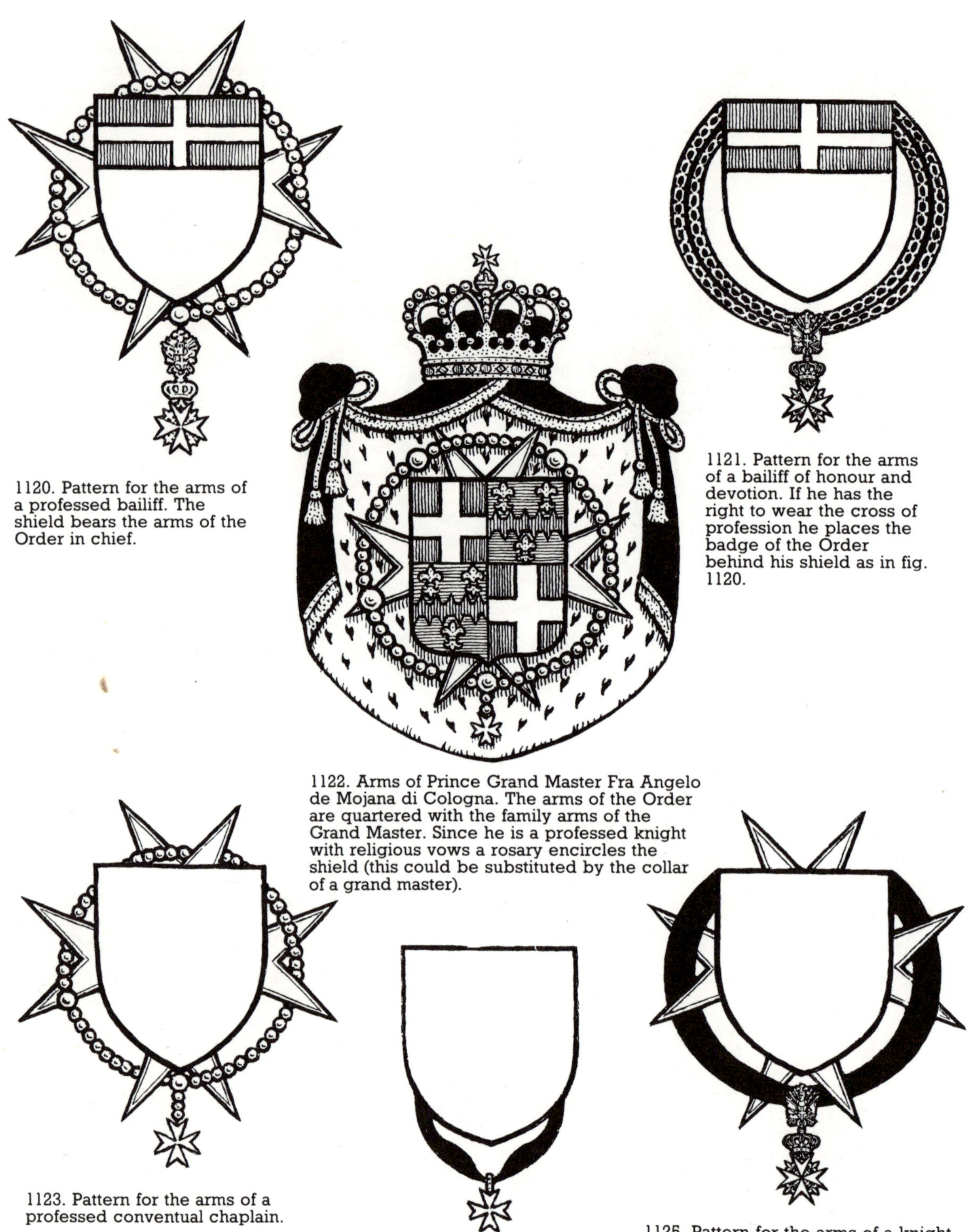

1120. Pattern for the arms of a professed bailiff. The shield bears the arms of the Order in chief.

1121. Pattern for the arms of a bailiff of honour and devotion. If he has the right to wear the cross of profession he places the badge of the Order behind his shield as in fig. 1120.

1122. Arms of Prince Grand Master Fra Angelo de Mojana di Cologna. The arms of the Order are quartered with the family arms of the Grand Master. Since he is a professed knight with religious vows a rosary encircles the shield (this could be substituted by the collar of a grand master).

1123. Pattern for the arms of a professed conventual chaplain.

1124. Pattern for the arms or monogram of a conventual chaplain ad honorem.

1125. Pattern for the arms of a knight of justice (with simple vows).

(Religious orders continued after colour section.)

HERALDRY IN THE ROMAN CATHOLIC CHURCH

1126. Pavilion or ombrellino. The emblem of a basilica. It is also used by the Cardinal Camerlengo during a vacancy in the Holy See. Compare figure 959.

1127. The arms of Pope John Paul I (died 1978). See figs. 44, 110 and 179.

1128. The arms of Pope John Paul II (elected 1978). The tiara is the emblem of the papacy. The three crowns symbolize the Church militant, penitent and triumphant, as well as the Pope's offices as priest, pastor and teacher of the faithful.

1129. The arms of the papacy and of the Vatican City. The pontifical or papal insignia, the tiara and the two keys, are placed on a red shield. The keys are the symbol of St Peter, Christ's vicar on earth.

1130. The arms of the Belgian Cardinal Mercier, Archbishop of Mechlin (died 1926).

The shield of a cardinal is ensigned with a red hat with 15 red tassels on either side of the shield, hanging from a red cord piercing the brim. For a time the number of tassels was considered unimportant, but 15 tassels on each side became customary during the time of Pope Pius VI, 1775-1779, and they became the rule in 1832. Cardinals who are patriarchs, archbishops or bishops place the cross of their rank behind the shield. In 1969 Pope Paul VI ordered that croziers and mitres should no longer be used. See fig. 40.
However, a diocese may use the mitre, with cross and crozier, and an abbey may use a mitre with crozier.

1131. The arms of the German Cardinal Döpfner, Archbishop of Munich and Freising (died 1976). The shield is quartered of: **1** and **4** the Archdiocese of Munich and Freising, **2** and **3** the personal arms of the Cardinal.

1132. *Right:* pattern for the arms of a patriarch. The shield is ensigned with a green hat from which two green cords are suspended with 15 green tassels on each side of the shield. A double-traversed cross is placed behind the shield.

1133. Pattern for the arms of an archbishop. The shield is ensigned with a green hat from which two green cords are suspended terminating in ten green tassels on either side of the shield.

1134. Pattern for the arms of a bishop. The shield is ensigned with a green hat from which hang two green cords with six green tassels on each side. A bishop places a simple cross behind his shield.

1135. Pattern for the arms of an abbot and provost with a mitre and crozier. The shield is ensigned with a black hat with black cords and six black tassels on each side. Formerly an abbot or a provost had the right to use a mitre and crozier in his achievement. Nowadays a veiled crozier is placed behind the shield.

1136. Pattern for the arms of an abbot and prelate nullius. The shield is ensigned with the same hat and number of tassels as for a bishop. The achievement may use a crozier with a veil (sudarium) instead of a cross. An abbess or a mother superior are not members of the clergy. They may surround their shields (oval) with a rosary and place a veiled crozier behind it.

1137. Pattern for the arms of a prelate di fiocchetto. Of the four high ranking prelates of the papal curia only a vice-chamberlain still holds office. Formerly there was also an auditor general, a treasurer general and a majordomo to the Pope.
The hat is violet with red cords and ten red tassels on each side of the shield.

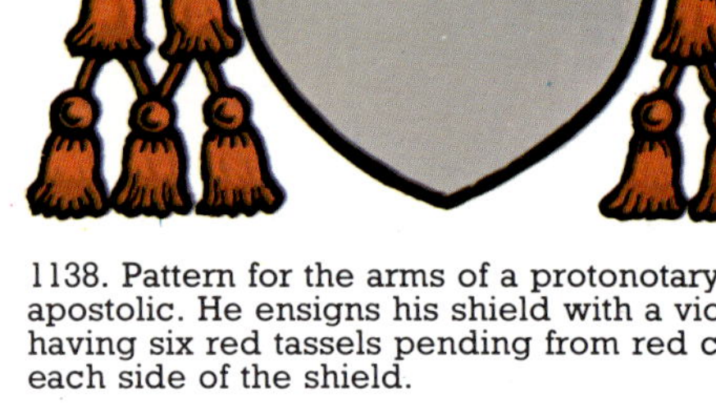

1138. Pattern for the arms of a protonotary apostolic. He ensigns his shield with a violet hat having six red tassels pending from red cords on each side of the shield.

1139. Pattern for the arms of a prelate of honour. He uses a violet hat with violet cords ending in six violet tassels on each side of the shield.

1140. Pattern for the arms of a chaplain to the Pope. The hat is black. The cords, with six tassels on each side of the shield, are violet.

1141. Pattern for the arms of a canon.

1142. Pattern for the arms of a dean and minor superiores. The hat is black with black cords and two black tassels on each side of the shield. The tassels can also hang side by side from a knot.

1143. Pattern for the arms of a priest. Hat, cords and the one tassel on each side of the shield are black. See fig. 38.

HERALDRY IN THE CHURCH OF ENGLAND

Archbishops and diocesan bishops of the Church of England may impale their arms with the arms of their see. Other bishops use only their family arms. All bishops place the precious mitre above their shields. The mitre of the Bishop of Durham is placed within a 'ducal' coronet (a crest-coronet), and a sword and crozier, crossed in saltire, may be placed behind his shield. This tradition goes back to the times when the Bishop of Durham was a count-palatine.
The arms of other bishops and sees may be displayed with two croziers crossed in saltire behind their shields.

1144. *Left:* arms of the Archbishop Lord Fisher of Lambeth (died 1961). His personal arms (argent, a fess wavy between three fleurs-de-lis sable) are impaled by the arms of the Archbishopric of Canterbury. The pallium, here used as a charge in the arms of the see, is often displayed below or above a shield when used in the arms of a Roman Catholic archbishop.
It is an external sign of dignity used only by residential archbishops.

1145. Arms of the Bishopric of Coventry.

1146. Arms of the Bishopric of Carlisle.

The mitre, symbol of episcopal dignity, is out of favour in the heraldry of the Roman Catholic Church, however the Church of England maintains the ancient tradition of placing a mitre above the arms of a bishop.
The same applies to the crozier, an emblem of episcopal jurisdiction, which is now used (veiled) only in the arms of an abbot in the Roman Church, while in the Church of England it is still used as an appurtenance to episcopal arms. See figs. 1135 and 1136.

1147. Arms of the Archbishopric of York. This is one of the two arms registered at the College of Arms.

1148. Pattern for the arms of a dean. Three red tassels on either side of the shield hang from purple cords.

Unlike the Roman Catholic clergy, in the Church of England clergymen of non-episcopal rank can use their own arms with helm, crest and motto.
In 1976 appropriate ecclesiastical hats were prescribed. These are all black, with cords and tassels in different tinctures, and may be used to ensign the arms of Anglican clergy in place of a helm and crest. The use of these hats is not obligatory and an Anglican priest who wishes to keep his own helm and crest may do so.

1149. Pattern for the arms of an archdeacon. Three purple tassels on either side of the shield are pendent from purple cords.

1150. Pattern for the arms of a canon, honorary canon emeritus or prebendary. Three red tassels hang from black cords on either side of the shield.

1153. Pattern for the arms of a priest. Two black tassels hang from black and white cords on each side of the shield. See fig. 1143.

1151. Members of the ecclesiastical household of a British sovereign use the hat of their degree charged with a Tudor rose.

1154. Pattern for the arms of a priest who is also a doctor of divinity. The arms of a doctor of divinity can be recognized by the skein of red which is interlaced with the cord of the hat of his degree.

1152. Deacons may use a black hat above their arms.

(Religious orders continued from fig. 1125.)

The Order of Malta (continued)

1155. Pattern for the arms or monogram of a knight of magistral grace.

1156. Pattern for the arms or monogram of a donat of devotion, 1st class. A donat of justice has the same arrangement as in fig. 1125 but with the badge of his degree pendent from the ribbon and the cross of three arms behind the shield.

1157. Pattern for the arms or monogram of a donat of devotion, 3rd class. The arrangement for the 2nd class is the same but the badge has a crown.

The Orders of St John of the Alliance of Niederweisel (1961)

The Protestant Orders of Sweden and the Netherlands were originally parts of the Bailiwick of Brandenburg (Johanniterorden).

1159. Gonfalon of the Swedish Order of St John. See fig. 971.

1158. Cross of the Swedish Order of St John (Johanniterorden i Sverige).

1160. Cross of the Dutch Order of St John (Johanniter Orde in Nederland).

1161. Arms of the Dutch Order of St John, granted 1971. The flag in fig. 1114 is used. See fig. 616.

The Johanniterorden

The Bailiwick of Brandenburg of the Chivalric Order of St John of the Hospital of Jerusalem (Die Balley Brandenburg des ritterlichen Ordens St Johannis vom Spital zu Jerusalem *called* Johanniterorden) started becoming independent from the Sovereign Order in the 14th century when the knights in the north-east of Germany were placed under the Markgrave of Brandenburg (1318). The real beginning of the Order was after the Thirty Years War when the Lutheran knights received seven of the thirteen commanderies and were given the right to continue to wear the eight-pointed cross and use the Order's titles. The Prince Elector of Brandenburg was declared Summus Patronus et Protector Ordinis. The Order is engaged in hospital and charitable work.

1162. Cross of the Order.

The Order has no arms of its own. The flag in fig. 1114 is used.

1163. Arms of the Herrenmeister (master) of the Johanniterorden, Prince Wilhelm Karl von Preussen. If the arms of the Hohenzollern family *(above right)* are not shown, the escutcheon quartered of white and black replaces the letters FR on the breast of the eagle. See figs. 507, 299 and 306.

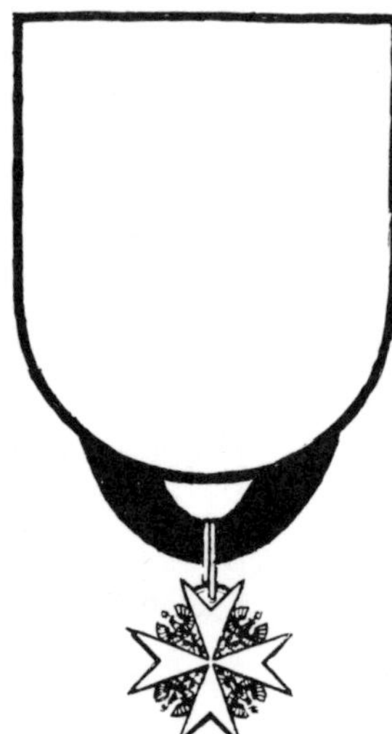

1164. Pattern for the arms of an Ehrenritter (knight of honour).

1165. Pattern for the arms of a Kommendator (knight commander).

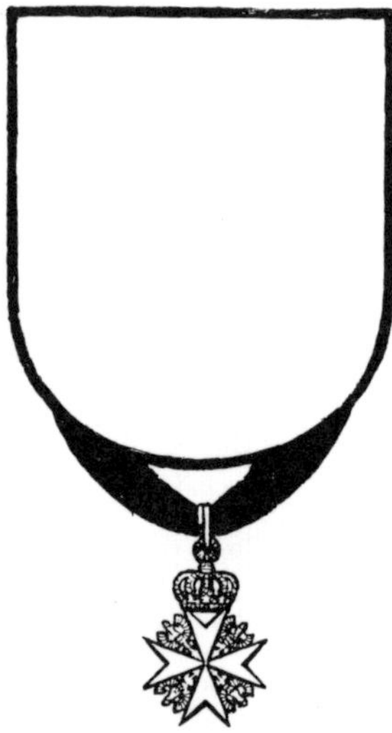

1166. Pattern for the arms of a Rechtsritter (knight of justice).

According to a history of the evangelical knights of St John, published in 1728, the simple cross of the Order on a red or black field could be placed in the arms of a knight of justice. In 1858 the chapter of the Order fixed the rules of how this should be done.

1167. von Blanckensee. Simple arms, probably including arms parted per fess or per pale, are quartered with a field charged with the badge of the Order.

1168. Baron von Türckheim. If the shield is quartered, an inescutcheon is used bearing the cross of the Order.

1169. Baron von Stackelberg. If the shield is quartered and already has an inescutcheon, a field bearing the cross is inserted above and below the inescutcheon.

1170. If the shield is parted per fess and in chief per pale, bearing an inescutcheon, a field charged with the cross of the Order is inserted above the inescutcheon.

The British Order of St John

1171. Pattern for the arms of a bailiff grand cross of the British Order of St John. Bailiffs grand cross and dames grand cross may use supporters to their arms. If they are not already entitled to supporters they may apply for a grant of these to Garter King of Arms, or to the Lord Lyon King of Arms if their arms are Scottish. They may also bear their arms with the arms of the Order in chief and place the Order's badge behind their shields. (Naturally the supporters do not have to be lions.)

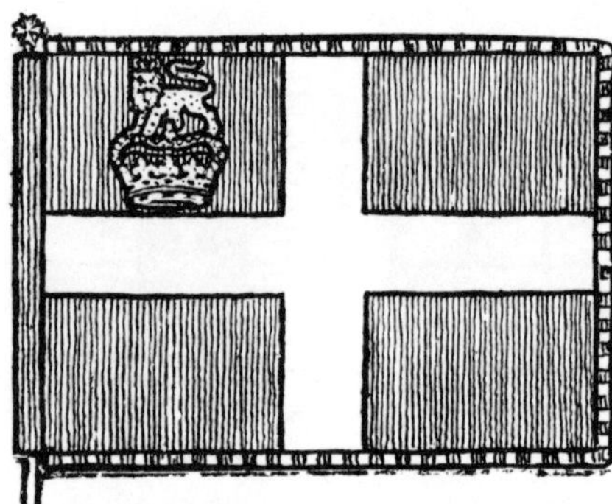

1172. The great banner of the Order. See fig. 964.

1173. The arms of the Order. The mottoes of the Order are Pro Fide and Pro Utilitate Hominum.

1174. The flag of the St John Ambulance Brigade.

1175. Arms of Prince Richard, Duke of Gloucester, Grand Prior of the Grand Priory of the Most Venerable Order of the Hospital of St John of Jerusalem, called Order of St John. See figs. 590, 964 and 965.

1176. Knights and dames, both of justice and of grace, and chaplains may display their arms on the badge of the Order. Members of any grade of the Order may suspend the badge of their grade on its ribbon from the shield.

Use of the Simple Cross of an Order

Members of a religious Order of Chivalry can display the simple cross of the Order somewhere next to their armorial bearings, wherever it looks best in the overall design.

1178. Arms of Baron van Haersolte van Haerst, a knight of justice in the Dutch Order of St John (died 1980).

1177. Arms of Diethelm Lütze, a knight of justice.

Three coats of arms, in different styles, of members of the Bailiwick of Brandenburg (Johanniterorden).

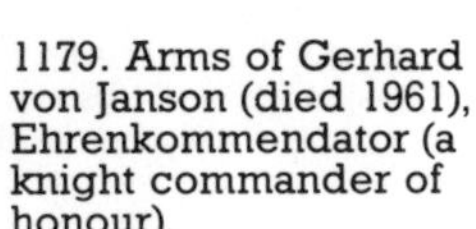

1179. Arms of Gerhard von Janson (died 1961), Ehrenkommendator (a knight commander of honour).

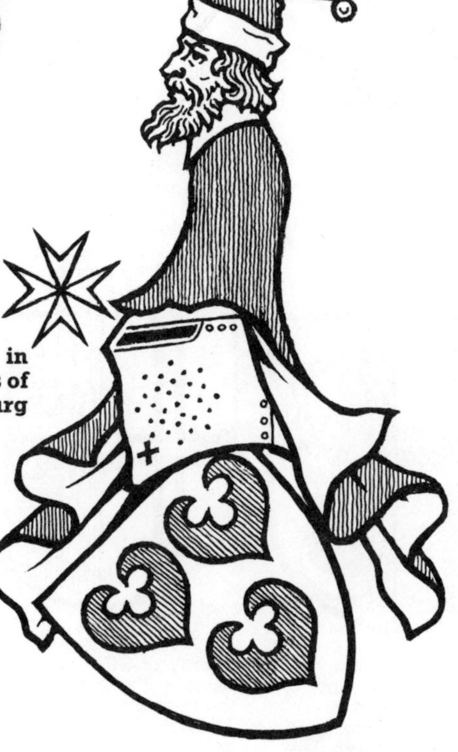

1180. Arms of Hans Ado von Seebach, a knight of justice.

German Civic Arms and Orders of Chivalry

1182.

1183.

1181. Heitersheim, in the county of Müllheim, Baden-Württemberg, in the possession of the Order of St John (Malta) from 1297 to 1797. It was the residence of the Grand Prior of Germany from 1428 onwards.

Bad Dürrheim in the county of Villingen, Baden-Württemberg. Both the town and the county bear a cross of Malta in their shield. This commemorates the presence in the area of an ancient commandery of the Order of St John, known in reports from 1257. The tinctures of the first field of the county arms are reversed probably to avoid having two coloured fields next to each other.

1184. Nieder-Weisel, in the county of Friedberg, Hesse, was the seat of a commandery of the Order of St John, known from before 1245. The ancient church belongs to the Bailiwick of Brandenburg since 1868.

1186

1187

1185. Neukölln, a West Berlin borough, was called Rixdorf before 1899. It belonged to the Order of St John from 1312 to 1435.

Bad Mergentheim in the county of Mergentheim, Baden-Württemberg. Both have the cross of the Teutonic Order in their arms. Mergentheim was founded by the knights in the 14th century and became the residence of the Hochmeister in 1526. Until 1809 the headquarters of the Order were in Mergentheim.
The inescutcheon in the arms of the county bears the arms of the house of Hohenlohe.

1188. Lövenich in the county of Cologne, North Rhine-Westphalia. The Knights of St John were the local masters from 1383 onwards. The cross of St Anthony recalls that Order's influence in the area.

1189. Gelchsheim in the county of Ochsenfurt, Bavaria. In 1401 it became the property of the Teutonic Order. The arms were granted by the German Master Walter von Cronberg in 1538.

1190. Waldstetten in the county of Günzburg, Bavaria. The cross recalls the relationship with the Teutonic Order's commandery of Altshausen.

1191. Marienberg, Westerwald, Rhineland-Palatinate. The cross recalls the relationship with the Teutonic Order in the 13th century. The inescutcheon bears the arms of the house of Nassau.

1192. Blumenfeld in the county of Constance, Baden-Württemberg, became the seat of administration of a commandery of the Teutonic Order in 1488.

The information on this page was collected from *Deutsche Wappen, Bundesrepublik Deutschland* by Klemens Stadler, Angelsachen Verlag, Bremen, 8 volumes, 1964-1972.

Swiss Civic Arms and the Order of St John

1193. Bubikon, Canton Zürich, uses the arms of the ancient commandery of the Order which, together with Wädenswil, was an estate at the disposal of the Prince Prior and Master of the Order in German lands in Heitersheim. See fig. 1181.

1194. Arms of La Chaux, Canton Vaud. In the 13th century the village belonged to the Knights Templars and it came into the possession of the Order of St John in 1298. United with the settlement in Cransaz, the commandery was headed by the preceptors of Vaud who were, until 1580, the patrons of Montbrelloz, Fribourg, and Saint-Jean de Grosset, Pays de Gex. The commandery was abolished during the Reformation.

1195. Reiden, Canton Lucerne. This was known as a commandery in 1284. In 1427 it was united with the commandery of Hohenrain. The officiating pastor of Reiden is, by virtue of his office, a chaplain of magistral grace of the Order of Malta.

1196. Contone, Canton Tessin. As early as 1367 the Order of St John owned a commandery and a hospital which belonged to the Italian Langue. In 1932 permission was given for the former commandery to use the cross of the Order in its armorial shield. The officiating pastor of Contone is, through his office, a chaplain of magistral grace of the Order of Malta.

1197. Montbrelloz, Canton Fribourg. From 1322 to 1556 the Order was the patron of the local church. It also owned a house in Montbrelloz which belonged to the Langue of Auvergne.
The rose in the arms commemorates the lords of Estavayer. Montbrelloz belonged to their territory in the 13th century.

1198. Villars-Sainte-Croix, Vaud. The Order of St John owned the ancient church and a hospital which is mentioned in records from before 1272. The buildings still existed as ruins in 1546. Both had been part of the commandery of La Chaux. Fig. 1194.

1199. Bardonnex-Compesières, Canton Genève. The Order of St John had a commandery here in the 13th century. The church of Compesières was given to the Order by Bishop Aymon de Menthoney in 1270. Bardonnex-Compesières uses as its arms the badge of the Order in a red field.

1200. Lonay, Canton Vaud. The commandery of La Chaux owned a great country estate and a hospital in Roman-Dessous. The arms of Lonay bear the arms of the Order of Malta in chief.

1201. Leuggern, Canton Aargau. The community uses the badge of the Order in a red field as its arms, in memory of the commandery which is mentioned in records from 1236. The officiating pastor of Leuggern is, by virtue of his office, a chaplain of magistral grace of the Order of Malta.

The information on this page is based on an illustrated article *Das Malteser Kreuz in schweizerischen Gemeindewappen* by F. J. Schnyder in *Archivum Heraldicum,* 1970 – Ao LXXXIV, Bulletin No. 2-3.

BADGES

The heraldic badge is distinctive of a person, a family, a clan or other corporate body and is independent from the coat of arms. It is normally used where armorial bearings would be unsuitable, especially as cognizances worn by adherents, retainers or followers. In this respect it can be compared with the cockade and cap badge of modern armies. Badges may also be displayed in conjunction with armorial bearings, for instance by members of an Order of Chivalry who include the badge of the Order in their personal achievements.

In the arms of Great Britain and Northern Ireland the plant badges of England, Scotland and Ireland are frequently shown in the compartment, see fig. 964, and thistles issue from the compartment of the arms of Scotland. The arms of Spain are accompanied by the columns of Hercules, badge of Charles I, and the yoke and the arrows, which were the badges of Isabella of Castile and Ferdinand of Aragon. See fig. 556.

1204. The white hart, badge of King Richard II of England, 1367-1400.

1202. A burning ragged staff with two water buckets was the badge of Gian Galeazzo Visconti, Duke of Milan, 14th century.

Collars of ancient Orders are mainly composed of badges. See fig. 900.

The crest badges of the Scottish clans are well known. They consist of the clan chief's crest encircled by a belt with his motto. Such badges, made of metal, are worn on the bonnet.

Badges were used mainly in southern Europe, France and Great Britain. In Germany and Scandinavia they were almost unknown.

In Great Britain the granting of badges was revived in 1906.

See also figs. 344, 386, 387, 398, 407 and 427.

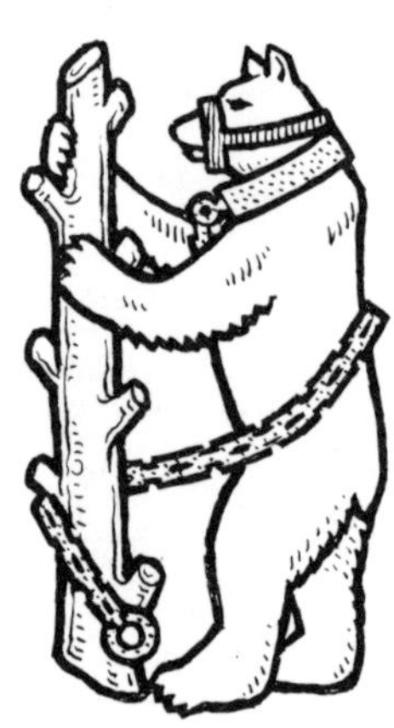

1205. Bear and ragged staff formed the famous badge of the Earls of Warwick.

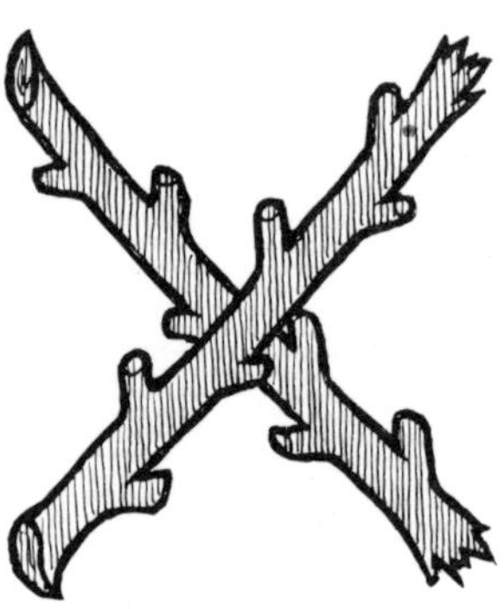

1203. Two red ragged staffs crossed in saltire was the emblem of the Dukes of Burgundy.

1207. Steel and flint, a badge of the Order of the Golden Fleece. See fig. 900.

1206. A white swan was the principal badge of King Henry V of England, 1388-1422.

1208. In England the astral crown is granted as a crest-coronet to institutions, and to people of outstanding achievement connected with aviation.

1209. Coronet for a British king of arms.

1210. Naval crown, granted in England as a crest-coronet to towns with naval associations and to distinguished sailors.

1211. Crown vallary, derived from defensive works (a fence of stakes).

1212. In England this is termed an eastern crown, in Scotland an antique crown.

1213. Palisado crown. This has the same origin (palisade) as the crown vallary. The terms are sometimes used interchangeably.

1214. Saxon crown. An ancient type of crown used in English heraldry.

1215. Coronet of a vidame (vice-dominus in latin), formerly an administrator of church property under a French bishop.

1216. The Celestial crown, probably inspired by St John's Revelation (according to which it should have twelve stars). See fig 158.

1217. Scottish crown for a county council.

1218. A crown used on a state coat of arms in West Germany (for instance Bavaria, Hesse and Rhineland-Palatinate). This is called a Volkskrone (people's crown).

1219. English crown for the arms of a rural district council.

ACKNOWLEDGEMENTS

It would have been more time consuming, maybe not even possible, to compile all the facts contained in this book, if it had not been for the generous assistance I received from many experts. I am extremely grateful to my friends of the International Academy of Heraldry who so patiently answered my inquiring letters, who sent valuable information or material to work with and who gave me the benefit of their experience and knowledge. I would like to express my gratitude to these gentlemen, of whom I must mention the following: Sven Tito Achen, A.I.H. (Danish heraldry). Roger Harmignies, A.I.H. (Belgian heraldry). H. Exc. Monsignor Bruno-Bernard Heim, titular Archbishop of Xanthus, A.I.H. (Church heraldry). Adam Heymowski, A.I.H. (Polish heraldry). Ladislao de Lászloczky, A.I.H. (Italian heraldry). Faustino Menéndez-Pidal de Navascués, A.I.H. (Spanish heraldry). Ottfried Neubecker, A.I.H. (German heraldry). Baron Hervé Pinoteau, A.I.H. (French heraldry). Gunnar Scheffer, A.I.H. (Swedish heraldry). H.S.H. Prince Karl zu Schwarzenberg, A.I.H. (Insignia of Rank of Princely Families of the Holy Roman Empire, Austria and Germany). O. Schutte, A.I.H. (Netherlands heraldry). Szabolcs de Vajay, A.I.H. (Hungarian heraldry).

I am also indebted to Frà (Marquis) Oberto Pallavicini of the Sovereign Military Order of Malta for sending me up-to-date material on the usage of heraldry by the members of the Order, and to F. J. W. Fabius for his information about the Teutonic Order in the Netherlands. I must also thank Serge de Nabokov for his kindness in providing me with good examples of Russian coats of arms. Last but not least my thanks to D. H. B. Chesshyre, Chester Herald, who willingly accepted the task of checking the parts connected with British heraldry.

C.A.v.V.

BIBLIOGRAPHY

Achen, Sven Tito: Danske adelsvåbener, Politikens Forlag 1973, København. Danske kommunevåbener, Saertryk af Hvem Hvad Hvor 1968, Politikens Forlag, 1967.

de Almeida Langhans, F. P.: Heráldica, ciência de temas vivos, Gabinete de heráldica corporativa, Lisboa, 1966.

Amman, Jost: Amman's Wappen-und Stammbuch, Frankfurt a.M., 1589, reprint von G. Hirth's Verlag, München, 1923.

Armorial General of the Noble Families of the Russian Empire, starting 1797.

Berghman, Arvid: Borgerlig Vapenrulla, med teckningar av Sven Sköld, Djursholm, 1950. Heraldisk Bilderbok, med techningar av Sven Sköld, Stockholm, 1951.

Bertini Frassoni, Conte Gr. Uff. Carlo Augusto: Il Sovrano Militare Ordine di S. Giovanni di Gerusalemme detto di Malta, Roma, Collegio Araldico, 1929.

Bolletino Ufficiale del Corpo della Nobilità Italiana, Anno I – N.1 – Giugno 1958.

De Boo, J. A.: Heraldiek, De Haan-Bussum, 1973.

Boutell's Heraldry, revised by J. P. Brooke-Little, Frederick Warne, London and New York, 1978.

Briggs, Geoffrey: Civic & Corporate Heraldry, Heraldry Today, 10 Beauchamp Place, London, S.W.3, 1971.

de Cadenas y Vicent, Vicente: Diccionario heráldico, Madrid, 1954.

Cappelen, Hans A. K. T.: Norske Slektsvapen, Den Norske Vapenring, ved Didrik Rye Heyerdahl, 1969.

de Crayencour, Georges: Dictionnaire héraldique, Bruxelles, 1974, complément, 1976.

Elvin, Charles Norton: A Dictionary of Heraldry, 1889, first published in this form by Heraldry Today, 10 Beauchamp Place, London S.W.3, 1969.

Ermerin, R. J.: La noblesse titrée de l'Empire de Russie, Librairie Emile Zeidler, Sorau, N.-L. (Prusse).

Fabius, F. J. W.: De Ridderlijke Duitsche Orde, van verleden tot heden, 1961.

Fourez, Lucien: Le droit héraldique dans les Pays-Bas Catholique, Bruxelles, 1932.

Franklyn, Julian: Shield and Crest, an Account of the Art and Science of Heraldry, MacGibbon & Kee, London, 1960.

Galbreath, D. L., Léon Jéquier: Manuel du blason, Editions Spes, Lausanne, 1977.

Gall, Franz: Österreich und seine Wappen, Wien, 1968.

Garcia Carraffa, Alberto y Arturo: Ciencia héraldica o del blasó, Madrid, 1957.

Genealogisches Handbuch des Adels, Adelige Häuser, B, Vol. I, 1954, Vol. VI, 1964. C. A. Starke Verlag, Limburg a.d. Lahn.

Genevoy, Robert: Monuments héraldiques au cimitière de Chaprais, a Besançon, Archivum Heraldicum, 1975, No. 3-4.

Gevaert, Emile: Héraldique des provinces belge, Vromant et Cie., Bruxelles, 1921. L'héraldique, son esprit, son language et ses applications, Bruxelles & Paris, 1923.

de Ghellinck Vaernewick, X.: Armorial & Historique des Alliances Contemporaines de la noblesse du Royaume de Belgique, illustrated by Roger Harmignies, Tradition & Vie, Bruxelles. 4 vol. 1962-1965.

The Grand Priory of the Most Venerable Order of the Hospital of St John of Jerusalem: Royal Charters (1955-1974), Statutes and Regulations of the Order.

Heim, Bruno-Bernard: Heraldry in the Catholic Church, its Origin, Customs and Laws, Van Duren, Gerrards Cross, 1978. Coutumes et droit héraldiques de l'Eglise, Paris, 1949.

Heimowski, Adam: Herby polskie w sztokholmskim Codex Bergshammar, Studia źródloznawcze XII, Instytut Historii Polskiej Akademii Nauk, Warszawa – Poznań, 1967. Polish Arms in Medieval Armorials, The Coat of Arms, vol. VIII, No. 58, 1964.

Hildebrandt, Adolf: Wappenfibel, Verlag von Heinrich Keller, Frankfurt am Main, 1909, Wappenfibel, Handbuch der Heraldik, bearbeitet vom Heroldsausschuss der Deutschen Wappenrolle, Verlag

Degener & Co., Inhaber Gerhard Gessner, Neustadt an der Aisch, 1967.

Hussmann, Heinrich: Über Deutsche Wappenkunst, Guido Pressler Verlag, Wiesbaden, 1973.

Imperiali, Marc M.: The Arms of the Genoese 'Alberghi', The Coat of Arms, vol. V, No. 39, 1959.

Innes of Learney, Sir Thomas: The Scottish Tartans, W. and A. K. Johnston and G. W. Bacon Ltd., Edinburgh, 1963. Scots Heraldry, Oliver & Boyd Ltd., Edinburgh, 1956.

Innes-Smith, Robert: An Outline of Heraldry in England and Scotland.

Joubert, Pierre: Les lys et les lions, initiation a l'art du blason, Les Presses d'Ile-de-France, 1947.

Klingspor, C. A.: Sveriges ridderskaps och adels vapenbok, 1890.

Konarski, S.: Armorial de la noblesse polonaise titrée, Paris, 1958.

Lindgren, Uno: Heraldik i svenska författningar, C. W. K. Gleerup, Lund, 1951.

Louda, Jiri: European Civic Coats of Arms, Paul Hamlyn, London, 1966.

Lukomsky, V. K. and Baron N. A. Tiepold: Russkaya geraldica, Petrograd, 1915.

MacKinnon of Dunakin, C. R.: The Observer's Book of Heraldry, Frederick Warne, London and New York, 1966. Scotland's Heraldry, Collins, Glasgow and London, 1962.

Manno, Antonio: Il Regolamento Tecnico-Araldico, spiegato ed illustrato, Roma, 1906.

Mannucci, S.: Nobiliario e Blasonario del Regno d'Italia, Roma, Collegio Araldico, vol. IV.

Mathieu, Remi: Le système héraldique français. Collection d'études historiques, dirigée par Jacques d'Avout, J. B. Janin, Paris, 1946.

Moncreiffe, Iain and Don Pottinger: Simple Heraldry Cheerfully Illustrated, Thomas Nelson and Sons, London, 1953.

Morini, Ugo: Araldica, Novissima Enciclopedia Monografica Illustrata, Firenze, 1929.

Neubecker, Ottfried: Kleine Wappenfibel, Rosgarten Verlag, Konstanz, 1966. Heraldik, Ihr Ursprung Sinn und Wert, mit Beiträgen von J. P. Brooke-Little, Wolfgang Krüger Verlag G.m.b.H., Frankfurt am Main, 1977.

Neues Siebmachersches Wappenbuch, Nuremberg, Bauer und Raspe, 1854-1976.

Pama, C.: Rietstap's Handboek der Wapenkunde, E. J. Brill, Leiden, 1961. Heraldiek en Genealogie, Uitgeverij het Spectrum N.V., Utrecht, Antwerpen, 1969.

Pedersen, Christian Fogd and Wilhelm Petersen: Alverdens flag i farver, Politikens Forlag, København, 1970.

Pinches, J. H. & R. V.: The Royal Heraldry of England, Heraldry Today, 10 Beauchamp Place, London, S.W.3, 1974.

Pinches, Rosemary and Anthony Wood: A European Armorial, Heraldry Today, 10 Beauchamp Place, London, S.W.3, 1971.

Pinoteau, Hervé and Claude Le Gallo: L'héraldique de Saint Louis et de ses compagnons, Les Cahiers Nobles, 27, 1966.

Pinoteau, Hervé: L'Héraldique Capétienne, en 1976, Nouvelles Éditions Latines, 1, rue Palatine – Paris 6 e.

Pye, Roger F.: Names, Arms and Cadency in Portugal, The Coat of Arms, vol. VIII, No. 62, 1965.

Ryckman de Betz, Baron: Armorial général de la noblesse belge, H. Dessain, Liege, 1957.

Schnyder, F. J.: Das Malteserkreuz in schweizerischen Gemeindewappen, Archivum Heraldicum, 1970, No. 2-3.

Schutte, O.: De Wapenboeken der Gelders-Overijselse Studentenverenigingen, Koninklijk Nederlandsch Genootschap voor Geslacht-en Wapenkunde, 'S-Gravenhage, 1975.

zu Schwarzenberg, Karl Fürst: Das Wappen der Fürsten zu Schwarzenberg, herausgegeben von den Schwarzenbergischen Archiven, Murau, Stmk, 1956.

Scott-Giles, C. W.: Augmentations for Loyalty, The Coat of Arms, vol. VI, No. 42, 1960.

Sierksma, Kl.: De gemeentewapens van Nederland, Utrecht, 1957.

Simon, Henry: Armorial Général de L'Empire Français, Paris, 1812.

Spreti, V.: Enciclopedia Storico-Nobiliare Italiana, Milano, 1928-1935.

Stadler, Klemens: Deutsche Wappen, Bundesrepublik Deutschland, Angelsachsen Verlag, Bremen, 8 vols., 1964-1971.

Stalins, Baron: Vocabulaire-Atlas Héraldique, Société du Grand Armorial de France, Paris, 1952.

Steimel, Robert: Kleine Wappenkunde, Steimel Verlag, Köln – Zollstock.

Ströhl, Hugo Gerard: Heraldischer Atlas, Stuttgart, 1899.

de Tamáska de Baranch, Endre: The Evolution of the Hungarian Coat of Arms, Sarasota, 1979.

de Thierry, le chevalier G. F.: Étude illustrée sur l'Histoire de l'Ordre Souverain Militaire Hospitalier de St Jean de Jerusalem, dit de Rhodes, dit de Malte, Mexico, 1961.

von Volborth, Carl-Alexander: Das Wappen, Stil und Form, C. A. Starke Verlag, 625 Limburg/Lahn, 1977. Heraldry of the World, 1973, Blandford Press, Poole, Dorset, reprint 1979. Johanniter Heraldik, Der Johanniterorden in Baden-Württemberg, No. 59, Stuttgart, 1979.

Wagner, Anthony: Heraldry in England, Penguin Books, 1953. Historic Heraldry of Britain, Oxford University Press, London, New York, Toronto, 1948.

Wappenbuch der Johanniter in Baden-Württemberg, geführt von Berthold Zilly.

Wappenbuch der Stadt Basel, edited by W. R. Staehelin, under the auspices of the Historical and Antiquarian Society in Basel, published by Helbing & Lichtenhahn, Basel.

Warnecke, F.: Heraldisches Handbuch, illustrated by E. Doepler d.J., C. A. Starke Verlag, Görlitz, 1880, reprint 1971, C. A. Starke Verlag, Limburg/Lahn.

Woodward, John and George Burnett, Woodward's a Treatise on Heraldry, British and Foreign, originally published in 1892, David and Charles Reprints, 1969.

Zappe, Alfred: Grundriss der Heraldik, C. A. Starke Verlag, Limburg/Lahn, 1968.

INDEX OF NAMES, ARMS AND DEVICES

References are to figure numbers.